*of book. Next
time I'll let you
know! Sorry!*

Johnny

FREE WILL?

An investigation into whether we have choice, or whether I was always going to write this book.

By Jonathan M.S. Pearce

Free Will? An investigation into whether we have choice, or whether I was always going to write this book.
Copyright © 2010 Jonathan M.S. Pearce
Published by Jonathan M.S. Pearce / Ginger Prince Publications
Printed by Lightning Source International

Printed in the United Kingdom and the United States (for US distribution).

Cover design: Jonathan M.S. Pearce

This publication has been submitted to the British Library in accordance with the Legal Deposit Libraries Act 2003 for listing in the British National Bibliography (BNB).

Trade paperback ISBN: 978-0-9566948-0-5

To Helen,
With all my love. A heartfelt hanks for all your support.
And cups of tea.

Further acknowledgements:

This book would not have been possible without the fantastic nights spent around the round table in the Cob and Pen debating all manner of things with fellow Tippling Philosophers: Rob Stroud, Andy Jordan, Mike Hollis and Peter S. Williams. The hours and days spent throwing emails at each other have certainly sharpened our wits. A huge thanks to Ben Wilson for his occasional chairing of our meetings, and, more importantly, for his vital editing and ideas.

About the author:

Jonathan M.S. Pearce is a teacher from South Hampshire, UK, who has dedicated many years to studying all manner of things philosophical and theological. Studying for a Masters in Philosophical Studies from the University of Wales, Lampeter, he also holds a degree from the University of Leeds, and a PGCE from Southampton. As a founder member of the Tippling Philosophers, a friendly group of disparate believers and non-believers (and sort-of believers) based in Hampshire, he is a big advocate of casual philosophy groups meeting over pints of good ale. He lives with his partner (and twin boys) and wonders how she puts up with him.

Author's Note

This book is intended to be an introductory "popular philosophy and theology" book rather them a heavy-going and totally comprehensive foray into the subject. My aim is that it is both easy to read and interesting, without being bogged down by philosophical terminology and pretension (though some terminology is inevitable and explained). I have listed all footnotes on the page on which they are found to avoid referring to the back of the book. Throughout the book, I have tried to link the philosophical and theological ideas, as is the wont of a Tippling Philosopher. Bible quotations are taken from the New American Standard Bible. There is a glossary at the back of the book so that the reader can reference certain terms that are new or forgotten to them. Many words in italic infer that they are in the glossary.

The book is set out as follows: Part I is a simple overview of the three main positions on free will in order to equip the reader with some tools to help grapple with the rest of the book. Part II looks at some of the core issues within the debate, such as consciousness, and the like. Part III delves much deeper into the three perspectives, using major works by a proponent of each perspective as a vehicle for investigation. Part IV is concerned with prophecies and their influence on free will in a religious context. Part V looks at how conclusions about free will might lead us to change our behaviour, and even our society.

I have not spent too many words considering the history of the ideas or who first developed them, since it really doesn't matter in this context. What matters is that the reader is interested and engaged. If they want to take the subject further, there are many good bookshops and university courses that offer a fantastic opportunity to delve more intensely into the depths of free will. Or lack thereof. There are many heavily philosophical and logical treatises that deal with this age old problem, and this book is not a similar attempt, but a lighter one that aims to provoke thought. This book is also not a biography of a freed killer whale.

CONTENTS

Introduction

Some years ago, after several impromptu high-brow discussions in the staff room (of the school where I teach), a colleague fell on the fine idea of starting a theology and philosophy club which could meet at a local pub. This club, soon to be called the "Tippling Philosophers", was to be styled on the "Inklings", the cosy group of theological writers such as C.S. Lewis and J.R.R. Tolkien who, likewise, used to meet over a drink and discuss all manner of things that exercised their grey matter. Our first meeting of five furtive philosophers took place at the round table in the "Cob and Pen", and covered many topics, as we dipped our feet into the realm of ideas. After several ales, and a good deal of head-scratching, I happened upon a revelatory thought. Sometimes in life, we have brainstorming ideas that switch on the light bulb in our heads, and words such as, "I've just come up with a new theory!" spring forth in a fountain of originality.

However, originality is hard to come by these days, which is no surprise, since humans have been thinking non-stop throughout their long and industrious history. If you think you've had an original thought, it's almost guaranteed that the Greeks have already thought about the same thing. It's as if no one in Ancient Greece went to work; as though they sat around all day pondering.

So what was this thought I had? Well, it was something I labeled (with some degree of attempted irony) the Perfect Order of Proceeding Events theory. Or POPE theory for short. My friend and colleague, Rob, was supporting his theory of the existence of God by explaining that if you see the universe, since the beginning of time, as a set of dominoes falling against other dominoes in a cause and effect relationship, then someone must have pushed the first domino. That is to say, if a butterfly flapped its wings on one side of the world, the chain of events that this set in motion would be like falling dominoes, causing the proceeding events to take place.

This got me thinking, not so much about the existence of God at this point (this comes later), but that if we could see the universe as a set of cause and effect relationships, and *if* we knew all the variables – all the scientific laws and all the

1

molecules in the world – then we could effectively (theoretically) predict all events in the universe, from the beginning of time onwards. This, then, opened my eyes to the possibility that, if all things adhere to this strict causal reality and the laws of the universe, then we (humans and other animals) might not have choice as we know it. We might not, indeed, have free will. And if this was true, and we believed it to be true, what a very different perception of the world we would have.

This *Eureka!* moment got me really excited – it all seemed to make sense – and that night I returned home with a new-found philosopher's spring in my step. Unfortunately, as with most aspects of life, the internet had the answer, or at least the ideas and information, to quash my feelings of genuine originality. Furthermore, it was my trusty friend (well, usually, anyway...), Wikipedia, that introduced me to the fascinating topic of determinism (what I had defined as the POPE theory) – exactly what I had been explaining to Rob in the pub. And no doubt what Hume or Laplace (or other philosophers) had been explaining to their friends down the pub all those many years ago.

The more that I have researched this topic, the more I have found that it could potentially and drastically influence the way I look at the world, and the way I carry out my daily life. I don't profess to having found a definitive answer, only something similar to a faith statement, something that I believe. Even as I write this book, I am aware that my belief could change: I like to keep an open mind.

In this book, I want to share the journey that I have had so far, exploring the reason and rationale behind the events in our lives. By the end of the book, we might be somewhat closer to working out how life fits together. Or we could become even more puzzled. For some readers, you may already know much about these arguments, maybe subconsciously, maybe through your own research or sphere of expertise; for others, it may open your eyes to seeing that the universe, that life, may work in a very different way to that which you had thought. There is also a subtext running throughout this book as to how all of this relates to the notion of a god that might judge us on our earthly actions. In fact, this is not just a subtext, but an integral part of my journey. How do we understand religion in the light of varying degrees of determinism, and how do we then interpret any idea of a God that we may, or may not, already have? Does any of this knowledge undermine the argument for a personal deity? Or does it strengthen it? Or is it neither here nor there? Do we believe in prophecy, as claimed throughout the bible, and if we do, have we ever really thought about the consequences of prophecy, of having a future already determined, or is it one of those things that we accept (or not) without really questioning?

The main aim of this book, though, is to share my thoughts, and those of the TPs; to help you ponder; and to help us get back to being a little more Greek about things.

Jonathan M.S. Pearce

PART I - GETTING TO GRIPS WITH THE LABELS

1 – LIBERTARIAN FREE WILL

I'm free, to do what I want, any old time...
I'm free, to choose who I see, any old time,
I'm free, to bring who I choose, any old time,
Love me, hold me, love me, hold me,
I'm free, any old time to get what I want.
(The Rolling Stones)

Life is like a game of cards. The hand you are dealt is
determinism; the way you play it is free will.
(Jawaharlal Nehru)

What is free will?

As with any good bit of thinking, language plays an important role, and so we can start by defining our terms to agree what we are talking about. Free will is described by Dictionary.com (the lazy man's dictionary) as:

> *–noun*
> *1. free and independent choice; voluntary decision:*
> *You took on the responsibility of your own free will.*
> *2. Philosophy. The doctrine that the conduct of human beings expresses personal choice and is not simply determined by physical or divine forces.*
> (www.dictionary.com, 2009)

This, in the context of our daily lives, means that we have the freedom of choice; we have no constraints, as to whether, say, we chose a meat-feast pizza or a vegetarian pizza in a restaurant. Or, indeed, whether we were a meat-eater or a vegetarian. It is, then, a voluntary decision as to what choice we make in these situations. I could just as easily, theoretically, choose a meat-feast, as choose a vegetarian pizza.

In the age of Enlightenment, the 18th century period when reason formed the basis for authority and changed the world of philosophy and religion[1], William Belsham coined the phrase *libertarianism* to sum up this position of free will, to oppose its antithesis – determinism. This position entails that humans, as rational beings, exert control over their actions and decisions, and that, in the extreme, no-one is determined, and everyone is free to choose at will their actions, and their paths. The idea that most libertarians hold is that the human, in making a choice, is the originator of that choice. That means there is no need to look further back into the causal chain to discover reasons that created that choice – the human that made the choice is the location from where that choice originated as a mental event. This is important to note, since it implies that the mental event was not a chance event, it did not come about by sheer randomness, but somehow by the mental capacities of the person, thus allowing them to be responsible for the choice.

---

[1] And most other aspects of culture and life in general!

Intuitively, people will almost always declare they have free will. You would be hard pressed to find someone who would sit down at *Pizzeria La Causa Bella* and would say they had no choice in the pizza they were about to order. Most would agree that the larger the menu, the more difficult to make that free choice, though the capacity to make that choice might remain the same[1]. People certainly operate *as if* they had free will.

To shift the example, we might consider crime. Laws are created as if we choose freely to carry out morally 'bad' actions. Here is an excerpt from the UK Misuse Of Drugs Act 1971:

> **8.**
>
> *A person commits an offence if, being the occupier or concerned in the management of any premises, he knowingly permits or suffers any of the following activities to take place on those premises, that is to say—*
>
> *(a) producing or attempting to produce a controlled drug in contravention of section 4(1) of this Act;*
>
> *(b) supplying or attempting to supply a controlled drug to another in contravention of section 4(1) of this Act, or offering to supply a controlled drug to another in contravention of section 4(1);*
>
> *preparing opium for smoking;*
>
> *(d) smoking cannabis, cannabis resin or prepared opium.*[2]

In this law, it is implicit that any person can choose whether or not they supply a Class A drug from their house. Choosing not to – a free choice – will mean you are in no danger of being punished. On the other hand, by committing this

---

[1] This was theorised in The Paradox of Choice: Why More is Less by Barry Schwartz, who states that the more choice people have, the greater their anxiety (particularly as consumers). Most people actually find it easier and less stressful to choose from 2 available jean styles than 15. He has a good talk on TED.com - http://www.ted.com/index.php/talks/barry_schwartz_on_the_paradox _of_choice.html. (12/2009)

[2] http://www.statutelaw.gov.uk/content.aspx?LegType=All+Legislation&Year=1971& searchEnacted=0&extentMatchOnly=0&confersPower=0&blanketAmendment=0&so rtAlpha=0&TYPE=QS&PageNumber=1&NavFrom=0&parentActiveTextDocId=136 7412&ActiveTextDocId=1367412&filesize=260094 (08/2009)

offence, you are running the risk of suffering the consequences with some kind of indictment[1]. Thus, free will is inherently understood to be an integral aspect of our legal system, as well as our restaurant system. The vengeful side of punishment requires that the perpetrator of the crime actively chose to do the crime. But what happens if someone was forced to steal a loaf of bread at gunpoint (quite why, I don't know, but that is the nature of thought experiments)? Can we rightfully punish them for this "crime"? The element of free choice is arguably there – get shot or steal a loaf of bread – even though I would wager that most rational people would choose to steal the bread.

Therefore, punishment for crime hinges on the notion that the perpetrator chooses *freely* to commit the crime. Note that this is only the retributive aspect of the justice system, and this is not concerned with the value of punishment as a deterrent to future similar actions. The legal system would potentially break down if culpability was shifted from the individual to the determined functions of any given behaviour. I will mention this at more length in the determinist chapter in Part III, and in the closing section.

As far as society as a whole is concerned, free will is woven through everything we do. Merit is given to decisions well-made, and responsibility is apportioned to actions taken. For example, if an investor decided to invest in a risky venture that came to fruition and brought her untold financial success and public popularity, she would be lauded for her decision, and for the audacity to choose that path. Merit would be given and no doubt, accepted for that decision.

As with crime, society sees moral responsibility as intrinsically linked to free will. A philanthropist who decides freely to put his millions towards buying a huge tranche of rainforest to safeguard its existence for generations to come would be congratulated and seen as a fine moral pillar of society. In general societal terms, free will is important in determining consumerist activities. Competition, in economic terms, is integral to a buoyant capitalist financial system, and is dependent upon consumers being able to choose between goods, and for producers to vie for the preferences of consumers. Of course, the producers then manipulate variables

---

[1] This approach of influencing behaviour with offering consequences to actions is known as *consequentialism*.

such as price (two for one!), or extra desirable features (cheesy crust on this pizza!), to strongly influence the consumer's choice, thus moving the consumer away from an un-influenced, purely free choice. When you are next out, perusing the fine purveyors of whatever goods you are looking for, it might be worth considering how much free choice you really have, and what things are bending your will towards buying a particular item. Did you buy that chocolate bar because you really wanted it, or because it was on the end display at the supermarket, and highlighted with bright signs?

Free will is something, most humans would say, that makes humanity enjoyable, challenging and full of happiness, sadness, success and failure. The choices we make are the things that define who we are, what we achieve, and the situations we find ourselves in, whether we succeed in that business deal, or fail miserably. The paths we take are the choices we make.

But I don't think anyone would contend that our choices are not influenced to some degree by external factors. Extreme free will (über-Libertarianism, if you will) is not something that realistically exists in our world. Everything we do is influenced in some way, surely, by who we are and what we have learnt from our environment, and our environment itself. If we look back to our Dictionary.com definition of free will, it defines the belief that a freely-willed action is the result of a "personal choice and is not simply determined by physical or divine forces". However, implicit in this statement is the notion that there may well be influences, that the action may not be "simply", "exclusively" determined, but that free will works with some degree of determined external forces. Much more on this, and free will as a realistic ideal is explained in the chapter on compatibilism.

We might decide to summarise the spectrum of free will in a diagram. The Tippling Philosophers don't always have paper, so it needs to fit neatly onto a beer-mat (or cigarette packet, as long as we avoid discussions about free will and addiction). If we consider extreme beliefs about free will then our initial diagram looks something like this:

| LIBERTARIAN FREE WILL | DETERMINISM |

ABSOLUTE FREE WILL		NO FREE WILL

But this is a continuum of extremes. In between these two polarities, in the middle, lie many different versions and combinations of free will and determinism. Nevertheless, disciples of either libertarianism or determinism usually argue their position to the exclusion of the other. In other words, belief in libertarianism requires one to believe that determinism cannot and does not exist. And vice versa. Thus, one can declare that both are *incompatible* with each other, and a believer of this is referred to, naturally enough, as an *incompatibilist*. In addition, someone who believes in full free will, as I just mentioned, necessarily believes that determinism is incorrect. To throw in another label, as we love doing in today's society, this person is an *indeterminist*, with *indeterminism* being defined as the belief that determinism is incorrect. A believer in this might live at the extreme end of the spectrum, or they might occupy the middle ground.

The next chapter looks at the idea that determinism and free will can exist side by side, like an uncomfortably married couple.

2 – COMPATIBILISM

L'homme est né libre, et partout il est dans les fers.
Man is born free, and everywhere he is in chains.
(Jean-Jacques Rousseau)

Human freedom is not an illusion; it is an objective
phenomenon, distinct from all other biological
conditions and found only in one species, us.
(Daniel C. Dennett)

"To understand everything is to forgive everything"
(Buddha)

The next step along the line

As we move along our journey into the actually-quite-well chartered territories of free will, the next stop along the spectrum is compatibilism. "Why is it called thus?" I hear you cry. Well, the answer is simply that it is a theory which is compatible with aspects of both free will and of determinism. It is the seemingly counter-intuitive belief that free will and determinism are both viable positions to hold simultaneously. Furthermore, how you arrive at destination compatibilism varies greatly – there are many modes of transport that can get you there, and many different drivers.

If we refer back to our continuum, it now looks a little like this:

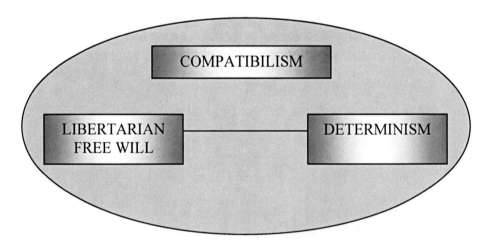

Compatibilism doesn't nestle between the two extremes, but encompasses them, due to the fact that adherents believe they can both exist, side by side.

Unfortunately, this is where the discussion gets a little more complicated, and this is where so much of the war for free will takes place. And the war takes place for so many reasons, not least because there is definitely an inherent feeling within most people that they have free will. Free will provides an oasis of purpose, and without it, we don't have the tools to achieve our goals or change our lives in any way; we merely become pawns in a cosmological chess game. This would be a scary thought for most of us, being played in a game of fate. But, just because this goes against our intuition, it doesn't mean we *aren't* merely pawns in a cosmological chess game. An ultimate truth doesn't necessarily have to be a comfortable one. That, though, is a debate saved for later pages. In the meantime, let us look at the characteristics of compatibilism, and how we can arrive at the point of giving it philosophical and theological credibility.

Given their acceptance of at least some degree of predetermined conditions in any human action, compatibilists are often called *soft determinists*. Thus, full determinism is called *hard determinism*. People's approach to compatibilism, as I have said, can be different, and much depends on the way in which free will is defined. Some people will assert that a free act is one that does not involve the influence of another person in the act. For example, to return to our pizza restaurant analogy, let us imagine the decision of Mrs. Scelta when looking at the menu. She looks down, sees all the different pizzas, and opts for the meat-feast. This can be seen by compatibilists as a free choice since she is not being coerced by another person to choose meat-feast, but does it at her own free will. Loosely, this choice is not as a direct result of anyone else, but the result of laws of nature, physics, the universe, and so on. Thus, Mrs. Scelta has free will.

On the other hand, if our Mr. Fato, the restaurateur, for some reason put a gun to her head and declared that she must choose a meat-feast pizza, then she is devolved of free will, and her choice is determined by the situation she is in (human coercion). Some might also include, in this version of human coercion, examples of internal compulsions from psychological disorders. These compulsions are behaviour- and choice-determining factors that forbid true free will to be employed (one example could be kleptomania). A common example given for the coercive approach is that of someone being in prison (due to its obvious notions of physical restraint), but can also be applied to any number of situations where there is an aggressor involved, such as being mugged, raped or kidnapped – your free will is evidently being curtailed. In many ways, this is connected to the consequentialist idea, that the subject has free will (theoretically) but faces dire consequences if they utilise this free will. In the case of someone in shackles in prison, then the free will aspect is more obvious, since there are not just the possible consequences (such as a bullet from a psychotic restaurateur) that constrain one's will, but the physical restraint as well. One does not have the choice of going to the pizza restaurant if one is locked up at Her Majesty's pleasure for life. Although with present prison overcrowding issues, perhaps that trip is never too far away.

Having said this, some people find this definition somewhat weak, and a real sidestepping of the philosophy involved. Whether one's actions are determined by human coercion, or natural coercion, if you will, is neither here or there – the action is still determined, and one's decision is still influenced by a set of pre-existing causal events.

What have the Scots ever done for us?

One man that had a lot to say on all things free will, was the famous Scottish Enlightenment philosopher David Hume. He was interesting in that he declared that liberty (free will) is actually dependent upon determined events – if our free will choices were not based on anything, then they are more like just random events. What's more, Hume believed that at any given point of action, we have the *potential* to do otherwise –

> *By liberty, then we can only mean* a power of acting or not acting, according to the determinations of the will; *that is, if we choose to remain at rest, we may; if we choose to move, we also may. Now this hypothetical liberty is universally allowed to belong to every one who is not a prisoner and in chains.*
> *(Hume, Ed. Selby-Bigge 1975A, p. 95)*

There are many criticisms of Hume's potential free will arguments. If Mr. Scelta is choosing his pizza and he is a vegetarian, then it is highly likely that, given the choice of the vegetarian or meat-feast pizza, he will choose the vegetarian. Now, potentially, he might choose the meat-feast, but that is not what usually happens. Even if he always chooses the vegetarian pizza, he has the hypothetical liberty to choose the meat-feast (as Hume would argue). This, though, is unsatisfactory since there is clearly a gulf between what one can theoretically do, and what someone actually does. If I hate the colour red with a vengeance, then I am clearly never going to buy a red jumper from the clothes shop, even though I theoretically could. My preference determines my choice, irrespective of what I *could* choose. The *actual* variables[1] and circumstances in reality define my actions, not hypothetical ones. This might be seen as a choice of potential actions, rather than a freedom of will, and a freedom of will is the Holy Grail here.

---

[1] Any influencing input in deciding something, from genetic influences, to environmental ones.

Hume claims that it is illogical to assert that the subject does not cause an action, but rather that it is freely caused *and* the subject is still responsible for it. He is closely knitted causality to free will, meaning that if the will for an action comes 'freely' from you, then free will is witnessed. But this kind of internal causation can still be claimed to be determined, as Kant explained: a clock does not have free will, even though its actions are all the result of internal causes.

We have, as we will return to again later, an issue with defining where internal determining factors become internal factors that can still permit free will choice; at some point there is an arbitrary line that one must draw to say "now you are definitely responsible for that". For example, assuming there are different degrees of kleptomania, then someone with acute kleptomania (100% on a scale of kleptomania) might be absolved of responsibility for stealing a jumper because they were simply bowing to overwhelming internal constraint. But what about someone with, say, 78% kleptomania? Are they personally responsible? Or are they still constrained by their internal issues, and determined, still, to steal? Perhaps there should be a sliding scale of responsibility to match a sliding scale of determined causation, internal and external. The problem with this is that, though logically sound, it is practically impossible to work out – you simply couldn't decipher internal and external influences on any one decision, certainly in such a situation as in a court of law. That said, it doesn't mean it is any less true.

Hume believed that man seeks society and sees other men as objects of either praise or of blame. Thus, the very nature of man necessitates us to be morally responsible:

> *Moral evidence is nothing but a conclusion concerning the actions of men, deriv'd from the consideration of their motives, temper and situation.*
> *(Hume, Ed. Selby-Bigge 1975B, p. 404)*

So it seems that for Hume, and other more recent compatibilists, free will is determined by one's beliefs and one's character. I have to be honest here, whenever I read anything about compatibilism, and whenever I speak to fellow Tippling Philosophers who have compatibilist leanings, I feel that underneath it all they, rationally, are really determinists. This determinism is so counter-intuitive, though, that perhaps people feel obliged to offer theories and ideas of compatibilism, of free will defining their actions. The argument boils down to how much determinism and free will interact – to what degree do they mix in order to allow for a morally responsible being? And this can be reduced further to a sort of matrix similar to the kleptomania argument mentioned previously, whereby people's responsibility is seen on a sliding scale that correlates with the amount of determinism involved in their decisions. How responsible is a child for torturing a cat, if you see his actions in the context of being determined by parents who have been violent to each other for the child's entire life, and who have abused the child, whilst also abusing drugs and living a life of desperation and misery? The child then has mitigating circumstances – but do these absolve his responsibility? And how about the fact that the subject is a child, rather than an adult – how does that affect choice and responsibility? How much external (and internal) influence mitigates a child's 'irresponsible' actions? It potentially becomes a formula, but a formula that no human could surely work out.

Let us look briefly at the UK Misuse of Drugs Act 1971 again. To remind you:

8.

A person commits an offence if, being the occupier ...
of any premises, he knowingly permits or suffers any
of the following activities to take place on those
premises, that is to say—

...

(b) supplying or attempting to supply a controlled
drug to another ...

Imagine a man called Doug who rents a flat. Doug suffered an appalling childhood: his parents abused drugs, and physically abused him, and then his dad left the house never to return, leaving an ill-equipped mother to bring Doug and his three sisters up. Doug suffered at school, because the lack of attention he had been given at home throughout his childhood, and his lack of literacy, had led him to communicate and seek attention in the only way he knew how – through troublesome behaviour. He couldn't access any lessons at school because his literacy was so poor, and so he was disruptive. These classroom performances led to his expulsion. He left school with no qualifications, and low aspirations, unmotivated to better himself, with very low self esteem. In trouble persistently with the law, and without the stability of a job, drug abuse added to the situation, with peer pressure and a feeling of such low confidence playing their part. Like father, like son, his genes also dealt him the characteristics of an addictive personality, ensuring he easily fell prey to the dangers of drug addiction. With a complete lack of money, low self esteem and no confidence in getting a job, Doug decided that the only way to make ends meet was to start dealing drugs – it was a world he knew, it was something he was confident he could be good at. He decided to package drugs in his house and sell them to his local estate. In the eyes of the law, with its absolute judgement, Doug is guilty of committing an offence. The law sees him as choosing to commit a crime, and therefore he is guilty. However, where we can see compatibilism, or more accurately, an understanding of determinism, creeping in is if the judge, when sentencing him, takes into account his background and the mitigating factors in his personal history. As a result, the judge decides to give him a lenient sentence, with a view to taking adult education courses and rehabilitation in order to try to determine that he doesn't do it again. So in the eyes of the law, and in the eyes of the public, though Doug did have mitigating circumstances, he was seen to have chosen his path, knowing the consequences. He is punished for his crime, though this is tempered by acknowledging that he did not have an easy life, and he was in a position to make him more likely to end up doing as he did than one of the jurors.

Critics often grumble that however much compatibilism seems to make emotional sense, it never seems to have the logical clout, or the scientific evidence to support it. This is backed up by views that great thinkers throughout the years have held: that compatibilism has to exist, because otherwise the door to hope and optimism is shut. In other words, as we shall investigate, determinism is nothing but fatalistic, nihilistic and somewhat depressing! Though this might be the case, it should not detract from the possibility that determinism might still be 'true'.

Taking these arguments for compatibilism into account, it is important to note that I have not yet brought in the modern philosopher's knight in shining armour, riding for compatibilism, Daniel Dennett. I am saving his arguments for compatibilism for the Delving Deeper section of Part III, where we can explore this idea in more detail.

Jonathan M.S. Pearce

3 – DETERMINISM

*Punishment as punishment is not admissible unless
the offender has had the free will to select his course.
(Clarence Darrow)*

*Everything is determined, the beginning as well as
the end, by forces over which we have no control. It is
determined for the insect as well as the star. Human
beings, vegetables, or cosmic dust, we all dance to a
mysterious tune, intoned in the distance by an
invisible piper.
(Albert Einstein)*

Jonathan M.S. Pearce

A massive set of dominoes

Having mentioned the word determinism plenty of times already in this book, it would be churlish not to explain what is meant by the word; a bit like reading the bible and thinking, "Who's this God fellow everyone keeps mentioning?" Determinism is the belief that all actions, all thoughts, everything that happens in this here universe, adhere to the strict laws of the universe, and are part of a causal chain of events. And when I say everything, I mean *everything*. Thus, the rules of chemistry, biology and physics provide the framework in which all events happen. And since this is the case now, it has also been the case since the beginning of time. Since the Big Bang (or whatever version of natural creation you might favour). Pick up your mobile phone. Go on, I guarantee it's not far away. Now drop it from your hand over the table, or airport lounge chair. I imagine you can predict what will happen – this sort of experiment has been carried out ever since you have been able to observe. The mobile phone reacts to the laws of physics, to gravity, and falls downwards. The predictability of this simple event is evident everywhere. Every time that we make a prediction for anything, we take in the variables that will be at play, and reason that something will happen in a certain way as a direct result of those variables. If something happens differently from our prediction, it will undoubtedly be as a result of unknown variables (or poor calculation). I have never yet seen earthly gravity suddenly work sideways.

Because of the very nature of the laws of science being reliable, and the physical constants[1] in the world working as they do, we can accurately predict what will happen in a simple science experiment. This is what I alluded to in the introduction to this book – the notion that I named POPE, that everything in life is eminently, theoretically predictable – i.e. we are

---

[1] A physical constant is a physical quantity thought to be constant, the same, in time as well as in nature. Such an example might be the speed of light, Planck's Constant, or the gravitational constant. Some people posit that if the constants were any different, the universe would not be anything near what it is today, and thus might not be able to support life. Some theologians have used this to point towards an intelligent designer of the universe who has fine-tuned the constants (the anthropic principle as it is often called), while others have refuted this (since using that logic entails that God has a greater interest in rock than humans, as the universe seems far more fine-tuned for rock than life).

theoretically able to predict everything. Now, I thought I was being quite clever in thinking about this all on my own, and neglected to consider that there have been billions of thinking homo sapiens existing before me, and a good many of them are far more intelligent than I'll ever be. A certain Monsieur Laplace, for example, considered this idea and even created his own demon to explain it. Yes, Laplace's Demon (though he did not see it as a demon, it was described as such by later writers) is a being that lives in a thought experiment and does a pretty good job of explaining to the layman exactly what determinism is all about. This demon that Pierre-Simon Laplace created in 1814 could hypothetically know the exact location of every atom, every molecule, in the universe and every force, every variable, acting upon every one of those atoms. Using the laws of Newtonian physics, Laplace thought that the demon could predict everything that will happen, and has happened. In his own words:

> *We may regard the present state of the universe as the effect of its past and the cause of its future. An intellect which at a certain moment would know all forces that set nature in motion, and all positions of all items of which nature is composed, if this intellect were also vast enough to submit these data to analysis, it would embrace in a single formula the movements of the greatest bodies of the universe and those of the tiniest atom; for such an intellect nothing would be uncertain and the future just like the past would be present before its eyes.*
>
> Pierre-Simon Laplace[1]

A key to the notion of determinism is the assumption that at the point of the Big Bang, there is a finite amount of matter and / or energy. This finite matter means that no extra 'stuff' can come into the universe *ex nihilo*[2] (out of nothing). Therefore,

---

[1] http://en.wikipedia.org/wiki/Laplace%27s_demon (08/2009)
[2] Ex nihilo – it is commonly assumed that something cannot be made from nothing, which is an argument that can be used to propose that the universe must have been created by an external being, or God, since the universe couldn't just pop into being. This argument of ex nihilo can, however, be used to argue against a Creator God – how could *he* be created ex nihilo? The theist answer is usually that he has existed

everything can be accounted for. To massively simplify this, one can see the initial finite set of atoms at the point of the Big Bang as, say, a domino at the beginning of a huge domino display. You know, the sort that you have seen on the news going for a world record. It has taken weeks to set up, and everyone hopes no clumsy sod will drop a doughnut on to set it off early. The Big Bang is when the first domino topples, and knocks the next one, which knocks the next one, and over time the dominoes fall in a predictable and spectacular fashion, playing out the history of our universe. The belief is that it is one massive set of dominoes acting in one huge causal chain, each preceding domino determining that the following one will fall, with the physical laws dictating at what angle they topple.

From a human point of view, let us take Mr. Scelta ordering his pizza, and the choice he makes (at point of time *t*) of saying to Mr. Fato that he is going to have a vegetarian pizza. Let that scenario run for a minute: Mr. Fato jots down the order and walks away, Mr. Scelta turns to his wife and smiles. Now let us rewind the tape back to the exact moment *t* when Mr. Scelta decides on his pizza choice. We have *exactly* the same set of atoms and variables in the world as the 'previous' point *t*, nothing has changed. With this identical world of every atom and force being the same, on the point of Mr. Scelta deciding what pizza to have, the "Needle of choice[1]" swinging, do you think that Mr. Scelta would ever, if we rewound the tape a hundred times, would he ever at that moment choose something else? I would tend to say that he wouldn't. In order to choose something else, I believe that the variables would have to be different; external factors out of his control would have to be different; previous events in his life might have to be different; atoms in his brain outside of his conscious control might have to be different. But if everything, down to the most minute subatomic particle is the same, he will always make that same decision. That is who he is, and that is why that decision is made so. He is determined, at that point, to always make that decision, all other things remaining equal.

---

eternally, and thus does not answer to the charges of ex nihilo. To which an atheist can argue that if you can argue that God existed eternally, you can posit that the universe / matter / energy has existed eternally. At which point, everyone should give up, and go down the pub for an ale and a chat about their favourite song to play whilst going on a road trip.

[1] See Part III, 1-Libertarian Free Will

It is also important to note here that a belief that things might be determined does not necessarily follow that they are pre-determined. Something being pre-determined implies that there is a sentient being that is determining things to turn out in such and such a way after prior thought and decision, such as a god[1]. This is not the case in simple determinism, which says that X, Y and Z were determined to happen because of all the variables and laws, but that there was not necessarily someone who set up the laws *so that* X, Y and Z happened. There, of course *may* be a sentient being programming the universe in such a way, but that is another belief entirely.

Talking of particles, it is interesting to note, unsurprisingly, that the initial big thinkers in the world of determinism were the Greeks. Of determinism, a chap called Democritus and another called Leucippus were big fans. They were paid up members of a club called the *atomists*. Well, they pretty much founded the movement in around 440 BCE. Democritus was a contemporary of the famous Socrates and the movement that the two were responsible for was so remarkably akin to modern science as to have been uncanny. I can imagine an event à la *Back to the Future* where they ended up with a school science text book from the future, and stole all their ideas from therein. Bertrand Russell (1946/1993, p.83) notes of the atomists:

> *Their point of view was remarkably like modern science...They believed that everything is composed of atoms, which are physically, but not geometrically, indivisible; that between the atoms there is empty space; that atoms are indestructible; that they have always been, and always will be, in motion...They were...strict determinists, who believed that everything happens in accordance with natural laws. Democritus explicitly denied that anything can happen by chance.*

The atomists tackled the issue of who started this world of atoms by saying that just as an initial causation must come from somewhere or someone, so too must a creator be answerable to this logic. By saying that a creator started the

---

[1] Though most Gods, against popular belief, don't cogitate or deliberate at all. Their thinking is very limited indeed, since they already know, being all-knowing!

causal chain begs the question about who created the creator? In the same way that people who believe in an uncaused causer, such as God, so the atomists believed in an uncaused first cause. Just not a God cause. It seems odd that in some ways we have advanced hugely over two millennia, and yet in others we are no further on than our toga-wearing, democracy-inventing, philosophising counterparts.

So, the atomists, as modern hard determinists think, left nothing to chance, as we shall now investigate.

It's all in the flip of a coin

One of the important considerations to take into account when discussing all things determinism is whether anything in the world is random, if there is chance in any of life's events. Some of this is answered in the next section on quantum physics. For the time being, I am going to look at commonplace perceptions of random and chance.

When Mr. and Mrs. Scelta were deciding on what to do that night (before encountering Mr. Fato at La Causa Bella), they thought that it would be a nice idea to go out for a meal since it's not something they often do. With that decision achieved, they then had the troublesome problem of deciding on where to go. "Shall we go to the Indian or to the Italian pizza restaurant that everyone is always talking about?" asks Mrs. Scelta to her salivating husband.

"That's a really tough call. On the one hand, we know the Indian always throws up good nosh, and on the other hand it would be nice to try something new for a change," replies the husband.

"In that case, since we can't decide, let us leave it to chance to decide. Do you have a coin? Go on, flip for it; heads is the Indian, tails is the pizzeria."

Agreeing that this would be a great way to 'randomly' decide which restaurant to go to, the husband retrieves a coin from amongst the lint in his pocket, and places it on his thumb nail, whilst planting the end of his thumbnail into the skin of his index finger, priming himself for the big flip. *Pizzeria. Come on. Tails. It's much cheaper...* he thinks. Releasing the pressure from his thumbnail, he flicks the coin into the air and lets it land on the floor, where it spins a couple of times and falls flat. A smile comes to his lips - it's tails.

To most people, this might seem like a totally random outcome. Let us return to our good friend Dictionary.com for a definition of random:

–adjective
proceeding, made, or occurring without definite aim, reason, or pattern: the random selection of numbers.[1]

---

[1] http://dictionary.reference.com/browse/random (09/2008)

Was the outcome for the coin landing on tails random? Did it have no preceding reason? I contest that this was, in this sense, random. This event, and this outcome, was determinable, predictable. If I, like Laplace's little friend, was able to know all the variables that were acting on the coin, then I would know exactly what side it would land on. If I could map out every contour of Mr. Scelta's fingers and thumb, and all the surfaces of the room even, if I could know the value of every single force that would come into play, the location of every air molecule, the architecture of the coin, the laws of physics that would dictate how the coin travelled through the air, and how it would react upon hitting the ground at such-and-such an angle (you get the point...), then I could predict exactly what side it would land on. This is a determinable, and hence determined, outcome. From all these known or knowable variables, it is then hard to agree that there was no preceding reason to the coin landing on tails. The coin landed on tails for many very mundane and physical reasons, and was not random in this sense. But to the human mind, this action is seemingly random. It has the illusion of being random, and that is good enough for the most of us.

What this illustrates is the difference between randomness and unpredictability. What may seem random most probably isn't, but it is more likely to be unpredictable to the observer. Probability, then, in the context of this coin flip, is reliant on the fact that there is imperfect knowledge of all the variables. Some determinists argue that there is no such thing, even, as probability, because they adhere to a narrow frequency interpretation of probability. This belief is the belief that there is only one possible outcome, which has been determined, and thus there is no such thing as probability. However, I would prefer to see it in the former context – that we don't have complete knowledge of the variables[1], and thus when flipping a coin, to the observer, there is a perceived 50/50 probability of flipping a tail.

When you look at coin tosses en masse, at a large number of them, they then exhibit probabilistic tendencies, they show trends. From these trends, people can extrapolate general probabilities, based on imperfect knowledge. Individually,

---

[1] This is known as the Bayesian interpretation of probability.

though, if we knew all the variables, all coin throws would be determinable – you could accurately predict their outcome.

Jonathan M.S. Pearce

What a naughty girl! I blame her parents...

As an anecdote that might well explain the nature of determinism, I will bring into play my daytime job – I work as a teacher in a primary school. The primary school is a fascinating environment to gauge how and if determinism works, as you see children from year to year reacting with and in their environment both at home and at school, and you also see the influence of nature, of their parents, of their genes. More often than not, (even though children are complex creatures, full of and victim to an incredible number of variables, not all of them obvious or known) one can predict their behaviour as a result of parental or extra-curricular influences, or one can guess those influences based on observing their behaviour.

In my experience, the children that behave badly (or indeed well, though sadly the better behaved kids get overshadowed by the worse behaved kids, as being well behaved is the expected norm) almost always seem to have mitigating circumstances. That is, for a particular 10 year old girl who exhibits bad behaviour such as shoplifting, carrying a knife, using abusive language and having a very low attention span (sadly, these things do happen at that age!), it is very easy to find reasons why she is acting in that manner. Quite often, you look at the parents (at whether they have similar traits to their daughter or abuse drugs etc.), or lack thereof, the socio-economic background of the family or neighbourhood, the instances of trauma in their childhood, their health and hygiene, the love and attention that they might or might not have received. Essentially, in my experience, one can almost always account for a child's behaviour by knowing the variables that have affected them throughout their life. With their genes, and their environment, and with the way their genes cause them to react to their environment in a certain way, and with their past experiences, they are *bound* to act in the way they are acting. As is everybody else. It is almost a truism, an obvious thing to say – we are who we are, and that is our biology and our experiences up to this moment. For that girl to have pulled a knife out in the local newsagent, I doubt that one single person will attribute that behaviour to either randomness, or the fact that she had just willed it without some kind of motive or background. It is more likely that people would look for the reason why she decided to do it. We all seem to live our lives in the knowledge that there are *causal circumstances* for everyone. That means that in any given decision, 1) the make up of the agent, and 2) the make up of the world at that moment, both define the choice made; and these two systems, together, make up the causal circumstance.

When I come across badly behaved or excessively needy children, I am saddened. I am saddened because they are generally dealing with their lot in the only way they know how – using the genes they have been dealt, and using the experiences that they have undergone up to that point to help them deal with any situation at hand. Children, so often, do not have the emotional toolbox from which to draw the correct tool to deal with a given situation in the way that one might hope. The simple reality is what differentiates them from the next person who is behaving well at that point is that the first child has been dealt a bum hand. Whether that is a poor set of genes, or a set of previous historical experiences that have had severely negative impacts on them, is neither here nor there. These are both sets of variables that are out of their control, yet determine how they interact with people and situations and 'choices'.

It is interesting to note that a fair bit of research has been done into environmental enrichment, which shows how the brain can be affected by the information processing it does in its immediate environment. Good research has been done with rats, but the same seems to happen in humans, as far as we can work out. Brains in a richer and more stimulating environment develop more synapses, and other brain mechanics, which result in a more complex brain. In other words, if you brought a child up in a bare-walled room with few or no toys, or anything of interest, the brain of that child would be less developed, less complex and smaller than the brain of a child brought up in a room with interesting and stimulating toys, walls and paraphernalia that promote interaction and information processing. Furthermore, it is thought that the stimulated brain is better at combating diseases and the conditions of aging in later life. These statistics bear out the theory:

Children that receive impoverished stimulation due to being confined to cots without social interaction or reliable caretakers in low quality orphanages show

31

severe delays in cognitive and social development. 12% of them if adopted after 6 months of age show autistic or mildly autistic traits later at four years of age. Some children in such impoverished orphanages at two and half years of age still fail to produce intelligible words, though a year of foster care enabled such children to catch up in their language in most respects. Catch-up in other cognitive functioning also occurs after adoption, though problems continue in many children if this happens after the age of 6 months.

Such children show consistent with research upon experiment animals marked differences in their brains compared to children from normally stimulating environments. They have reduced brain activity in the orbital prefrontal cortex, amygdala, hippocampus, temporal cortex, and brain stem. They also showed less developed white matter connections between different areas in their cerebral cortices particularly the uncinate fasciculus.[1]

---

[1] http://en.wikipedia.org/wiki/Environmental_enrichment_(neural) (08/2009) This quote from the article sites these sources:

Kaler, S. R. Freeman, B. J. (1994) "Analysis of environmental deprivation: cognitive and social development in Romanian orphans". J Child Psychol Psychiatry. 35: 769-781. PubMed

Rutter, M., Andersen-Wood, L., Beckett, C., Bredenkamp, D., Castle, J., Groothues, C., Kreppner, J., Keaveney, L., Lord, C. O'Connor. T. G. (1999) "Quasi-autistic patterns following severe early global privation. English and Romanian Adoptees (ERA) Study Team". J Child Psychol Psychiatry. 40: 537-549. PubMed

Windsor, J., Glaze, L. E. Koga, S. F. (2007) "Language acquisition with limited input: Romanian institution and foster care". J Speech Lang Hear Res. 50: 1365-1381. PubMed

Beckett, C., Maughan, B., Rutter, M., Castle, J., Colvert, E., Groothues, C., Kreppner, J., Stevens, S., O'Connor T, G. Sonuga-Barke, E. J. (2006) "Do the effects of early severe deprivation on cognition persist into early adolescence? Findings from the English and Romanian adoptees study". Child Dev. 77: 696-711. PubMed

Chugani, H. T., Behen, M. E., Muzik, O., Juhasz, C., Nagy, F. Chugani, D. C. (2001) "Local brain functional activity following early deprivation: a study of postinstitutionalized Romanian orphans". Neuroimage. 14: 1290-1301. PubMed

Eluvathingal, T. J., Chugani, H. T., Behen, M. E., Juhasz, C., Muzik, O., Maqbool, M., Chugani, D. C. Makki, M. (2006) "Abnormal brain connectivity in children after

The importance of the environment on a child (and an adult) cannot be overstated here (as we know from research into emotional intelligence), and prove to be vital ingredients in determining the outcome of a child's future.

All this leads us to examine how we react to the knowledge of these variables. Such fascinating themes emerge in the well acclaimed novel (and adapted film) by Bernhard Schlink – *The Reader*. The book revolves around a teenage boy brought up in 1958 post war Germany. The boy starts a passionate affair with a 36 year-old tram conductress. Some months later, she disappears as he spends more time with his school friends. Some years later, as he attends law school, he observes one of the war trials taking place, and sees this lady in the dock as being one of a group of guards responsible for the death of 300 Polish women in a fire in a church. He comes to realise that she cannot read, and understands why she made him read so much to her. However, her inability to read plays a major part in making her the most culpable in the group for the deaths of those prisoners. Hanna, the lady, does not reveal her illiteracy out of shame, much to her disadvantage. The really interesting theme of this book, for me, is how it deals with moral responsibility, and how this is seen when we know more about the perpetrator of any given crime. We spend many chapters feeling sympathy for this woman, understanding her, somewhat, and then we find out the horrific act that she was involved in and was culpable for. The narrator, older and reflecting on it whilst at Auschwitz years later, states:

> *I wanted simultaneously to understand Hanna's crime and condemn it. But it was too terrible for that. When I tried to understand it, I had the feeling that I was failing to condemn it as it must be condemned. When I condemned it as it must be condemned, there was no room for understanding. But even as I wanted to understand Hanna, failing to understand her meant failing her all over again. I could not resolve this. I wanted to pose myself both tasks –*

---

early severe socioemotional deprivation: a diffusion tensor imaging study". Pediatrics. 117: 2093-2100.

> *understanding and condemnation. But it was impossible to do both.*
>
> *(Schlink 2008, p. 156)*

This truly insightful quote really exhibits the difficulty that one has in retributive punishment, in punishing people for vengeance, if we understand the mechanisms that made them commit the crime in the first place. To simplify her predicament, could she have refused to accompany the prisoners? Could she disobey SS orders? And knowing her inability to read, how did this interplay with her culpability? Moreover, if she had been a less amenable character, but that we could know that her less agreeable characteristics were as a result of definite things (her strict and obscure upbringing, and a genetic predisposition from her father to be a control-freak), does this make her any more or less culpable? Do we have any more or less sympathy for her? Is she any more or less responsible for her actions? These make for very interesting thought experiments, and can really make us think about how we view punishment and moral responsibility, and certainly something over which I will be spilling ink later in the book.

Wear your genes on your sleeve

And that brings us nicely onto the importance of genes. Genes are the building blocks from which we are made. Within all cells, there are chromosomes which contain genes (all the genes in the chromosome(s) are known as the genome). A gene is made up of DNA[1] which is coded in certain ways, depending on what the gene does. The vast majority of organisms have a large set of genes – long strands of DNA. Something obvious that a gene might define is eye colour, but sets of genes may define a personality trait. All characteristics of an organism are known as phenotypes, whether they are physical or non-physical. Genetic mutations that can lead to evolutionary activity happen when these genes are replicated (copied), and minor mistakes can be made in the copying of these incredibly complex sequences (these new types of gene are known as alleles). Alleles sometimes, but not all of the time, result in different traits. Genes themselves don't often cause a particular trait per gene, but combinations of genes give phenotypic traits. These traits mingle, in humans, when the sperm, with the genome of the father, combines with an egg, with the genome from the mother. Thus, at inception, we really are the product of our parents – our looks and our initial characteristics are determined by the codes within our cells, making us, initially, who we are.

The argument remains over whether we are the product of nature or nurture; genes or environment, which has been argued ad nauseam over the last hundred years or so. The most commonly accepted answer is both. And to someone who is born to their two parents, and then lives with those same two parents for eighteen years has a very strong chance of being, characteristically, very like their parents. The nature *and* the nurture are being provided, essentially, from the same source. There is not an awful lot of chance of turning out particularly different from your parents in this situation, unless you have a particular combination of genes[2] that might make you fairly different from your individual parents. Either way, you are fairly

---

[1] Deoxyribonucleic acid which was discovered in the 1940s, primarily made of four proteins, ascribed the letters A, C, G and T.
[2] This is where recessive and dominant genes come into play – but I have not the urge to give a full biology lesson here...

determined here. As they say, the apple does not fall far from the tree.

If you fancy popping down to a shop, of a Saturday, to buy a lottery ticket, one has to mark off six numbers on a ticket of 49 numbers (in the UK). These six numbers give you a chance of one in 13,983,816 of winning by having your 6 preferred numbers being randomly chosen. That means with 49 numbers, there are 13,983,816 different combinations of six numbers. That is quite huge, with a very short set of numbers. Now, if we take the human genome as having somewhere around 25,000 genes, then the combinations are staggering, especially in combining the two parental genomes. In fact, original estimates were that we had some 100,000 genes, since we imagined ourselves to be so much more complex than other animals. However, we probably have only a third more genes than a simple roundworm. That said, there are still some estimates as high as 42,000 genes for the human genome. Each of these genes have coding parts (that determine what the gene does) and non-coding parts (that determine when the gene is expressed, when it is to kick into action, so to speak). Interestingly, genes only comprise about 1-2% of the human genome, with the rest being made up of "noncoding regions" which may determine when, where and how many proteins are made.[1] It's actually these proteins that do a lot of the leg-work in creating our organic structures and functions. Over to the experts:

> *The constellation of all proteins in a cell is called its* **proteome**. *Unlike the relatively unchanging genome, the dynamic proteome changes from minute to minute in response to tens of thousands of intra- and extracellular environmental signals. A protein's chemistry and behavior are specified by the gene sequence and by the number and identities of other proteins made in the same cell at the same time and with which it associates and reacts.*[2]

---

[1] Human Genome Project information from
http://www.ornl.gov/sci/techresources/Human_Genome/project/info.shtml (11/2009)
[2] ibid.

Now, if you imagine this huge set of variables in the body, and superimpose them onto the even more massive set of variables that is our environment (billions upon billions of atoms and molecules and forces), then you have a truly incredible set of variables that influence our lives. One can certainly understand the differences between people, or the differences between similar people based upon differences in environment. This partially explains the differences that can occur in identical twins (who have identical genomes) that live in the same house, and have the same parents. Even minute differences in the environment, from the womb onwards, can have large impacts on the outcome of the character, personality and general make-up of the twins.

As I have said, genetic influence doesn't necessarily depend upon individual genes. Not at all. In fact, if you were to talk to the average geneticist, they would say that the most annoying term used by the media, when writing about the genetics industry, is the term 'gene for'. This is a headline winner, used often in such a way that "Scientists have discovered the gene for bad breath / tennis proficiency / sexuality / mathematical ability / dress sense" (delete as appropriate). In reality, of course, phenotypes are determined by numbers or combinations of genes. For example, it is thought that height in humans is determined by over one hundred genes, thus rendering the term 'gene for height' incorrect. However, just because there is more than one gene, and often a complicated and as yet unknown quantity or combination of genes, it does not mean that phenotypes are not genetically determined. It simply means that working out exactly what determines the phenotype is a wholly more substantive and complex task.

There is something called genetic determinism that posits that an organism is entirely dependent and resultant on the genes (and proteins) that they are dealt. At first glance, this is easily dismissed, but I think people are often too hasty to dismiss it. A genetic determinist would state that an organism's set of genes dictate entirely how that organism will turn out, as might be evident for certain hereditary diseases, but also for their behaviour. However, the importance of environment, and how that can shape the outcome of an organism, is clearly evident. If we took Mr. Fato (the restaurant owner) and rewound his life, picked him up, and put him in and had him grow up in an orphanage in downtown Cairo, we can imagine that, though

37

he would be the same person in many respects, exhibiting many identical characteristics, we would predict that he would also be different in many ways. The experiences that he would have being brought up in an orphanage in Cairo, and then maybe living on the streets (and being influenced by the role models in his life there), would have a profound affect on his personality, of who he becomes. The same man, being brought up by his caring immigrant Italian family in the safe and welcoming environment of a Cotswold village might produce someone very different. Who we are, what makes us the people we see ourselves as, is a combination of our genes and our environment (and what we learn from it).

In a chicken and egg scenario, it is clear that when we are talking about a human, it is the genes that come first. The embryo develops, and though we do experience things in the womb, we already have our genetic blueprint, and out we pop with a toolkit to face the world. So from our inception, it is our genes that dictate how we act with our environment, it is the genes that come first. There is a finite regression, when we look at an adult, that ends on rewind with a set of cells and genes. Each experience after our inception has an outcome that is decided by our genes and what we have learnt from life before, and all those experiences were decided by our genes and we had learnt from life before, and...so on and so forth. It is the genes that end that regression, and it is the genes inside you that dictate whether you will react excessively angrily to your football team's loss at the weekend, or not. So, in one sense or another, and with some caveats, one could say that we are genetically determined.

"It's OK sir, there's always Quantum!"

For some time, now, it has been evident that there is a new kid at science school, and being the new kid from the Big Bang, everyone else in this relative backwater school thinks he is cool. And his name is Quantum. You'll hear the teachers all saying "Quantum this" and "Quantum that"; he's starting to get in all the teams and all the clubs; and quite frankly he's getting a little too big for his boots.

You see, when discussing determinism and free will and suchlike, it is virtually impossible to get through a lengthy conversation without the mention of quantum physics. For those of you that don't know your quantum physics from your elbow, let me attempt to explain. The blind leading the blind.

Way back yonder, in the time of Sir Isaac Newton, there was a scientific chap called ... Sir Isaac Newton (though he probably wasn't a Sir by then). He had the fortune to be sitting under a tree when an apple fell on his head, as we all know[1]. This was great, because it gave him the opportunity to realise that terrestrial gravity extends in an inverse square proportion, naturally. This enabled him to theorise about universal gravitation and its effects on the planetary system. A long way down the line, and with no small dollops of help and brain activity from such clever-clogs as Albert Einstein[2], we arrive at the general theory of relativity. This basically describes gravitation in terms of space and time (also known as space-time – a similar concept to ham-cheese, which should be a new sandwich filler[3]). It forms the basis of most cosmological theories, including black holes and gravitational lending. However, in recent years, where once general relativity was thought to be the foundation of physics, now, a second pillar has been built – quantum physics. General relativity does a very good job of explaining how physics works on a large scale, but as soon as we were able to observe how atomic and subatomic particles interacted, we realised that general

---

[1] Actually, it most probably didn't, but he did watch an apple fall from a tree, and it (or descendents of this tree) still exists, according to the King's School in Grantham or the National Trust's Woolsthorpe Manor, depending on who you believe.

[2] Einstein published his theory in 1916, and it still stands today.

[3] Strangely enough, my friend has recently told me that this is actually a sandwich filler in Denmark!

relativity couldn't answer all the questions. I say *we*, but of course, I had nothing to do with it. To this day, it is still unknown how the two will be reconciled.

The major issue here is that, in quantum mechanics, one cannot specify the velocity and location of a subatomic particle with 100% certainty, and there are issues with the fact that observing a particle seems to have an effect on the particle itself. This is known as the Heisenberg Uncertainty Principle, indicating a possible inability to accurately predict such particles. It is now thought that all known objects obey the laws of quantum mechanics, and that mechanics of general relativity, classical mechanics, is simply quantum mechanics, but on a much bigger scale[1].

What this, in the form of the Copenhagen interpretation[2], means is that there is indeterminacy to quantum mechanics. This interpretation by a Danish physicist, sets to answer the criticism that the reason there is indeterminacy is that we simply don't know all the facts yet, and it stipulates that the universe is probabilistic, and not deterministic. However, being a theory (or an interpretation) it is open to debate, and there are other interpretations (many and varied), some of which are consistent with determinism, such as the Bohm interpretation. David Bohm, a British physicist, had different ideas, declaring that there might well be hidden variables that we just don't know about, and this is a valid, if controversial, alternative to the Copenhagen interpretation. Einstein, who was one of the founders of quantum mechanics himself, was a critic of indeterminacy, being an advocate of determinism to the point that he declared, "God does not play dice with the universe." Einstein and Neils Bohr, the Danish physicist, debated the seeming existence of randomness in systems for years.

Ted Honderich (2002), a British philosopher, states that there is a fundamental issue with the Copenhagen Theory inasmuch as it:

> *...has been on the table for about 75 years. In that time, no evidence in a standard sense has been produced for there being any such chance events.*

---

[1] Please note that this is a truly simplistic view being given here!

[2] Interpretations can often differ wildly in accounting for the evidence that we have accumulated. Different interpretations can lead people in completely different directions.

There is no direct and unequivocal experimental evidence at all [his emphasis]...- That is really a remarkable fact that needs to be paid attention - 75 years is a long time in science.

(Honderich 2002, p. 73-74)

Honderich also ponders why we have not seen these chance events manifest themselves in macro-reality – why has quantum indeterminacy not caused a spoon to levitate, and so on? He also asserts that, as determinist physicists might claim that there are hidden variables to quantum physics, so it is the same for Free Willers, who must maintain there is a hidden variable that allows them to sneak in a mechanism that accounts for free will in the system of a decision in a causal network.

As with most types of philosophy, you can regress the arguments back further and further until you reach an axiom, or a first basic assumption – almost like a faith statement. René Descartes (a Frenchman who sparked off heated debate about the mind-body problem[1]) boiled everything down through what were known as his six meditations (which set out to discard anything that wasn't absolutely certain, in favour of expounding that which can be known with absolute surety), to the famous phrase "cogito ergo sum" or "I think, therefore I am". You can doubt everything in life, but by being able to think, by being able to doubt, you are proving that you, yourself, exist. This, of course, does not mean that the body definitely has to exist, since the senses are known to be unreliable. Therefore, the only indubitable thing is the thinking mind. Descartes explains this using the wax argument, whereby you can observe a piece of wax, noting its characteristics, such as texture, colour, size, smell and suchlike. If you move the wax towards a source of heat, these characteristic traits of the wax change entirely. Yet, to the thinking person, it is still a piece of wax. This shows that your senses cannot reliably grasp what the nature of the wax is; this is something that can only be achieved by the mind.

In the case of the argument for determinism, with regards to the uncertainty principle, we need not go so far. However, I would state, as my own faith statement, that there is a unified theory that connects relativity and quantum mechanics,

---

[1] We'll look at this a little later.

somewhere, lurking in the shady realms of the science resource cupboard. I believe that in order for the universe as we know it to work reliably on classical physics, the theories of classical physics need to, themselves, be built of reliable bricks. This is often known as a unified field theory, wrapping quantum and classical physics up in one cosy blanket. Without this, then, physics, and science in general, become a disjointed and unwieldy affair. This is the Holy Grail for scientists that will lead to, if it exists, a 'Theory Of Everything', which has been the lifetime ambition of clever people such as Stephen Hawking. Many scientists are working on this, but as yet, it remains elusive. Personally, I think it exists, and I think quantum mechanics will be united with its cousin in a fashion that makes clearer sense of what is happening around us.

So why is quantum mechanics so important? Why do we care about Heisenberg?! Depending on how you view it, quantum mechanics can be either overrated in its appeal, or absolutely vital. One could argue that, if certain things, on occasion, are seemingly random at subatomic level, and the probabilities so tiny as to not affect the science of the more human scaled things, then what is there to worry about? The indeterminacy of subatomic particles is clearly not affecting the determinacy of relative physics, so there is no issue. Part of me thinks that this is fine, that there is no need to entertain the idea of subatomic uncertainty, of minute randomness. On the other hand, does this render Laplace's Demon impotent? By not knowing the exact velocity and location of a photon at a given time under observation, does this make him not quite as clever as we thought he was? Or since the demon would not be observing photons in order to affect them, and cause them to be uncertain, by simply being able to calculate their velocity and location from mapping them out from the Big Bang with his inordinately large calculating capacity, does he actually bypass the uncertainty principle? To be honest, it would take a much greater brain than mine to answer these questions.

In the free will debate, quantum indeterminacy is used by some people in claiming that it plays a role in decision making and brain computation. Somehow, it is argued, this allows for free will to flourish. The fact is, this is simply an idea, perhaps a straw eagerly clutched, with no real knowledge of how it can realistically be applied. The problems that such controversial theorists have to come up against are firstly that it implies indeterminacy giving man control over his own behaviour. Nest is the fact that there is no agreed mechanism or manner in which quantum mechanics can actually affect the human brain and thought –

> *The temperature, time, and length scales of the human brain are far above the temperatures and scales at which quantum decoherence occur making it questionable whether quantum mechanics plays any role in the functioning of the brain at all. To deal with this problem, some physicists most notably Roger Penrose argue that microtubules rather than neuron and synapses are important in cognition, a position that most neurologists find absurd.*[1]

The other issue that quantum faces, within the context of consciousness and the brain, is the fact that quantum physics does not, as any theory of consciousness struggles to do, explain how we have a feeling of experience. It cannot explain how I have an experience of the colour red and so on (these experiences are known as *qualia*). This will be expanded upon later, where its relevance will become clear.

But perhaps one of the most powerful arguments about quantum indeterminacy, and how it cannot affect determinism in a causal chain of events is as follows. Doug had a choice over whether to do X or Y. Determinism would posit that Doug had no choice to carry out X in always choosing Y, whereas free will would state that Doug chose to carry out X, but could also have chosen Y. Now, assuming that quantum indeterminacy is true, then not everything that happens is physically and knowably determined – some of the most minute things are indeterminately caused. So, does this mean that Doug could have chosen Y, with the addition of indeterminacy? No. In both versions of determinism, the variables that input into his 'decision' are out of control of Doug. Either X was carried out as an action as a result of a 100% causal chain, with no aspect of indeterminacy, or X was carried out as a result of a mixture of a causal chain and the indeterminate behaviour of subatomic particles. In both options, the 'decision' made is still made as a result of a previously determined causal chain, it just so

---

[1] http://ww.knowledgerush.com/kr/encyclopedia/Quantum_indeterminacy/ (08/2009)

happens that in one of the options, part of that chain includes quantum indeterminacy (a bit of random). Thus, you can say that quantum indeterminacy *caused* the decision to be made in such a way. In both methods, Doug has no free will, his options are determined, whether one of those options had an aspect of randomness in its chain or not. Someone that accepts quantum indeterminacy into their version of determinism can be called a *near-determinist*. For Doug to make a cup of tea based on variables that were built upon some random subatomic movements still does not mean he has control over those variables involved in deciding to make the tea.

So it seems to me that quantum mechanics doesn't necessarily present as much of a problem to the argument for determinism as some people grant it. Quantum mechanics prevails as a universal hope for many scientists to answer many conundrums in science, but also pops up in inventive ideas, science fiction and new technology. I have to say that I can just imagine a meeting in the Pentagon one day between the President of the United States and his war cabinet and other important bigwigs.

"Mr. President, we have tried everything. We started off with troops, then we tried hearts and minds, and we have trained up their armies for five years, and educated their children, but they still don't seem to like us," says one uniformed man.

"What can we do to cure this Middle Eastern problem, then?" replies the President.

"Well sir, we are left with only one option. We have developed a quantum computer. We are in the process of putting in all the options that we could think of into the Middle East model to see what comes up as the best idea, including buying all of Afghanistan a pair of Nike trainers, opening a cheese factory in Nazareth (Cheeses of Nazareth...) and only allowing trampolines to be used in Iraq on a Tuesday. The quantum computation will be done in record time, and we should soon have a policy answer."

"So you don't need me to tell you what to do? You just ask a computer..."

"Sir, it's not just *any* computer, it's a quantum computer..."

Quantum could well be the future, but as it is now, scientists and philosophers are trying to shoe-horn it into anything they can get their minds on. Quite often, it is certainly possible that they are wide of the mark.

Jonathan M.S. Pearce

PART II – WHAT ARE WE?

Before we delve deeper into the three approaches to free will that I have started to explain, it would be prudent to look at more fundamental building blocks that underpin much of how we view the field. It is like trying to explain how an engine works without knowing how combustion works; like learning to cook without knowing anything about taste.

Er, what is causality?

Yes, this is a term that I have previously mentioned, but one that we perhaps take for granted. Causality is the relationship between two events – the cause, and the effect, whereby the effect is a direct consequence of the first event, the cause. This sounds a lot simpler than the whole subject really is. In its simplest form, a cue ball in billiards being hit by the player may hit a red ball in such a way that it causes it to roll off into a pocket. The cause for this would be seen to be the cue ball, and prior to that, the player. But if we consider something like the credit crunch, sweeping the world in 2008 and 2009, then to find the cause for this would be somewhat harder. One might hear the statement that "too much borrowing was the cause of the credit crunch", but although this was a contributing factor, there were many other causal factors, such as the supply and demand of the housing market, the devaluation of the pound, the emergent markets in the East, the risky lending strategies of the world's banks, and so on. The cause of the credit crunch was multifarious, having many different aspects from many different sources.

Let us look back to the coin flip that we talked about earlier. If the coin lands on tails, and we ask ourselves "what caused it to land on tails", would we be able to answer simplistically? The reality is that every variable from the position of each air molecule, to the force and direction of force exerted on the coin by the flipper, to the forces of friction when the coin hits the floor has a causal influence on the coin. This network works co-operatively to cause the coin to land on tails.

This is what can be termed as the *causal circumstance*, as previously mentioned[1]. So, although the outcome appears random to the human eye, and effectively without cause, the intricacies of the causal chain, of the causal circumstance, are knowable to Laplace's Demon.

So, as philosopher Daniel Dennett (2003) asks, can we therefore posit that the death of JFK, if we regress the causal chain backwards, was caused by the Big Bang? In fact, is *everything* the result of the Big Bang? This is where we need to investigate the difference between *necessary* and *sufficient* conditions. You see, all the events that led to JFK's death were sufficient to create the situation where he died, but it is possible to think of another possible world, parallel to ours, where maybe JFK's best friend was left-handed and not right, or was a woman and not a man, and he was *still* murdered. In this case, it was not *necessary* that his best friend was right-handed, because JFK was still murdered in the world where his friend was left-handed. Consequently, the variable of the handedness of his friend is merely sufficient, and not necessary. Statements may also be conditional such as "If shape X was a triangle, it would have 3 sides" but this does not mean that X being a triangle actually caused it to have 3 sides, since it is a definition of condition.

As Dennett (2003) points out, there are often problems in working out causality in a given situation. Here he gives a version of a famous thought experiment:

> *Everybody in the French Foreign Legion outpost hates Fred and wants him dead. During the night before Fred's trek across the desert, Tom poisons the water in his canteen. Then, Dick, not knowing of Tom's intervention, pours out the (poisoned) water and replaces it with sand. Finally, Harry comes along and pokes holes in the canteen, so that the "water" will slowly run out. Later, Fred awakens and sets out on his trek, provisioned with his canteen. Too late he finds his canteen nearly empty, but besides, what remains is sand, not water, not even poisoned water. Fred dies of thirst. Who caused his death?*
>
> *(Dennett 2003, p.74)*

---

[1] See **What a naughty girl! I blame her parents...**

In this example, it is virtually impossible to find what most people would see as the cause. The cause of his death was thirst, and the cause of his thirst was... well, one could argue that deep into the night. It can be a philosophical quandary trying to work out causes, and sometimes, there simply is no (easy) answer.

The implications of this are that it is very difficult to know, to really know, the causes within a causal chain, with our limited knowledge. Perhaps even Laplace's Demon would not be able to differentiate necessary variables from merely sufficient variables. So it seems that a deterministic universe can still contain (unanswerable?) questions of causality, but still remain determined. *Determinism* does not equate directly to *causality*. Not knowing what caused something does not equate to it not being caused, and not being determined.

Jonathan M.S. Pearce

My intentions are noble, Madam.

We've looked a little at causality – what causes things to happen – so it would be a good time to think about *intention*. When we talk about willing certain actions, we more often than not infer an idea of intention onto the events; we believe that we intend to do certain actions before we do them. Having an intention is defined by the Oxford Dictionary of Philosophy (2008) as:

> *...to be in a state of mind that is favourably directed towards bringing about (or maintaining, or avoiding) some state of affairs, but which is not a mere desire or wish, since it also sets the subject on a course to bring that state of affairs about.*

However, there is the issue that arises between accidentally doing something, and doing it intentionally. Moreover, there is the matter of automatic actions, such as if you were playing football and wanted to kick a ball that was 10 metres away, is the movement of running intentional? Is placing one foot in front of another intentional? Is the act of breathing faster intentional? And so on. The very presence of volition[1] might also be beyond a person's control, which interferes with the notion of intention. In most cases in people, someone's intention is seen as the causal thought process that precedes any consciously willed action.

As hinted previously, automatic actions are often perceived as less intentional, and bodily actions are often placed under a larger intentional umbrella of action, as in the football example. When we make a cup of tea, we see that as an intention: "I intend to make a cup of tea," we might say to ourselves. We most certainly don't consciously say (and thus explicitly intend), "I will straighten my arm and extend my index finger to press the button to turn on the kettle, and then I will bend my arms and hands and fingers in such a way as to operate the cupboard door, so I can peruse the cups in order to select my preference (although, it'll always be the one with the naked lady on, whose clothes were meant to disappear when you put hot

---

[1] Volition being the act of will to do something, rather than the intended physical movement it might cause.

50

liquid in it, until on its first day, my Granny put it in the dishwasher so now she is permanently disrobed).”

Desires also confuse matters, since they can be similar to intentions, but have a longer term approach that encapsulate many intentions and actions. In desiring to become healthier, one may intend to buy green tea, and make green tea instead of fully caffeinated tea with full fat milk. The two are clearly different here. If there is a long period of time between intention and action, then *plans* can be differentiated from *intentions*. “I plan to get a dog next year” is somewhat different to “I am going [intending] to the dog home now to buy a rescued puppy”. The plans pave the way for the later intentions, making them much more likely to occur successfully, but not actually causing the behaviour to happen.

So when talking about intention, one is talking about conscious thoughts that precede the action carried out by someone.

Jonathan M.S. Pearce

Is everything just stuff?

I feel it is now important to consider the following question: From what point of view do you view the world? In other words, what is your worldview? I ask this, because what we think and believe is going on around us in our universe depends almost entirely on the foundation layer of how we view the universe.

The initial choice we make, often before even thinking about whether or not a god exists out there (or in us, or that we are made of) is whether we believe everything in the universe to be of physical matter or whether we allow for the existence of anything *supernatural*. This position of *naturalism* entails the belief that nature is all there is, that everything is physical and material. This would therefore exclude the belief in God or gods, ghosts, magic, miracles and the like. This overall view is sometimes called *metaphysical naturalism*. This worldview leads on to what is known as *methodological naturalism* which is essentially the methods taken on by virtually all scientists the world over, since it underpins our approach to and our understanding of science.

> ***Methodological naturalism,*** *sometimes called* ***scientific naturalism,*** *is an epistemological[1] view that is specifically concerned with practical methods for acquiring knowledge, irrespective of one's metaphysical or religious views. It requires that hypotheses be explained and tested only by reference to natural causes and events. Explanations of observable effects are considered to be practical and useful only when they hypothesize natural causes (i.e., specific mechanisms, not indeterminate miracles). Methodological naturalism is the principle underlying all of modern science.[2]*

Thus, if a naturalist lost their car keys, they would straight away rule out the possibility of a poltergeist misplacing them. Likewise, a naturalist would look at religious miracles and say "they couldn't have happened", claiming that a more likely

---

[1] Epistemology, by the way, is the study of knowledge, in case you were wondering, or the dictionary was too far away.

[2] http://en.wikipedia.org/wiki/Naturalism_(philosophy) (09/2009)

explanation is that they were false claims, were not witnessed accurately, were not understood properly or were hallucinatory visions, amongst other options. Therefore, someone's underlying naturalism can mean that they, methodologically, rule out the possibility of a God, or certainly one that interferes on earth, and with the system of the universe (although it can still allow for deism, the God of the philosopher, that starts the ball rolling at the beginning, but does not interfere thereafter). Most people, in the hustle bustle of their daily lives, are fairly naturalist. There are not many things in your daily life that you put down to supernatural, or non-scientifically rational reasons. Any product you have bought, any new invention, is tested scientifically, and as far as I know, the methods for their research and development and for their manufacture are soundly natural and scientific. Supernaturalism is reserved for only those special moments, it seems.

However, many people, when looking at their core beliefs, would not strictly[1] come under the umbrella of naturalism. For example, anyone believing in a God that interferes in our lives on a physical or spiritual level would not normally be considered a naturalist. Furthermore, if you believe in the existence of a soul, then you are a generally considered to be outside the realms of naturalism. Consciousness, too, is another area of interest when discussing naturalist worldviews, as we will also discover in the coming sections.

As science has advanced, there has been a subtle shift towards naturalism over the centuries. Some people even argue that science, or scientism, is the new kind of religion, that all our answers will come from the realms of science, and our quest for knowledge.

Let us talk a little about the notion of a soul, since it can have an effect on whether one believes that decisions are determined or not, and after all, that is what this book is about.

---

[1] although there is such a thing as religious naturalism.

Jonathan M.S. Pearce

He's a soul man...

The word soul is an outstandingly commonly used word for something that is so outstandingly unknown and undefined. Switch on the radio and you can be assured that you will soon enough hear a song that refers to the soul in some way, and I am not just talking about soul music. It permeates through popular culture all over the world so much so that I would dearly like to know the statistics of the amount of people who believe that humans have souls. I get the feeling that there are quite a few people in the world who would readily admit that they believe in a soul. But, I wager, a hefty proportion of those people would not be able to adequately define and explain what a soul is. In addition, I imagine that they would not be able to explain how it interacts with our earthly bodies, with our minds and with our intentions. I find it staggering that a thing of such unknown quality can be so widely accepted as a concept. And, more importantly, there seems to be absolutely no scientific evidence whatsoever for its existence.

So why do we generally believe, as a species, in something that doesn't necessarily have much of a concrete, evidential foundation? Part of the problem in answering this question comes in defining the term 'soul'. What is a soul? A soul can be many different things depending on where you live and what religion or beliefs you adhere to. To some, a soul is simply an interchangeable word for a form of spirit. To others, it entails much more. Without considering why almost all cultures believe in a soul to some degree, and what this belief entails, it is important to note that most religious notions of a soul (with notable exceptions) are entangled with the perceptions of life and death.

The soul is commonly seen as the essence of human life[1] or a sort of sentient spirit that exists outside of the body. One reason that these types of ideas are so attractive to humans is because it seems to allow the possibility that we can go on living after death. Throughout the ages, humans have been obsessed with death, and we have generally been afraid of it in one way or another. All our efforts, and all our trials and

---

[1] What differentiates us from animals that entitles us to a soul? Or if some animals have souls, where do you draw the line in allowing certain animals to have them, but not other? The debate over whether animals have souls is one for another time!

tribulations could possibly amount to naught unless something existed that prolonged our essence beyond our deaths. Enter stage right the soul.

The soul has the great quality of making us immortal, and that is why, in my most humble of opinions, it is such a universally popular concept. Without even bringing religion into it, you can see the benefits to humanity in believing in the existence of a soul. It allows us the possibility to give purpose to our lives, beyond the daily drudgery; it comforts us when children and babies die without experiencing life as they should; it affords us justice when we see a person so woefully treated in their lives as we imagine them balancing out the unfair life they have had with riches in an afterlife... and so on. But just because it is so attractive, does not mean that it necessarily has to exist. Indeed, that is the very reason it might have been invented! I, for one, would love to have a soul, I would love to be assured that some part of me will exist eternally after I die, or get reincarnated into something else, but, alas, I have never been shown any kind of evidence, any kind of proof, that such a thing exists. This is the power of faith that many people have, and this is the power of faith, in a funny kind of way, that I have in methodological naturalism. I have this faith because throughout my life science and the natural laws of the universe have been adhered to, to my observations[1]. It also seems to me that there have been a great many cases of things that were once inexplicable now being explained through the increase in our knowledge, and the improvements in science.

In religions such as the Christianity, souls receive judgement for that which you do in your earthly life. God either punishes you, or rewards you, for the deeds that you do in your life, and this works as possibly the greatest (historically) consequentialist[2] approach to behaviour management in the history of the world. If you steal that loaf of bread, you will burn in hell forever. Well, I guess I might just go hungry, thanks. I remember visiting the cathedral in the French town of Albi which contains a painting called *The painting of the Last Judgement* (1474-84) (which originally covered more than

---

[1] And at the end of the day, these are the only ones that I can be sure of!

[2] As explained in the final section of the book, this is the idea that behaviour can be controlled by having consequences to certain actions. If the consequences of stealing are burning in hell, then you might think twice about stealing.

200m²). It is a marvellous piece of medieval propaganda that evokes the notion of the classic three-tier structure of heaven, earth and hell. I wonder how a non-literate French peasant would have felt walking into this magnificent building and being confronted with a painting bigger than their house which pictures, at the very top, out of reach and almost out of sight, heaven in all its beauty and purity. In the middle strata, earth stands with people going about their daily lives. And at eye level, and right across the church is hell; people getting boiled alive, monsters of disgusting natures disembowelling and suchlike – it really is horrific. And this represents what will happen to your soul if you sin. Truly powerful stuff, and I urge anyone passing by to visit it.

Aside form being the vehicle with which to evaluate[1] good behaviour, many people actually believe the soul is the locus of human will, the place where will originates, amongst other things. St. Augustine, one of the biggest early influences on Christian theology, stated that the soul was a "special substance, endowed with reason, adapted to rule the body". More modern Christian philosophers have elaborated, saying that souls have thoughts and can feel, that they can believe and commit purposeful actions. However, none can quite agree on exactly where they come from and how they pop into existence, and so there are several differing theories.

Also, the Christian notion of the soul differs among the Christian family, although most believe that the soul is mortal, restored after death by resurrection. Whenever I discuss the notion of the soul with other members of the Tippling Philosophers, there are varying ideas of what the soul is and what it does. Some theories, which are reflected by most mainstream theistic scholars, claim that the soul is a learning sentient entity. In order for this to be the case (past the obvious question of evidence for such a claim), there has to be some discussion over how the soul learns, and whether there are any rules to learning such as might be applied to human (and animal) brains in educational psychology. A teacher such as myself doesn't spend years learning about the pedagogy of teaching to think that it isn't based on some kind of social and biological science. If the soul does this learning as well, then it too must adhere to some kind of educational science, to laws

---

[1] A cynic might say "scare you into"…

that dictate how well it learns. Subsequently, it follows that we then have to entertain the notion that the soul is determined by influences of the past (its learning) and how it learns. In effect, all that a believer in a soul is doing, when positing it as a vehicle for free will, is deferring the problem one layer back to the soul. The soul is equally as victim to the variables that are out of its control, namely the prior learning of the soul (which must then influence its 'decisions') and its 'make-up'. In other words, if Mike, at Tippling Philosophers, decides to offer to buy a round for the boys, then on this model the choice to buy the round doesn't come from his mind, but originates in his soul. However, if the soul has spent all its life being sentient and learning, then it will have experienced life, learnt to be kind, and found out what the benefits to buying the boys a drink might be. This learning that the soul undergoes influences the fact that it makes that choice. At the point of Mike making the choice to buy a round, there are variables for both he and his soul that are outside of their control. Of course, the soul is argued to be a combined entity with the person, but the point remains.

Additionally, what is the soul made of? If it exists, it must exist in some format, and that format must adhere to some kind of rule that keeps it together, otherwise a soul will not have the identity of a soul. A soul must be able to be identified *as a soul*, otherwise it just isn't a soul. So what are the properties that define a soul, and what defines those properties? By claiming the existence of a soul, one is opening themselves up to far more unknowns and questions than the simpler and more plausible option of a soul not existing.[1]

In relation to our notions of free will, how does a soul affect what we have talked about? It appears, to me at any rate, that the soul offers a 'get out of jail free card' to proponents of free will. Without explaining how the soul works, without offering any viable evidence, people posit that it is the root of free will decisions, of intentions. In order for this to be anywhere near an acceptable explanation, I would ask that there be some enlightening of the mechanisms in our earthly bodies that interact with the soul, of how the soul realistically negotiates our intentions and will.

---

[1] Ockham's Razor, as you will see, is a theory which posits that the most simple, efficient and adequate explanation is often the correct one.

I think that Dennett (2003, p. 290) sums it up with aplomb:

> *Frankly mysterious agent causation, quantum indeterminacy in the faculty of practical reason, moral levitation performed by immaterial souls or other spectral puppeteers – at best these doctrines cajole us into diverting our attention from a difficult puzzle and fixating on a conveniently insoluble mystery.*

In the face of an unknown quantity, I would be happier to assume that souls do not exist, and if by some magic they do, I would then posit that they have no affect on our decision-making processes. If anything, Aristotle was closest to the mark in his deliberations of what a soul is, arguing that a thing's soul is in what it does and is not a separate essence from the body. A human's soul is the actuality and totality of the human in *being human* – thinking, being rational, using the intellect, but also doing things. The soul of a hammer is in the hammering, and when the hammer is destroyed, it can no longer hammer, and thus has no soul.

So, I would have to admit that I am not a soul man. The burden of proof, for someone who believes that the soul enables free will, is on them, not just to show that the soul exists, but to explain how it affects free will and intentioned actions.

Consciousness explained?

We have touched lightly on naturalism and the soul, so it would be rude, and a little short-sighted, to forget to mention consciousness. Consciousness is another sticky bog that perhaps potentially undermines any concept of determinism. Unlike the soul, we know consciousness, at least in some way (and possibly not the way we imagine at all), exists. We feel it all the time – back to our Cartesian arguments of thinking, and therefore being. It is incredible that our consciousness is the thing we spend the most time with and yet it is the thing in biology that we understand the least. It can be described as the subjective experience of thoughts, feelings and sensations – of our mind. But that is about where agreement ends amongst philosophers of the mind.

As we were discussing earlier with either naturalism or supernaturalism being foundation blocks to thinking about our beliefs, there are similar issues that we need to consider before we investigate consciousness further – materialism and dualism. There is a version of naturalism known as *materialism* that dictates that everything in the universe is made of matter, including consciousness. A materialist worldview asserts that consciousness is a physical thing that adheres to the laws of science like everything else in the universe. The belief that consciousness is a purely natural, physical phenomena is sometimes known as *monism* – as opposed to *dualism* which asserts that mind and body are separate. A monist, as a result of materialist methodology, could claim that the brain pretty much equals consciousness, and that consciousness adheres to the physical laws of the universe, being essentially a 'physical' phenomenon. The other option of materialists is that consciousness is somehow resultant from biological processes, and is made up of something that is still physical, and adheres to physical laws. The history of the term materialism has been interesting. Originally materialism, according to Descartes, was a very "matter-driven" theory. So when electromagnetism and gravity popped along, the idea of materialism was somewhat blown out of the water, and had to grow to encompass the new states. Personally, I think *physicalism* is a better term to use, since we can posit that consciousness is a state that adheres to the laws of physics, but that we don't properly understand that state yet. Much like people did not understand gravity or electromagnetism way back yonder, we do not fully understand the physics of consciousness.

The dualist, although they might possibly accept that the consciousness adheres to natural laws, believes that consciousness and the brain are separate states; the brain is physical, but consciousness is mental, it's out there beyond the confines of the physical brain. It is another state entirely that needs explaining.

From my experience in Tippling Philosophers, and from seeing many vociferous debates among philosophers of the mind, the mind-body problem embodies some of the most closely fought battles within the realms of philosophy, science and religion. It is something that everyone can engage with, because almost everyone believes that they have some kind of consciousness. I have lost many hours of good sleep throwing emails back and forth with other members of the group in an often exasperated, and angry keyboard-tapping fashion.

The big issue with consciousness, as I mentioned earlier, is that although it is an obviously existent thing, in one form or another, we aren't exactly sure how it works. There are, according to the experts, different types of consciousness: the experience we have of the physical sensations around us (*phenomenal consciousness*), and the verbal representations of our internal reasoning (*access consciousness*) such as perception, introspection and remembering. This latter is most connected to decision-making and intention. There are many interpretations of consciousness, and how the mechanism of the brain 'interacts' with it. For example, one such suggestion is that our senses build up a model of the world around us, a sort of simulated representation, and we make sense of all the data with our brain. Many say that there are philosophical issues with separating the consciousness and the body out, and that humans should be seen as a unified entity.

Language certainly plays a pivotal role within the realms of consciousness, with some arguing that only humans are conscious and only recently so, as a result of the evolution of complex linguistics. I would probably not go so far, but I certainly herald the importance of language both to consciousness and to humanity as a whole. It is very difficult to investigate consciousness and the mind due to the entirely personal and subjective nature of the beast, and our complete inability to access the consciousness of others. However, I would agree with most that the consciousness of animals is far less complex than that of humans, with the main reason being their comparative inability to communicate in such a complex manner. If an elephant was hungry and wanted to eat, I imagine its thought processes would be, internally, primarily pictorial and 'urge-like'. On the other hand, a human has a consciousness full of internal dialogue and nuance, which can only be expressed with complex linguistics. "Ooh, I could murder a an ice cream, maybe with a chocolate flake and raspberry sauce, although it plays havoc with my sensitive teeth, so maybe I'm better off settling for a large frothy latté (even though they're extortionate and it's weeks from payday)." As we can see with this conscious thought, the complexity of the nuances, constructions, the weighing up of the pros and cons and the mental images are a world apart from what an elephant must experience. Our conscious experience is intrinsically linked to our linguistic ability, which also reflects the complexity of our society. In fact, our opposable thumbs and our ability to communicate are the most important factors, to my mind, of our success as a species, allowing us to handle tools and work co-operatively, as well as weighing up choices and decisions, opportunities and costs. Our language allows us to empathise and conceptualise to a degree almost infinitely higher than any other organism.

A further debate often arises here about what comes first, thought or language, and many philosophers and linguistic experts have proposed different theories. I am attracted to the belief that the two are coextensive – that one cannot exist without the other. In other words, a human could not understand the concept of unrequited love, or philosophy of the mind, without having the language to support these concepts, and more basic language builds itself on more basic concepts so that over the millennia, humans have built brick by brick, a complex understanding of the world around them. With each new concept comes new language – new words – and these enable the person to investigate the concepts that exist higher in order above the last learned concepts. This sort of theory is borne out when considering feral children. Research into feral children has shed light on this area and the "Critical Period Hypothesis" has been put forward to explain that after a certain age, if a child has not learned to speak, then it becomes incredibly hard, if not impossible to learn language thereafter (somewhere between the ages of 5 and puberty). For example, a feral child is one that has been brought up by animals or suchlike that has not had the opportunity to learn and neurally develop the organisation of language. If they are reintroduced to society post-puberty, they will find it almost impossible to then learn language and effective human communication. With this, they can also not comprehend the higher order concepts that many humans live with, and are inspired by. The subject of this book, for example, would be way beyond the comprehension of such a person, and an internalisation of language seems very much to be the golden key. From this, we can deduce that such a child would have a much less nuanced, more animalistic life; they would be much less party to the world of choice and free will that most normal humans are used to. The influence of language has a huge impact upon the lives and society of modern humans, and the way we create intentions, desires, plans and actions.

So, what are the main arguments for a monist approach to consciousness, and what are those for a dualist approach? To look at monism, it is probably wise to start in the realms of neuroscience. Indeed, most neuroscientists seem to be proponents of monism. As one can imagine, the unfortunate property of investigations into consciousness is that they are very difficult to do, since you cannot, in the modern world of human rights, simply dig around inside someone's head whilst asking how it makes them feel. I'm not sure, even for a few thousand pounds, that I would accept someone poking my opened skull with a metal rod whilst having to describe to them how it inhibits my sense of self.

What is evident in clinical studies, is that the smooth running of the brain is essential for the sound running of consciousness. Problems like strokes and brain damage cause a loss of aspects of consciousness. When the brain has the misfortune of going into a vegetative state (with its lack of consciousness), it still operates its basic automatic functions. However, patients exhibiting such a vegetative state also have an impaired connectivity between the deeper and upper margins of their brains. Consciousness does seem to be rooted in several parts of the brain, and affecting these different parts with various methods can affect consciousness in different ways (such as memory recall, or the ability to resolve time). There are necessary parts of the brain required for consciousness (though on their own, they may not be sufficient). Problematically though, with there being no clear definition of exactly what consciousness is and does, then there is no clear test for consciousness, and therefore no clear understanding of from whence it comes.

Without getting bogged down with either neuroscience or philosophy of the mind, there are physical theories of the mind, saying that consciousness is somehow a physical property of the brain, that our hardware creates what we know as conscious sensations. One such theory is known as *functionalism* which tries to eliminate the need for a mental consciousness, seeing it more as a function of the brain, such as cleaning the blood is a function of the liver. For example, being in pain from burning the hand is the causal function of the brain in taking in the nerve and sensory inputs and showing the behaviour of swearing and pulling the hand back. This is sometimes seen as being separate from both physicalism and dualism.

Returning to the notion that certain, more complex animals have consciousness, many believe that the more complex the animal, the more complex the consciousness, such that monkeys and dolphins would have a more complex consciousness than hedgehogs and robins. This suggests that consciousness has a real, tangible function; that it is a direct result of evolutionary processes. If so, what would these functions be? Well, many functions could be suggested such as planning, learning, problem solving, the imagining of alternatives and so forth. These are the things that make humans what they are, and the things that give us an (evolutionary) advantage over other species around us. Our ability to live and work co-operatively has allowed humanity to spread so successfully around the world that in the last sixty years the world population has over doubled to almost seven billion, reflecting our conscious ability to manipulate technology and each other. These evolutionary functions to consciousness hint strongly at its possible physical nature, developed over millennia of adaption and natural selection.

As far as dualism is concerned, there are many proposed versions of consciousness and how it exists in a separate format from the body / brain. Some certain types of dualism state that consciousness, though effectively separate, still emerges from the physicality of the brain. Such an example of this is the fascinating theory known as *Epiphenomenalism*, which claims that consciousness is nothing but a reflection of what the brain has already decided to do. It is as if your brain has decided to act, and then at the same time, or just after, it sends impulses to the consciousness that give the impression that the consciousness is intending the actions, but in reality they have already been determined by the brain. An example here would be Andy, at Tippling Philosophers, deciding to get the second round in[1]. His thinking "I'd better get a round in before last orders" might well have been a decision that his non-conscious brain had already taken, and his thoughts are merely a later reflection of that, a by-product of his non-conscious machinations. Thus, in this case, consciousness is nothing but an illusion of control over the body, and simply appears to be a sort of fictional movie of what is going on, shown in the internal cinema of the mind, but not the actual reality. A good explanation is given by Julian Baggini in *The Pig That Wants To Be Eaten*:

> *Let's say you're trying to work out a solution to a tricky logical or mathematical problem. Eventually, the eureka moment comes. In this case, surely the actual thinking has to play a part in the explanation for your actions?*
> *Well, no. Why can't I believe that the conscious experience of thinking is just the by-product of the computing that is going on at brain level? It may be the necessary by-product. But just as the noise that a boiling pot of water makes is an inevitable by-product of the heating without that meaning it is the noise that cooks the egg, so thought could be the necessary by-product of neural computation that doesn't itself produce the solution to the problem.*
> *(Baggini 2006, p.62-63)*

The most commonly accepted version of dualism is known as *interactionism* which proposes that there is an interacting causal chain between brain / body and mind. Such an example would be the chef in the Bella Causa Pizzeria preparing a pasta meal, cutting some parsley, and then cutting his finger. His

---

[1] I'm not entirely sure that this is a realistic scenario…

cries of pain can be heard in the restaurant outside. This makes the owner put down the bottle of wine that he is pouring. Feeling a sense of fear that something really bad has happened in the kitchen, he runs back to the kitchen. Here we have a physical event causing a mental event, which causes a physical event and a mental event. There is clear interaction here between the mental and the physical, and vice versa. This is generally the position that people hold, especially people that haven't ever really pondered how consciousness or causality works. This version of events is taken for granted, and supposed in all our conversations about why we do things and why something happened. In a way, this becomes the crux of the free will debate – can this version of events be correct?

Arguments for dualism or against dualism range in form, but I will try to sum some of them up here. The first, and perhaps one of the foremost arguments to support dualism is the idea that mental and physical qualities are very different. This is known as dealing with *qualia*, which are the subjective sensations associated with a mental experience (the phenomenal aspect of consciousness). For example, what it feels like to look at your newly painted burgundy wall, or what it feels like to cut your finger, or how nice it feels to see your family again after climbing Mount Everest. These feelings seem to be extremely difficult to express in physical terms. In a physical sense, we can know all there is to know about, say, a dog, but we would never know what it *feels* like to be a dog. This theory was expounded by a chap called Frank Johnson who created a thought experiment called Mary's Room. Imagine that there is an amazing neuroscientist, specialising in the neurophysiology of vision, who is made to learn all about the world from a black and white room, using a black and white television. She acquires all the physical information there is to know about situations when we see things of colour, such as ripe tomatoes. She understands the wavelengths of colours as they hit the retina and interact with the central nervous system, and understands the processes of the vocal chords contracting to produce the words "The sky is blue", and so on. When she is released from the room and sees, for example, a ripe tomato, in colour for the first time, does she learn anything new? It is posited that if she experiences something new and different, that this is the experience of qualia, that they cannot be physically learnt without experiencing.

One problem with this thought experiment is the premise that all can be learnt without experiencing. This is simply a dubious premise. As Daniel Dennett[1] would say, Mary would simply not have the full knowledge of visually seeing red. A complete understanding would simply allow Mary to know how and why she would experience qualia. In this way, we can state that someone in Mary's position would not be able to ski in that room, that the *act* of skiing gives over new information and ability[2]. This is like fishing with a three-inch holed net and then claiming that 2 inch fish don't exist because you have never caught any. We have in no way established that knowledge can be entirely learnt discursively – through reason and theory alone. We must remember that memory is a physical function within the brain, and it is memory that is involved so much in this process. If she has no memory of red, then she does not know all there is to know about red. Having the memory of going to the restaurant, for Mr. Scelta, is a different physical situation from being told what it is like. Moreover, the thought experiment itself is often critiqued as being a thought experiment with severe limitations and with several doubtful logical issues[3]. Qualia are a veritable battleground of philosophical forays, flanking manoeuvres, frontal assaults, and defensive trench lines that philosophers have commanded. There are a whole host of philosophers who believe that these subjective experiences can either be described in physical terms, or that they do not actually exist as we perceive them. Either way, dualism is not necessitated by the idea of qualia.

Additionally, there are some physical phenomena that contribute to a physicalist understanding of qualia. Firstly, pain asymbolia is a condition that occurs when there is damage to specific parts of the brain. This causes the victim to lose all subjective responses to pain, so that they might know the difference between hot and cold, or when a needle pricks the skin, but have no subjective experience of the pain. In other words, they have no qualia of pain and this is resultant from a physical condition in the brain. Nerves in the brain can be

---

[1] Dennett (2006)

[2] This is known as the Ability Hypothesis.

[3] There are also a good few other theories, such as the Acquaintance Hypothesis and the New Knowledge / Old Fact View that support physicalist approaches to qualia. See the Stanford Encyclopaedia of Philosophy http://plato.stanford.edu/entries/qualia-knowledge/#4.1 (11/2009)

severed to cause this exact phenomena, and patients can still feel the pain, but not have the experience of that pain – painless pain!

Another physical condition, known as synaesthesia, also defends qualia as physically rooted phenomena. This is a neurological condition whereby stimulation of one sensory pathway leads to involuntary stimulation of one or more other sensory or cognitive pathways. In other words, synesthetes can, for example, smell or hear colour, experience colour with letters or numbers, experience time in three dimensions (such that 1986 seems further away spatially than 1994), experience sound with visual stimulation and so on. There are scores and scores (over 60) of different manifestations of this condition, and it can be a naturally existing condition, or be brought on by drugs, stroke or temporal lobe epilepsy, among other things. Therefore, the extra qualia experienced by synesthetes are entirely grounded in a physical condition, and strongly points towards qualia being physical phenomena, not necessitating dualism.

Perhaps telling in the debate is that dualism itself doesn't actually offer an explanation in the knowledge debate of qualia, as dualists spend most of their time trying to undermine physicalist arguments, rather than providing decent ones of their own. As The Stanford Encyclopaedia of Philosophy says:

> *There has not been much discussion of the knowledge argument from a dualist perspective. This is unsurprising given the small number of contemporary philosophers who defend a dualist position.*[1]

Another argument, first used by C.S. Lewis concerns itself with naturalism, and is known as the argument from reason. He states that in order for a human to claim whether something is true or false, they must use a rational source. He then claims that no merely physical material constitutes a rational source. He follows that no assertion of what is true or false can originate from a source that is purely physical. Since human minds are capable of such assertions, he concludes that human

---

[1] See the Stanford Encyclopaedia of Philosophy
http://plato.stanford.edu/entries/qualia-knowledge/#4.1 (11/2009)

minds are not merely a physical source, that dualism thus exists.

Let us now postulate on some of these arguments for dualism a little further and see if we can come to some kind of general conclusion, although it is vital to note that I have not mentioned all the arguments, since some are difficult to express succinctly, and others are very philosophical indeed, but not without their issues and detractors. With regards to interactionism, where the mental and physical interact with each other in a causal chain (remember the clumsy chef), there are some issues concerning laws of science. Conservation of energy is a fundamental law that asserts that, in a system, energy cannot be lost or used, it just changes format. Thus, pushing a trolley up a hill converts kinetic energy to heat and potential energy and so on, but the total amount of energy in that system remains the same. In an interactionist system, there is causal power going in and out of the system. In other words, when the Mr. Fato decides to put the bottle of wine down, there must be some use of power or energy to flick the switch that actually makes him start to put it down, to flick the first domino, if you will. There would have to be some kind of energy being taken out of the system, or being put into the system from the mental sphere for this to be possible, and this is a controversial notion. If an intention such as "I am going to stand up and walk across the room now" has no force, as it is mental, how can it make a neuron physically fire, to make the muscles act towards standing up and moving across the room? Along with issues such as how exactly physical memories are created with regards to consciousness, it leads scientists to strongly question exactly how, if the physical and mental are so different, they interact. There seems to be no plausible explanation so far, but that of course does not mean it is necessarily impossible. There are some tentative replies to this problem, but none of them can explain *how* interactionism actually works, and thus this remains a big thorn in the side of dualism. As ever, quantum mechanics is called in as one of the possible defences.

With regards to ideas about feeling, intuitively we just 'feel' pain without any necessary spatial location, and this is sometimes levelled at physicalists as an argument for dualism – pain might not have a spatial location. Yet, we know that nerve endings transmit this pain to the brain, to a certain part of the brain and then we feel this sensation, perhaps meaning that the 'feeling' of pain is physical after all.

One particularly common refutation of dualism is the argument from brain damage and neuro-scientific tinkerings. Throughout the years of scientific advancement, especially in the realms of neuroscience (a still relatively unknown field – people just don't let you delve into their brains like they used to), it has become absolutely clear that there is a definite causal connection between damage to the brain and deterioration of mental facets. As I alluded to earlier, we can accurately predict the psychological impairment that will be caused by certain types of brain damage. We know this through monitoring the victims of various accidents, but also (sadly) through messing around with the brains of monkeys for cheap thrills and scientific discovery. Nowadays, with a new system of affecting the brain known as transcranial magnetic simulation (TMS), we can momentarily stun or slow areas of the brain (without long term effect) and see the ramifications of this to our consciousness. This is truly an exciting time for brain research. One very powerful lecture I once watched online[1] was given by Jill Bolte Taylor, a neuroscientist, who went through the horrible process of having a stroke. The amazing factor of this talk is that, as a neuroscientist, she was able to analyse exactly what she went through as the haemorrhage impaired her brain activity and her consciousness. There resided, in this episode, a clear correlation between physical brain and consciousness, and she was perfectly placed to understand it. She felt as if she was connected, through one side of her brain and at the exclusion of the other hemisphere, to the physical world of energy. I strongly advise anyone to watch this extraordinary twenty minute emotional and enlightening explanation.

Of course, one can refute the connection of brain to consciousness (as in brain *is* consciousness) by claiming that the brain isn't simply the direct source of consciousness, but is more like the hardware that interprets the consciousness. In the same way that if you damage the circuitry in a computer, then you will have an impaired reading of any software that you might want to load onto it. The software might represent our consciousness, while the hardware of the computer might be our brain – the interpretation of the software (consciousness)

---

[1]http://www.ted.com/talks/lang/eng/jill_bolte_taylor_s_powerful_stroke_of_insight.ht ml (09/2009) Well worth watching, as are so many of the videos on TED.com.

gets corrupted when the hardware (brain) is damaged. This is quite a nice analogy, and seemingly fits, but it isn't necessarily backed up by any proof. There is no analysis of that which is mental, and no knowledge of physical mechanisms that react with the mental that allow this analogy to hold any kind of explanatory power whatsoever.

To me, the most influential argument against dualism comes from biology. To the very best of our knowledge, humans (and, indeed, every other animal) begin their existence from entirely physical and material sources, from a single material cell. Throughout the course of human development, nothing is added to our being from outside the realms of the physical world, and our development can be viewed in explicable terms of natural selection and biological evolution. When we look at conception, fertilisation, and gestation and so on, there is no mental input from anywhere that can explain the development of a mental aspect to humanity and our consciousness. This period of development is created through the input of nutrition which is accounted for, and so any explanation of dualism needs to overcome this hurdle.

One might counter this approach by saying that since we have no way of knowing or measuring the mental sphere, then we naturally do not know if there really is any input from the mental sphere. Interestingly, though, if one considers the nature of frozen sperm, eggs and, more importantly, embryos, then we have a hugely problematic situation for dualists. Where does the mind reside when life forms are being cryopreserved? Do the minds hang around in a mind pub while the freezing process (which is technically infinite with modern freezing techniques) takes place, checking their mind watches every five minutes in boredom? "Come on body, I haven't got all the time in the world to hang around doing nothing. I need to learn things, and decide stuff!" says the dislocated mind. We can transfer pretty much every organ in the human body, usually involving freezing, and one assumes we could technically, if we wanted, transplant a brain. If we did that, where would the mind go? Would it stay with the old body or continue residing in, or connecting to, the brain that is transferred? Already we know we can transplant human brain tissues, and more radically, entire bird brains have been transplanted successfully. In a dualist world, we would seriously be messing with our (or the birds') sense of 'I'. This is not the case in a physicalist world. To add to that, scientists have been able to, with the help of a physical laser, create 'learned memories' in fruit flies[1] that affect their behaviours. In the experiments, once the laser has altered their neurons, the flies avoid a stream of air as if they had bad memories associated with that stream. Scientists were able to isolate the correct neurons by observing other flies brains for changed neurons when they flew into the stream and were electrocuted (not fatally). Eventually, the flies learnt to avoid the stream so as not to get stunned. The memory was then 'lasered' in, in common parlance, to other flies' neurons, and they behaved as if they had been electrocuted, evading the stream. These flies had not actually been electrocuted, but behaved as if they had been. This implies, then, that memory itself is a physical thing, and it would follow that other things that 'feel' mental are simply manifestations of physical networks.

This has similar implications for those who believe that each human (and perhaps animal?) has a soul. Since some 41,000 frozen embryos[2] were transferred into patients in Europe in 2001 alone, where are all the souls residing whilst their human body counterparts are sitting on earth, frozen? If you believe, like many Christian theologians do, that souls are learning sentient aspects of human existence, what do they do in this limbo? What do they learn? It certainly never manifests itself in the later lives of these humans who once spent time frozen as embryos. Again, proponents of the human mind and soul as separate to body must, in order to defend their theories, be able to tackle these fundamental questions. It is no good simply positing theories because they sound nice, and because we, as humans, like the idea of a soul or separate mind.

Finally, a much used philosophical technique, *Occam's Razor*[3], can be utilised in support of physicalism. Occam's Razor stipulates that when there are two theories that compete for the same outcome, the simplest one of the two is more preferable. The principle suggests that the preferable theory should contain as few assumptions as possible, and still maintain a good explanatory scope whilst not contradicting any

---

[1] As ever, with these things, the New Scientist magazine is invaluable. See http://www.newscientist.com for some great research.

[2] http://en.wikipedia.org/wiki/Controlled-Rate_and_Slow_Freezing_in_Cryopreservation (10/2009)

[3] Also known as Ockham's Razor.

observed facts. When looking at dualism versus physicalism, Occam's Razor would posit that dualism and monism are competing for the same outcome, but dualism contains more entitics and assumptions, such as a mentalistic entity. Using this approach, monism is the more clearly explanatory option to maintain. To add to that, it might be worth noting that the biggest ever survey of mainly professional philosophers was done in November 2009 showing that only 25.8% of philosophers leaned towards or accepted non-naturalism and only 27% of philosophers leaned towards or accepted non-physicalism[1]. I would hate to rely on evidence from popularity, but it shows that physicalism is fairly consistent with modern, mainstream philosophy.

There are other questions that require answering within a dualistic framework, such as whether we cease to exist when we are unconscious, what the properties of being unconscious truly are, and what form consciousness takes (ectoplasmic, consciousness as a mental state or something that simply cannot be described in any physical terms, and therefore cannot really be described at all)? In addition, there is the interesting idea, as Baggini (2006) summarises when he poses the thought experiment involving somebody who is dying in body, who decides to have a brain transplant, and transplants her brain into a healthy body. This poses the question that if a person can exist, and feel like they are still *them*, in another body, then the feeling of self is in the brain. The brain is the organ that *is* the self. Thus, you could theoretically simply hook up your brain to some simulated sensory organs and it would still feel like *you*. But is this really the case? It certainly suggests that if the consciousness is separate to the body, then it is joined inexorably to the brain, that the brain is the vital organ for both dualist and monist theories. Killing the brain kills the consciousness, the mind, one way or another. It is as though, in a dualist sense, our mind is connected to the brain by a vital, invisible chord. Personally, this just seems a little bit too far fetched in comparison to the idea that consciousness is physically created *in* or *by* the brain. And not necessarily in one particular place, but as a sum, maybe, of parts and networks that can be analogised in this way:

---

[1] http://philpapers.org/surveys/results.pl (03/2010)

Think of a chat show on radio. The programme is put together by a team of people. It is broadcast across hundreds, perhaps thousands of miles. The words of the host spark off thoughts in the minds of thousands of listeners. Some respond and phone into the programme. Where is this whole phenomenon of the chat show located? If it does not have a single physical location, what does that say about physical identity and personal communication? Can it be that our identity is not contained within a physical location, but is formed by networks of significance?

(Thompson 1995;2006, p.114)

Having paddled around in the pool of the mind, where does this leave us? Well, personally, I tend towards the ideology of monism, mainly due to the biological argument being so logically strong, and also with the problems that dualism has with overcoming the hurdles involved with a separate mental system interfering causally with a physical system (and the issues with the conservation of energy). However, it still remains for both sides of the argument to fully explain exactly how consciousness really works, whether in a two-tiered reality or on a simpler, physical plane. More importantly still, and often cited as the crux of the debate, is that no one has yet produced a concise and accurate definition of what consciousness actually *is*. Together with the potentially unskilled methods we use to observe our own consciousness and feelings of selfhood, we have a practically spurious starting position from which to try and answer the conundrum of the mind-body problem.

The way I see it, our consciousnesses adhere to the rules of science, and are answerable to physical laws. I don't think that consciousness *is* the brain, but that it is a physical by-product of the brain that is not, as yet, fully explicable. Perhaps it is best explained as a conglomeration of a series of very complex variables and networks combining all our sensory organs and processing abilities. However, I don't think that inventing the mental sphere, outside of physical realms, helps the matter in any way, but simply confuses it. Nevertheless, the belief in a soul and in dualism doesn't necessarily exclude determinism, since one can posit that both immaterial souls and minds can be thought to exist, but not to have any causal influence, or themselves are determined. Sort of like tagging along for the ride.

Essentially, when investigating the consciousness, it seems that the most likely candidate for explaining consciousness is a physical, or physically dependent one. As a result, consciousness fits into a seemingly deterministic framework. Although many free willers will try to use consciousness as a magic oasis of free will, there has not once been a satisfactory explanation of how it provides free will, and how it can cause physical actions if it is an entirely different state.

So, to recap, we have seen that quantum uncertainty may not exist and if it does, does not affect determinism with regards to making decisions – the variables are out of one's control whether they involve aspects of random or not. Random (aside from our quantum discussion) does not exist, only the lack of knowledge of variables. The soul most likely does not exist, since there is no evidence for it or explanation of its mechanism and how it interacts with the physical body. If it does exist, it must adhere to its own set of laws and rules that enable it to be in the form and have characteristics of a soul. It seems an unlikely vessel for allowing free will. Then we have consciousness, which is most likely derived from or equated to the physical brain, which is biologically and physically determined, it seems.

Does this mean that free will is hard to come by? We shall investigate further.

PART III - DELVING DEEPER

Having painted a delicate picture of the continuum of will with light philosophical brushstrokes, it is important to delve a little deeper into the three basic areas in a more critical fashion. I will be looking at a few of the main defenders of these areas and critiquing some of their views in a hope to get a slightly better understanding of both sides of the fence.

1 - LIBERTARIAN FREE WILL

*There are those who think
that life has nothing left to
chance take,
A host of holy horrors to
direct our aimless dance.*

*A planet of playthings,
We dance on the strings
Of powers we cannot
perceive
"The stars aren't aligned,
Or the gods are malign..."
Blame is better to give than
receive.*

*You can choose a ready
guide in some celestial
voice.
If you choose not to
decide, you still have
made a choice.
You can choose from
phantom fears and
kindness that can kill;
I will choose a path
that's clear
I will choose freewill.
(Rush)*

Jonathan M.S. Pearce

Is it good and proper to use the Kane?

The American philosopher Robert Kane presents himself to be an interesting defender of free will. This is primarily because he is a naturalist – one that believes in a materialist and non-supernatural worldview, that everything can be understood in scientific and natural contexts. His well received 1996 book *The Significance of Free Will* provides a serious attempt to defend the notion of free will from a naturalistic standpoint. Kane is not without his critics (isn't that the case for everyone?), but let us first set out his basic position before seeing if it holds any merit.

Kane sees a necessity to prove free will because he links it strongly to responsibility, or what he terms Ultimate Responsibility. Only with the acceptance of the idea that (as Dennett 2003 puts it) the "buck stops here", in the human mind, can we accept that humans have the Ultimate Responsibility for their actions. If there is any way that reason for actions can be abrogated elsewhere, to other factors, then Ultimate Responsibility is also devolved to other factors, and a human is bereft of the responsibility that Kane believes humans should, and do, have. Here is an oft quoted Kanism:

> ..."the power to be the ultimate creator and sustainer of one's own ends or purposes." This power is connected to the ability to make choices or decisions by virtue of the fact that choices and decisions are the formation of intentions.
>
> *(Kane 1996, p. 23)*

He claims that, at the end of the day, we have that power, and by natural means, without the interference of the supernatural or otherwise. Kane sees the decision making process as a set of inputs leading to an output, almost seeing our brains as a computer, and somewhere between that input and output the influence of free will acts. It is here that he sees indeterminacy acting, when choosing or intending to do something in a rational way. Of course, it cannot be a part of the input, since that would then determine the decision, so it must be part of the process, between input and output. In one such way he sees this working, Kane gives the example of a businesswoman on her way to a career-defining meeting when she sees an assault in the alley – what does she do, and how does this decision manifest itself? He claims that the struggle for a decision of what to do here, the choice between going on to the meeting, or involving herself some way in resolving the assault, sets up two connected but different neural networks, and their chaotic activity acting with each other causes internal conflict and the nature of a 'tough decision to make'. But many critics of this approach point out that although neural networks acting 'chaotically' together may give the impression of randomness, they are actually deterministic, though they give the impression of chaos.

> *The "chaotic activity" Kane mentions here is deterministic chaos, the practical unpredictability of certain sorts of phenomena that are describable in plain old Newtonian physics. As Kane recognizes, two networks interacting chaotically would not in themselves create any indeterminism, so if there is any "indeterminism that make it uncertain", it has to come from elsewhere.*
>
> *(Dennett 2003, p.105)*

There are many examples that can be given to illustrate this, from, as Dennett uses, the "chaotic" Hyatt New Departure Ball Bearing exhibit at the Museum of Science and Technology in Chicago that is actually very fine tuned and entirely deterministic, to many computer hardware and software models that in their complexity, appear chaotic. But in reality, they are strictly deterministic.[1]

So what is this other aspect of the decision making process in the human brain that allows the possibility for indeterminacy in Kane's model? Well, this is where quantum randomness is sent in, to rally the libertarian troops to make a charge on determinism.

---

[1] Chaos Theory that is often mentioned in popular science and maths circles is a theory that stipulates that a system has such a massive set of variables that it is as good as unpredictable, *even though the variables are deterministic.* The weather is a good example. Predicting it any more than five days in advance is futile, though with computing power and knowledge cast enough, it could theoretically be done. In that way, chaos is almost a misnomer since there is no random in the system.

In a model where you have inputs and an output to decision making, you wouldn't want to have a computation that rigidly gives the same output when you put in similar inputs. When getting up every day, if you always made the same thing for lunch, then life would be a little more uninteresting (although, it must be said, that this kind of routine in people's actions is very evident, and does reflect a sort of input / output regularity – get up, make tea, eat toast with strawberry jam, clean teeth, get dressed, choose tie, lock door etc. etc. This is life for many people). However, every day, though it may seem the same, throws in different variables, and all your experiences from the day before will change who you are to the slightest degree at least, as well as all the different variables on the day, whether the weather, news on the radio, menstruation (always a variable worth considering, I find), or running out of sugar.

In order to satisfy true indeterminacy in the process, Kane envisages a randomizer, but, importantly, one that is resultant upon the person themselves, not just complete randomness. A randomness that takes place purely by chance takes responsibility away from the doer. Before we talk about this source of indeterminacy, let us ask how often Kane thinks we engage this sort of thought process, one where we have Ultimate Responsibility.

Kane seems to see these critical moments of real deliberated choice as infrequent even though they are vital. More common are instances of snap decisions. For example, Mr. Scelta's choice to have a vegetarian pizza, when asked by Mr. Fato, the proprietor, is instinctive and very quick indeed. Without hesitating, he says he wants the vegetarian option. On face value, this is not a huge moral question, and not much of importance rests on it. But the decision itself is based on much more deliberated and important decisions at previous times. In this instance, there is no need for Mr. Scelta to declare, "Well, Mr. Fato, you see, by choosing the meat feast, I am condoning the intensive farming of sentient creatures, and their hurtful mass deaths in the abattoirs to which they are crammed into a truck and sent. As a result, I would like to choose the vegetarian option, due to its more ethical nature, and the overall consumption of water in arable farming is less dramatic than for livestock farming. Having been a vegetarian for 19 years, I have also developed a preference for the taste of vegetarian dishes too." This dialogue, internal or otherwise, is unnecessary since the brain can process all this information instinctively, at the blink of an eye, and in a determined fashion. However, Kane would emphasise that the determined inputs to this instinctive snap decision were dependent upon previous, more complex and rational, free will decisions. Thus, in effect, they are under the mandate of Ultimate Responsibility.

Kane calls these less frequent, but character defining decisions *Self Forming Actions* or SFAs, the output of which inform future decisions deterministically. In other words, these decisions determine your sense of self, your future actions and decisions. Now equipped with these SFAs, and defining your own future and motivations in action and decision, you are a morally and ultimately responsible being. The crux of the matter as far as SFAs are concerned is the idea that a person, at the time of making such a choice, has *alternative possibilities* (APs), meaning that "the agent *can* (has the *power* or *ability* to) do A and *can* (has the *power* or *ability* to) *do otherwise*" *(Kane 1996, p. 33)*. What Kane is saying, is that at the point of making a decision, a person really can do either choice. Mr. Scelta really could have, 19 years ago, decided to be a vegetarian, and really did have the ability to deny himself that choice, and remain a meat eater.

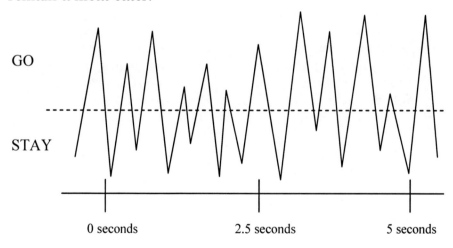

The Quivering Needle hovering between Go and Stay[1]

---

[1] This is a reworked but almost identical version of Dennett's figure, reprinted with kind permission of Daniel C. Dennett.

Dennett has investigated the way Kane looks at these moments of SFA decision, in trying to see whether the actions are indeterminate or not. Using a quivering set of fate's scales that he has borrowed form 19th century William James' free will kitchen, he sets up the following model. When making an SFA decision, say to Stay or Go (Dennett 2003), imagine that over a 5 second period of deliberation, the needle of choice is flipping between the two choices as the mind investigates the reasoning for either choice. The jagged graph of choice would look something like the diagram on the previous page.

In this representation, would there be any moment of alternative possibility? Would there be any moment where there is perfect free will deciding upon whether to Go or Stay? If the time of decision is taken at 2.5 seconds, then the decision is determined at Go, and if taken at 5 seconds then it will always be at Stay. Where, then, can the indeterminacy come? When, of course, is the key word – Kane is looking at us being able to decide the *time* of the decision. Dennett sees this as when one can press the "Now!" button to activate the decision, and Kane needs this decision to be up to the decider:

> *...suppose a bystander yells just as you are about to press the Now! Button, startling you and thereby hastening your press by five milliseconds, causing your press. Is the decision no longer yours at all? After all, the crucial part of the cause, the part that determined whether to Go or Stay, was itself caused by the bystander's yell (which was caused by the seagull flying by so close, which was caused by the early return of the fishing fleet, which was caused by the resumption of El Niño, which...was caused by a butterfly flapping its wings back in 1926)...The butterfly's moment of freedom back in 1926 isn't what gives you free will today, is it? Kane's libertarianism requires him to break the chain of causation in the agent and at the time of the decision...If it really matters, as libertarians think, then we'd better shield your processes of deliberation from all such external interference.*
>
> *(Dennett 2003, p. 123)*

I apologise for the lengthy quote, but Dennett sums it up so well here. Now we get into difficult territory, because at what point can you realistically make decisions without any external influences? What degree of external influences can we accept before we say 'enough's enough, any more and the decision is not *ours*'? The philosophical brain starts going into overdrive. Thus, Kane is needing the decision not just to happen in *you*, but to be defined *by you* at a time that is, in effect, undetermined (using the model I have just shown). The problem is, in order to *be yourself,* you have to understand *who you are,* and who you are is determined by your experiences up to this point, and your bodily make-up, and so the issue of external influences, or internal influences, indeed, is back.

Kane seeks to address this issue, by declaring that we have simultaneous reasoning going on – he calls it parallel processing (Kane 1996, p.231) – that our brain, when deliberating say on Stay or Go, has reasoned both options and has taken ownership over those reasonings to separate them from previous external issues. The brain has honed two arguments, if you will, and they are both effectively competing for the decision. Given that the brain has weighed both of these options up, and has seriously entertained the idea of either of the outcomes (the verdict of choice), then the decider is still responsible for the outcome, even if there is a bit of 'randomness' or 'indeterminism' in the actual method of deciding between the two – i.e. the time.

To put this back into an example, so that this doesn't just sound like theoretical mumbo jumbo, let us look at whether Mr. Fato, our pizza restaurant owner, wants to run away from his business to another country to avoid paying taxes (Go) or to remain at its helm and steer it through financial difficulty to the other side (Stay). A tough moral decision indeed. Under Kane's theorising, he has two conflicting but parallel reasoning processes interacting with each other, and these are *personally* rationalised by his brain with only very limited external influence, and any major influence in this rationality is from previous SFAs (Self Forming Actions - examples of personal choices dependent on free will, such as this one). Whilst these two choices are vying for acceptance, quantum indeterminacy as an aspect of Mr. Fato's calculating brain possibly causes the timing of a choice between these two options and one is chosen

– Mr. Fato decides to brave it out, and keep the restaurant open, much to the Scelta's delight.

However, as far as this sort of theory goes, there are several issues in my mind. Firstly, it is potentially dependent on quantum indeterminacy which, as I have discussed, is something that I have an issue with, especially as a harnessed mechanism of the brain, a randomizer. This puts far too much emphasis on some kind of random, whether one can have ownership over that randomness or not. A number generator in the brain just seems, well, anti-libertarian. There is also the fact that much of the important work of processing the arguments for each choice is done by the subconscious brain, and thus is not at the mercy of the conscious "I". This means that the conscious "I", even assuming Kane's theory is correct, has a minimal part to play in the vitally important decisions of our SFAs.

Therefore, it seems to me that Kane, and many other libertarians, are really clutching at straws when trying to find the originating mechanism for free will. Where does this magic ownership over choices come from that we all would love to have. And how much work does our subconscious brain do, unbeknownst to our "I"s, when we are making decisions? Even when we feel we are rationally weighing things up freely in our thoughts, where do the actual thoughts and rationality come from that allows us to make these decisions?

Rationality comes from the neurons in the brain. The left and right hemispheres of the brain are responsible for different aspects of how we rationalise. The anterior cingulate cortex and the dorsolateral prefrontal cortex, for example, are engaged when we make decisions and evaluate probability. Interestingly, these areas, when we are spoken to by a perceived expert, activate less – we don't rationalise information when it is given to us by a perceived expert[1]. This is perhaps why confidence tricksters have so much success, because we believe them to be experts in what they are talking about, and turn off our rationalising mechanisms. More fool us. Thus, libertarians are faced with the problem that the very mechanisms that they use to rationalise and help them decide, are themselves biologically deterministic, operating unknown to our conscious "I", computing away under the auspices of our subconscious.

---

[1] http://www.timesonline.co.uk/tol/news/science/article5962749.ece (10/2009)

Kane, in trying to rationalise his own libertarianism, is simply opening up the argument to many other deterministic issues, and not offering any credible explanation for the mechanism of free will. Evidently, this is from a naturalistic worldview, and from such a worldview, I see it as nigh on impossible to entertain a viable thesis for the mechanism of free will. To allow free will to hold tenure, one must start to entertain the ideas of a dualistic consciousness, or a soul, being involved in the mechanism of making a freely willed decision.

That being said, and before dealing with the other options, let us first see how Libertarianism interacts with the notion of a divine being that judges our every action.

Jonathan M.S. Pearce

Free choice and God

In order to investigate the idea that a divine being may be judging our every decision, it is important to first explain what I mean by a divine being. This is worth, in itself, many hefty theological and philosophical books, and I have neither the time nor space to discuss it here. For ease of discussion, I will predominantly talk about the Abrahamic God of Judeo-Christian nature. However, I will endeavour to also talk of Eastern theology (amongst others), in order to explore these concepts at a little depth, and for some good measure of interest.

Being born and bred a Westerner (as in Western Philosophy, not as in one who embraces globalisation and strategic empire-building wars) of British origin, I am geographically accustomed to the influence of Christianity, and the Christian understanding of God, who, for sake of argument, I will now call...God (all other gods I will not capitalise, just to clear things up. No offense to their pride and sense of importance if they exist, being misfortunate enough, as I am in their eyes, to have been born in an area that is not under their sphere of influence).

In fact, as we will see in more detail throughout this book, the very existence of a personal god can be argued through the existence, or lack thereof, of free will. Furthermore, there is the highly important notion of a theologically determined set of events, and what the consequences of this might be, which I will also be dealing with.

Many believers use the bible as a tool to work logically *from*. The bible is their axiom – "its truth is taken for granted, and serves as a starting point for deducing and inferring other truths"[1]. In other words, the bible is true, and from the bible, one can infer other 'facts'. In this case it is the fact that the bible necessitates the existence of free will, and since the bible is true, there must, therefore, exist free will. This, naturally, begs the question about the veracity of the bible in the first place.

---

[1] http://en.wikipedia.org/wiki/Axiom (08/2009)

God as an exerciser of free will

Firstly, let us look at whether God himself has free will at his disposal. This is important because one of the primary characteristics of God is that he is perfectly free, not being constrained by the sorts of influences that humans are. It is often said that if God created all things then every thing that he created must have some attribute of his. Man has free will and, therefore, one of God's attributes must be that of free will. Of course, this might be a *circular argument, begging the question* of whether we have free will ourselves. The bible is littered with examples of where God supposedly chooses people, things, cities and tribes. Here, in Numbers 16:6-8 God chooses who will be holy:

> *"Do this: take censers for yourselves, Korah and all your company,*
> *and put fire in them, and lay incense upon them in the presence of the LORD tomorrow; and the man whom the LORD chooses shall be the one who is holy. You have gone far enough, you sons of Levi!"*

In Deuteronomy 16:5-7 we have God choosing a place, assuming that God, in human, anthropomorphic terms, deliberated over where the best place might be, and then chose accordingly:

> *"You are not allowed to sacrifice the Passover in any of your towns which the LORD your God is giving you;*
> *but at the place where the LORD your God chooses to establish His name, you shall sacrifice the Passover in the evening at sunset, at the time that you came out of Egypt.*
> *"You shall cook and eat it in the place which the LORD your God chooses. In the morning you are to return to your tents."*

And in John 15:16 we have Jesus talking to his disciples, declaring that he has chosen them, implicitly assuming he deliberated, and may have had other choices, but freely weighed up that the 12 he had in mind were the best choice:

> *"You did not choose Me but I chose you, and appointed you that you would go and bear fruit, and that your fruit would remain, so that whatever you ask of the Father in My name He may give to you.*

Although it is more difficult to look at texts dealing with Jesus, as one can get into deep theological arguments over whether Jesus was fully man, and thus choosing was done in a human context, it is important to look at the way God is described as choosing in biblical texts. As mentioned before, there is a definite human, anthropomorphic character to God (not unusual in the Old Testament, as he, in various books, is described as having eyes, ears, a nose, a mouth, a finger, a hand, a back, loins and feet to name but a few pieces of the anatomy) that imparts the image of God sitting in heaven and deliberating, pondering what the best course of action would be, and then *choosing* accordingly. Of course, the classical notion of God is that he is omnipotent, omniscient and omnibenevolent: all powerful, all knowing and all good. With this is the understanding that he is prescient – meaning that he knows events before they happen. The problem here then comes with the texts indicating that God chooses. If he is prescient and omniscient, then he knows all the options, and he already knows all the answers, he knows the best and optimal decisions without having to deliberate. God does not need to sit and work out, mentally, what is the best option, does not need to calculate who the best choice of person is to do his bidding. God simply *knows* – there is no choosing then. In Deuteronomy 7:6-7,

> *"For you are a holy people to the LORD your God; the LORD your God has chosen you to be a people for His own possession out of all the peoples who are on the face of the earth.*
> *"The LORD did not set His love on you nor choose you because you were more in number than any of the peoples, for you were the fewest of all peoples..."*

it is written as if God pondered the best choice for, wait for it, his *chosen people* – the Israelites. He chose the Israelites over and above all other peoples of the world, over the Aborigines, over the Chinese, over and above the Meso-Americans. And one assumes that this was a choice of free will. Yet, in a sense, it wasn't, since God always would have known he would choose them, and if full blown omniscience is agreed, then would know all the outcomes. Thus, this aspect of God tangibly choosing anything is rendered somewhat redundant.

Let us look at God as having libertarian free will from another angle. In Titus 1:2, Paul tells us that God cannot lie:

> *in the hope of eternal life, which God, who cannot lie,*
> *promised long ages ago*

So, if we believe in the theology and writings of Paul, the backbone of Christianity, then we have to assume that God cannot lie. So he cannot choose to lie. This already constrains what God can choose to do; we are starting to see aspects of God that determine his actions and choices. Theologians will try to sidestep this conundrum by claiming that God has the free will to lie, but since it is not in his nature, he is just simply never going to lie. Others say that he cannot sin, but sin does not apply to him. This is simply denying free will in all but name, and one feels left a little short-changed.

Furthermore, if God is the standard set for goodness, the benchmark, as is often thought, then it is necessary that he is good. One anecdote that I have read that explains this concept in simple terms is that of a king that wanted to have a standard measurement for distance for his kingdom to use. To decide what the standard measurement for a foot (in length) would be, the king's measurers measured his foot. How long was it? Well, a foot, naturally, because it was the standard by which all other distances were measured. This analogy works well for the standard, then, that God has to set for goodness. He is 'necessarily' good, and can't be anything *but* good. If God is necessarily good, then it follows that he cannot have libertarian free will – he is constrained by having to be good. He cannot, theoretically, choose to do something bad.

Martin Luther, in response to Erasmus (the Dutch Renaissance humanist scholar and theologian), wrote in his *The Bondage Of The Will* that will is in bondage to sin. This definition of free will means that God does not have free will inasmuch as God is not bonded to sin, but quite the opposite. What's more, according to Paul (who said in Romans 6:7 "he who has died is freed from sin") people who die and go to heaven are freed from sin, but potentially from the will, too. Does this mean that free will is not available to those in heaven? However, this is changing the goalposts since this is not the usual definition accepted for free will.

God also suffers from something that, at first sight, seems obvious and self-evident. If one agrees that God has been eternally existent, then one can get into some very interesting discussions about the personality of God, God's very own nature. Has God ever been able to change his nature or character? Does God even have a character? As humans are born and grow, we develop our personalities, and our characteristics change and grow. However, we are (arguably) always fighting our genetic traits, or the influences of the environment around us. There is still, no matter who you talk to, the fact that we have a core being, a sense of self or "I" from which we cannot seem to stray too far from. Does God have this? Does God have a set character? If he is eternally existent, how was his character defined? Can he define his own personality? This is connected to the idea that God can't lie, as previously stated, but is larger than that, with more far-reaching consequences. Is God bound by his always good nature to be completely constrained in who he is, and what he can choose? I would actually argue that God is, himself, fully determined, if you take into account the all-powerful, all-loving, all-knowing nature of God. He always, in setting the benchmarks for those characteristics, and in the same sense that he cannot lie, has to act in the maximally caring way for his entire existence. But caring to whom? Being more caring to humans might well be at the cost of another species, and being more loving to the lion or giraffe, might be at the expense of human success and happiness. I will return to this idea later (I can feel your excitement building already). So God can no more do 'bad' as change his own character. He is eternally stuck with being who he is, and cannot change in any way, since he must always be maximally good. Perhaps he could change what it means to be maximally good, by shifting the goalposts, just so as to allow a bit of variety in his existence. However, one then has the age-old debate of whether God creates moral absolutes (and they are therefore subjective to God), or whether good is objectively good, irrespective of what God says[1]. If God said the Holocaust was good, would that make it good? Or is it objectively evil, no matter what God says (and therefore begging the question of whether we need God for morality)? Or is it, indeed, neither good nor evil, but just is? I can feel the chins being rubbed in thought.

A British cognitive scientist called Donald Mackay looked at a logical problem that an omniscient God would face, in relationship to being bound by his omniscience to act in a particular way. This problem is born out of the issue of whether one can predict one's own actions. John Barrow, in his 1999 book *Impossibility*, talks about how God could not predict his own actions if he wanted to be contrary, based on Mackay's logic. In other words, God, as a superbeing of omnipotence and free will, cannot choose to be contrary. Imagine that a certain Mr. Scelta has the full knowledge of the brain and the universe, like Laplace's Demon[2], so that he could work out where he would want to go for a meal – the Italian restaurant or the Indian restaurant. Now, if he wants to be a little "perverse" and decide to choose exactly the opposite of what his predicted calculations state, it then becomes logically impossible for him to predict where he wants to go for a meal because he is choosing against his prediction. Conversely, if Mr. Scelta decides to conform to what his predictions state, to go to the restaurant that his calculations of all the variables computes, then he will predict correctly. Mr. Scelta's successful prediction of his future actions depends upon him not being contrary, and not deciding to choose the opposite of what his predictions calculate. To choose the opposite is logically impossible, given the knowledge of the prediction as a part of the system of variables.

As Barrow (1999) states:

> *Let us look at what sort of dilemma this creates for our Superbeing. If he stubbornly chooses to act contrary to what his predictions say he will do, he cannot predict the future, even if the universe is completely deterministic. He cannot therefore know*

---

[1] This was first examined in Plato's dialogue Euthyphro, and is known as the Euthyphro Dilemma.
[2] See Part I -3 Determinism.

> *the structure of the Universe. Omniscience is logically impossible for him, if he wants to be contrary. But if he doesn't want to be contrary, then he can be omniscient No being will not do what he predicts he will do!*

So God can be omniscient, but he is restricted in the power to be contrary. Or God can be contrary, and therefore be restricted in the power to know everything. Thus, it is logically impossible for God to be omniscient and omnipotent. This has some interesting implications for those who have the classical view of God; that he is omnipotent, omniscient and omni-benevolent.

There are some arguments to support the fact that God has free will, but they all seem to fall logically short of any kind of convincing status. For example, one might say "I don't believe it's possible for an entity to give/grant an ability that it doesn't already possess, i.e., how can God give man free will if He doesn't have it?" as I saw on one forum[1]. This simply begs the question of whether humans themselves have free will – a dangerous assumption from this forum member!

So, what can we conclude from these observations? God's own character means that the assumption that God has libertarian free will is fraught with issues, and that, realistically, God is not just a little determined. Not only are his actions seemingly constrained, but his ability to shape his own character, and his own 'destiny' is apparently non-existent.

---

[1] http://www.mwilliams.info/archive/2003/07/does-god-have-free-will.php (08/2009)

Humans as subjects of God, and choosing wisely

As with society in general, the personal idea of God has integrated into it the necessity for humans to be able to exercise free will. The mission statement of Christianity, if you will, is to engage willingly in a loving relationship with God on a personal level. It is a choice thing – you can choose not to, and follow the path of an unbeliever, or you can choose to accept the word of God, and receive the riches of a successful afterlife. Here is an example of how God insists on people choosing options he sets out (not exactly libertarian, but there you go) in 1 Chronicles 21:9-12:

> *The LORD spoke to Gad, David's seer, saying,*
> *"Go and speak to David, saying, 'Thus says the LORD, "I offer you three things; choose for yourself one of them, which I will do to you."*
> *So Gad came to David and said to him, "Thus says the LORD, 'Take for yourself either three years of famine, or three months to be swept away before your foes, while the sword of your enemies overtakes you, or else three days of the sword of the LORD, even pestilence in the land, and the angel of the LORD destroying throughout all the territory of Israel.' Now, therefore, consider what answer I shall return to Him who sent me."*

This is clearly a difficult choice, but illustrates the importance God puts on humans to select a correct path. David clearly has a tough one here, and much death from pestilence ensues. Job goes further still in claiming that our souls can choose (Job 7:14-15):

> *Then You frighten me with dreams*
> *And terrify me by visions;*
> *So that my soul would choose suffocation,*
> *Death rather than my pains.*

It is another discussion altogether as to whether we do have souls or not, but as to whether our souls can actually exhibit sentient decisions outside of our body, this is surely pure conjecture, lacking in any kind of evidence. This simply pushes the argument as to whether free will exists into another dimension, and simply complicates the issue, as previously discussed.

Moral responsibility is something that is communicated throughout the bible and that hinges on the decisions made by individuals. Here Job has some very insightful stuff to say (Job 34:4):

> *"Let us choose for ourselves what is right; Let us know among ourselves what is good."*

Thus, this links the decisions we make as humans to our morality, inferring that we exercise our free will in order to achieve what is right or wrong. Or, conversely, what we know to be right or wrong will influence our free will. The bible also indicates that a person learns from what is around them, throughout their formative life, so as to be able to make more informed free will decisions, and this obviously implies that a person is subject to external conditions that influence their decisions. In the following case, it is the knowledge of what is right or wrong (Isaiah 15:15-16) that influences free will:

> *"He will eat curds and honey at the time He knows enough to refuse evil and choose good.*
> *"For before the boy will know enough to refuse evil and choose good, the land whose two kings you dread will be forsaken."*

Thus, time (and the implied moral education of the boy) determines his understanding of morality, and, therefore, his ability to act morally. Again, we are moving away from a libertarian approach to free will. The choice of people to do what is deemed as morally wrong, to choose to do bad things throughout their lives, will reflect badly on judgment day. Peoples' actions will be judged, and the choices they made will have repercussions for eternity. Here is what Hosea (9:7) had to say:

> *The days of punishment are coming,*
> *the days of reckoning are at hand.*
> *Let Israel know this.*

*Because your sins are so many
and your hostility so great,
the prophet is considered a fool,
the inspired man a maniac.*

If we assume that we have free will to make our choices, and then we also know that the choices we make have serious repercussions, then this will affect our choices that we make. If I was to walk down the street, and I saw a nice, shiny, new chopper bike – one that I had been hankering after all of my formative years – and no one was around, then I would have the free choice to decide to either steal it, or walk innocently by. This is a free will decision, based on no consequences. And based on no consequences, who knows, I may steal it. However, if I knew that by stealing this most stylish of be-pedalled vehicles I would suffer the consequences in my afterlife, that I could be victim to eternal torture as a result of my freely chosen action, then I would probably not do it. Thus, the consequences of stealing it will determine my decision; my free will is constrained. Remember, here, the painting on the walls of Albi cathedral of heaven and hell: the consequences illustrated would have influenced many a French peasant's decisions.

Now, the usual retort to this position is that I still have the free choice to choose to steal the bicycle, irrespective of the consequences. I can still choose to steal the chopper, and I would simply accept the consequences. But, how free is this choice really? Let me explain with the taxman analogy:

A taxman walks up to the owner of La Pizzeria Bella Causa, a Mr. Fato, and declares, "Mr. Fato, you have the choice to either pay £25,000 in taxes this year, or you can choose not to. You are free to choose."

"Excellent," replies the restaurateur, "In that case, I choose not to pay them. What a great tax man you are!"

"Aah, Mr. Fato, don't be too hasty, my friend. If you choose not to pay the taxes, we will lock you up for the rest of your life. So what will your choice be?"

Mr. Fato looks puzzled. "So you are saying that I am free to choose not to pay, but if I do, then I will end up in prison for the rest of my life?"

"Yes," says the tax man, smiling, "You are free to choose whichever option you want."

"That is not a free choice," Mr. Fato exclaims, "If I choose one option, I am punished harshly for it, so I am always going to choose the other option. This is not free choice, you are forcing my hand!"

"No I'm not, you're free to choose."

"This is not a free choice!" cries the pizzeria proprietor, realising his dreams of a holiday in Fiji were quickly slipping into the government's pockets.

As a result of this sort of analogy, it may be necessary to redefine free will as not the realistic position of free choice, with its inherent influences, but the potentiality for free will, the theoretical ability to choose freely. Yet, to me, this is unsatisfactory. This is not free will as we would realistically use it. As we will see later, this is consequentialism – the influence of future consequences in determining our present actions: a potentially powerful motivator of decisions.

Free will and the problem of evil

The problem of evil exists as a major thorn in the side of Christians the world over, and there are parts of the bible that are dedicated to investigating why evil takes place in the world, such as in the case of Job in the Old Testament. The problem of evil manifests itself as follows:

The classic view of God is that he is omnipotent (all-powerful), omniscient (all-knowing) and omni-benevolent (all good). Since there is a large amount of suffering (evil) in the world, there needs to be an explanation. This is because, being all-powerful, God should be able to do something to lessen or stop the suffering. Since God is all-knowing, he should know how to lessen or stop the suffering. Since God is all-loving, he must be opposed to the suffering. This suffering exists, from murder, to rape, to cholera, to cancer, to tsunamis, to being burnt alive in a forest fire slowly and painfully. Therefore, God is either: not all-powerful; not all-knowing; or not all-good (or even all three)[1]. Many brain cells have been over-used, and pen nibs blunted over settling this issue from Greek times to now, and the argument still rages like a burning inferno of defenceless deer. It would take me many chapters to debate the matter, so I am going to look at one relevant answer to the conundrum offered by many a theist[2]. The reason offered for much of the evil in the world is that in order to have the full benefits and power of free will, evil must exist. If God was to restrict us from committing acts freely by only allowing us to commit acts with benign outcomes, then we would live a straight-jacketed existence without a full and proper free will at our disposal. A life like this is often compared to living like robots. Is it better that we live in a world where there is no free will, but no suffering, or a world such as the one we live in, with some good degree of (apparent...) free will, but a whole plethora of suffering? And, generally, the theist has to conclude that the value of free will is higher than the value of having no suffering. To put it another way, the cost of living a life full of evil and suffering is less than the cost of living an evil-free but straight-jacketed existence. It is worth more to humanity and God that

---

[1] It is thought that this was first put forward by the Greek Epicurus, and the trilemma is called the Epicurean paradox.

[2] A believer in a (usually) personal God.

we have free will, than there is a burden and a cost of suffering. If, however, we don't have free will, then the amount of suffering in the world is abhorrent when we understand that the nature of God is all-good. Consequently, we can see the importance of free will to the average theist's understanding of God, and God's characteristics.

It is interesting that we spend more time on earth trying to inhibit each other's free will through the creation of rules and laws, and through conquering and controlling others. Religions themselves are often charged by non-theists as being tools of control, inhibiting people's free will for the better good. Well, if free will is so valuable, why do we, religion, and God spend so much time trying to limit it? If it is so much more valuable than the lack of evil, then why is it constantly minimised? God, in the bible, through Levitican and Deuteronomical laws, has hundreds and hundreds of rules to set out exactly what we should not do. If you are going to go to that extent of creating so many hundreds of rules, then why let us have the free will in the first place? Does the good from free will outweigh the bad that comes from it? That is very hard to answer, but well-worth thinking about on a rainy Sunday afternoon after church.

It would be prudent to also mention that there is some debate as to exactly how free will would look in heaven. For so much value to be put on free will, for it to be the crux of humanity, one would assume it would have to exist in heaven, otherwise heaven would just be a straight-jacketed version of earth (making earth a 'better' place to be than heaven), and this begs the question of: If you can do it in heaven, why can it not be so on earth? How can you have full free will in heaven, but not the suffering to go with it? Unless heaven is still full of suffering, but that is somewhat counterintuitive. The inference from Paul's Roman 6:7 quote is that there is freedom from sin in heaven, and on some definitions, this means that heaven might not contain free will. If this is the case, then free will can't be all it is cracked up to be, so why bother insisting it takes place on earth, with all the ensuing evil? There are definite contradictions afoot, methinks. The notion of free will being apparent in heaven is one of the strongest arguments that refute positions of Christian philosophers such as Richard Swinburne. It is often argued that evil is the by-product of allowing people to exercise their wills freely, and that suffering, as harsh as it sounds, helps to build a greater character in those involved. However, to logically allow for free will to be possible in heaven without there being evil, it means that it must be logically possible for God to create that on earth. Swinburne sees this heavenly ability of free will and no suffering as a reward for those who achieve salvation through Christ on earth. However, it is difficult to weigh up the suffering of six million Jews and these countless others dying from the choices made by other people, in the light of it being beneficial to the characters of countless others. This seems like a fairly heartless appraisal of free will and suffering, and seems desperately harsh on those who suffer when God could create a world where free will can exist without suffering, where six million Jews do not have to suffer from the decisions made by an oppressive regime outside of their control. Therefore, it appears that God wants to allow suffering as the collateral damage for testing to see who can 'choose' salvation through Christ. This is perhaps one of the most costly tests that one could ever imagine. All the pain and suffering, all the evil on earth (which could logically not exist on a heaven-like earth) existing because God wants to test who will follow and love him, and who will not. Either this is potentially egocentric, or slightly sadistic.

To recap, the evil in the world is as a result of our misuse of free will. And when we do misuse it, as often we do, God then punishes us. This is amply evident in the bible because God kills a good few million people in the Old Testament alone, for various reasons. This has often been likened to analogies such as God giving a razor blade to a two-year-old. Ex-preacher turned atheist, John Loftus, explains this analogy with aplomb:

> ...*giving us free will is like giving a razor blade to a two-year-old child. Razor blades can be used for good purposes by people who know how to use them, like scraping a sticker off a window or in shaving. That's because adults know how to use them properly. We could give an adult a razor blade. We cannot give a two-year-old one, for if we did, we would be blamed if that child hurts himself. Just like the younger child should not be given a license to drive or left unattended at the mall, so also if God gives us responsibilities before we can handle them, then he is to be blamed for giving them to us.*

Jonathan M.S. Pearce

Loftus talks about such ideas that if, in his omnipotence, God is caring enough about humanity, he could easily turn any bullet that is fired from a gun in malice towards another innocent human to jelly, or any baseball bat to "toilet roll". Thus, without harm being done, God could still punish the intent. As for why we (and all plants and animals) suffer so greatly from the vagaries of nature, and natural disasters, no decent answer has ever been given in the light of God's supposed three characteristics. Hundreds and thousands of people die from a tsunami, and we have to assume that it was not within God's power to create a life-giving planet without plate tectonics. Could this imply that he is not very powerful, then?

Another issue with this argument is that the existence of free will for humanity is incredibly anthropocentric (i.e. placing humanity squarely and egocentrically at the centre of everything that matters). How can it be fair that, since there has been a military coup in Madagascar over the last year, the biodiversity of the country has been decimated by the local population and their exercising of free will under a collapsed government? The locals have run riot and logged the beautiful rainforest, and killed much of the animal life for bushmeat. The wood is being shipped to China, who have exercised their free will in demanding it, and the illegally caught bushmeat is taken out of the national parks for food. Who suffers? Not us, not the humans who are freely willing. Those that suffer are the animals and the ecosystems in which they live. These animals themselves are deprived of their 'free will' and they suffer and die for the gift that was given to humanity. If God was omnipotent and omni-benevolent, then he would surely at least allow the animal life not to suffer from our decisions. Where is the free will of all the collective animal and plant life that suffers as a result of man-made pollution and climate change? Why is it that free will is all about us, all about offering humanity the chance to decide freely, when it inhibits all other living creatures on earth? How unfairly favoured we are! The cost of our highly valued ability to choose is, more often than not, carried on the shoulders of those animals that are not granted the 'God-given' gift of free will. And they have nothing but their lives with which to barter.

x

Free will in other religions and Eastern Philosophy

There is a diverse approach to aspects of free will in Eastern philosophy and theology. More of my reflections on Eastern philosophy will come in later sections, as they provide a more appropriate laboratory in which to investigate our Eastern cousins and their thinking. Obviously, Eastern philosophy encompasses an almost impossibly wide range of diverse belief systems, but I will try to pick out a few pertinent ideas.

Suffice it to say that in both Hinduism and Buddhism, free will is not seen in a completely libertarian context as there are deterministic influences aplenty. In the karmic elements of Buddhism and Hinduism, Jainism and Sikhism, free will is afforded importance, since it is seen that one's actions in the past indebt a payment in the future. Thus, we should be free enough in order to commit present actions that will either be rewarded or punished accordingly in future lives. Swami Vivekananda, an important figure in the revival of Hinduism in the late 19th century, and a major proponent of Yoga and Vedanta (a philosophical tradition of Hinduism), illustrated that in his 19th century society, the discussions of free will were at the forefront of philosophical thought:

> "Therefore we see at once that there cannot be any such thing as free-will; the very words are a contradiction, because will is what we know, and everything that we know is within our universe, and everything within our universe is moulded by conditions of time, space and causality. ... To acquire freedom we have to get beyond the limitations of this universe; it cannot be found here."
>
> *(Swami Vivekananda, reprinted 1977)*

The transcendental aspect of his beliefs is here laid bare, forming from the notion of a lack of free will. It is said, though, that this does not necessarily imply a lack of free will, but a sort of middle ground, and that he believed that choice can change karma.

Buddhists do not believe in a polarised version of free will, but again free will is important, particularly in their concepts of karma, although in Buddhism, the repercussions are more concerned with our present life. Buddhism does decree that a belief in absolute free will is simply wishful thinking, since we are victim to circumstance and physical needs.

Islam's position is very similar to the other two great monotheisms (religions that exclusively believe in only one God) of Judaism and Christianity. There is a comparable notion that we are morally responsible, and our actions will be accounted for on the Day of Judgment. Here, we see that Allah punished people who chose to deny his "favours":

> *"Allah coins a similitude: a town whose people that lived secure and well content. Its provisions came in abundance from every quarter, but its people denied the favours of Allah, so He afflicted them with famine and fear because of what they used to do."*
>
> *(Surah al-Nahl, 16:112)*

Here is another verse that implies through the word "seek" that humans have the ability to choose (although you could also claim that them seeking is simply a position of carrying out that which has already been ordained for them):

> *"Whoever seeks the harvest of the hereafter, We shall give it to him in abundance, and whoever seeks the harvest of the world, We give him a share of it. But in the hereafter he shall have no share."*
>
> *(Surah al-Shura, 42:20)*

One of the early movements of Islam (the Mu'tazilites) philosophised over the free will debate, and decreed these three dogmas:

> *1. God is an absolute unity, and no attribute can be ascribed to Him.*
> *2. Man is a free agent. It is on account of these two principles that the Mu'tazilities designate themselves the "Partisans of Justice and Unity".*
> *3. All knowledge necessary for the salvation of man emanates from his reason; humans could acquire knowledge before, as well as after, Revelation, by the sole light of reason. This fact makes knowledge*

obligatory upon all men, at all times, and in all places.[1]

It doesn't take much explanation to see the importance of free will to their doctrines. Well, it pretty much *was* their doctrine.

Judaism differs, though, in the belief that free will is intrinsically linked to the soul, since it is the only aspect of humanity that is not linked to cause and effect. Thus, inherent in this view, is the understanding that the soul exists, and that part of the soul resides with God, who in his uniqueness is not influenced by causality. Essentially, though, given the foundations that Christianity has in Judaism, the argument of free will plays out pretty much the same, and there is no great distinction between the two religious disciplines.

Zoroastrianism, based on the teachings of Zoroaster some five hundred years before Jesus, has many similarities to Judaism, Christianity and Islam, as well as Hinduism (some say that many of these religions borrowed aspects of Zoroastrianism to develop their own religion and theology). Its approach to free will is fairly libertarian, since man is born in a sinless state and has complete freedom of will to shape his destiny by co-operating with good and evil. Judgement of the soul takes place after death, whereupon paradise or hell awaits.

So what have we learnt here? Primarily, that free will, in its libertarian extremes, has issues, both in humanity, and in the notion of a god. The dialogue that can be seen between theologians of all major religions shows that the notion of free will is one that promotes problems, and at the very least, soul-searching debate. To me, it seems that no such thing exists in this polarised state – there is no über-libertarian free will, only free will with an as yet undisclosed dollop of constraints determining the outcome to some degree. But to what degree?

---

[1] http://en.wikipedia.org/wiki/Kalam (08/2009)

Jonathan M.S. Pearce

2 – COMPATIBILISM

*"Human freedom...is an objective phenomenon,
distinct from all other biological conditions and found
in only one species, us...Human freedom is real – as
real as language, music and money – so it can be
studied objectively from a no-nonsense, scientific
point of view."*
(Dennett 2004, p.305)

"We must believe in free will, we have no choice"
(Isaac Bashevis Singer)

Jonathan M.S. Pearce

And in the compatibilist corner, weighing in with an evolutionary argument, is Daniel Dennett!

One of the most famous big guns in the compatibilist camp is Daniel Dennett, a prominent philosopher who covers many disciplines. Remember, compatibilism is the idea that free will can exist side by side with determinism in some way or another. Dennett argues many of his points from a naturalist viewpoint, using the tenets of Darwinian evolutionary theory. In his book *Freedom Evolves*, Dennett sets out an argument that he confesses some might find controversial. In fact, many critics of his theories accuse him of still being a determinist in all but name. The tack that Dennett adopts is to attack the assumptions made in the questions about free will and determinism, thus not necessitating having to answer the problems but shifting the paradigm. Dennett claims that the way we view free will has to change, in the same way as if we used to think falling in love was the result of being shot with cupid's arrow until a scientist came along and showed us that this was not actually how it happened. Dennett says that some would say that this shows that love does not exist, maybe a necessary fiction, but others would say that love is real, along with falling in love, and that it is just different from what people used to think it was, it just doesn't involve "flying gods"[1]. He sees everything in the context of evolutionary thinking, and this covers all things from cells to choosing freely. Because our humanity relies so much on the moral responsibility of choosing freely, so the idea of free will is so important for humans to investigate and understand. To exist without intention and knowledge of consequence to their actions makes a human not a human, not a person as we know them. We are intrinsically entwined with the idea of free will and intention, that one without the other is like a ship without water.

Dennett sees free will as not something that exists in a causeless environment – it exists in conjunction with it, and even necessitates causality to exist. For choice to be uncaused, renders it next to useless, simply random. Choice has to have the parameters and the foundations of variables in order to be meaningful. To put this in context, if Mr. Scelta and his wife were deciding on what to do for the night, without the luxury of

---

[1] Dennett 2004. p. 222-223

the usual variable inputs (the things that influence decision making), the choice would be random. They might decide to go naked skiing after robbing a bank, even though that would not be possible to do in the English Summer evening on the South Coast. You see, without the determining inputs of knowing where they were, what they could realistically do, the legal and financial restraints, what they enjoyed doing on a mid-week evening, then the decision becomes random, unconnected and meaningless. The constraining inputs *do* add meaning and context to any decision, and thus they become necessary in order to have a decision of any realistic use.

Dennett continues by looking at the scenario of Laplace's Demon and inferring that he really doesn't have too much against the theory per se. He believes that the job the demon would have to do of knowing all those variables and calculating them in order to use the calculations to predict future actions is so incalculably complicated as to make his ability to comprehend anything impotent. Dennett sees that the perceived options that humans have give them enough elbow room to act as, well, humans, and not as automatons.

One interesting point of thought that is inspired from his writing is that of reason, our human ability to reason. If we were merely automatically responding to given situations, we would be nothing more than simple animals, which can be seen to be biological machines. When an input to their senses happens, the animal reacts in a determined manner – it doesn't reason what it should do, weighing up the pros and cons of carrying out a given action, imagining the future if it carried out action X, and if it carried out action Y, and then choosing between them. Most animals will simply do X or Y, depending on their biological programming. A woodlouse won't wonder whether to look for food under the shelter of a nearby log, or whether to walk a bit further into the sunshine to look for an alternative, and potentially abundant source of detritus. It is a situation action machine[1]; it doesn't ponder a SWOT[2] analysis

---

[1] A machine (animal) that operated with acting on a set input with a set output. E.g. 'If I smell nectar, I fly towards it" (if bees had a sense of 'I'). This is opposed to a prediction-value machine that weighs up the value of one choice over another based on predictions etc., such as a human reasoning between two complex choices.

[2] For those not well versed in business jargon, a Strengths, Weaknesses, Opportunities, Threats Analysis is a way of weighing up the pros and cons of any (business) decision.

of there being a greater chance of being spotted by a predator in the open, weighed against there being a potential greater source of food by venturing into the unknown open. It is simply programmed to stay in the dark where it is safer and moister, programmed through evolutionary processes whereby the woodlice that did venture out invariably dried up or were eaten by predators.

Humans are different; they can weigh up, using their more complex brains (and, hugely importantly, their grasp of language and tools), the pros and cons, and the likely proposed success rate, of settling on the fertile pastures across the river, as opposed to continuing to live in the rocky and difficult terrain this side of the river. As Dennett declares:

> *Gary Drescher (1991) calls this architecture a situation-action machine and contrasts it with the more expensive, more complex choice machine, in which the individual creation generated its own reasons for doing x or y, by anticipating probable outcomes of various candidate actions and evaluating them in terms of the goals it also represents.*
>
> *(Dennett 2004, p. 46)*

Humans have rationality, and what use would this be if we did not have a practical application for it? In situation-action machines, the machines, or organisms, are programmed (and therefore continue to exist) to avoid harm, or fate, as some might say. These organisms avoid the harmful effects of any number of causes. More sophisticated organisms can invent and choose more sophisticated ways of avoiding this harm. This plays out in reality as a simple organism being programmed to do harm avoiding action X if cause A happens. A more complex human would reflect rationally, "Would it be better to carry out action X, Y or Z to avoid harm from cause A?" Though the cause A may be determined, there is an element in X, Y or Z that hints at free will. Dennett seems to ascribe to the notion that if there are a variety of causes to a fate-avoiding action, then we use our practical rationalising to avoid the harm, and freedom has been utilised.

Thus, evolutionary processes have harnessed free will and put it to use in combating fate, in avoiding harm to the organism, to the self. But really, Dennett is suggesting that free will, as we know and understand it, needs to be redefined, and in the way that we understand it, it is an illusion. But because we observe freedom as a fact, because it is ingrained in our causal timeline, because it is self-evident, then we can accept moral responsibility and the consequences which come with it. Our need for morality has necessitated our need for free will. His central doctrine is the understanding that free will has naturally evolved. Dennett's naturalist worldview, he claims, is totally compatible with the idea of free will. However, one must then understand that his explanation of free will is not quite what the average punter would ascribe to. From his point of view, it seems that freedom is more about the ability to think about our actions in a moral framework, than the *actual* ability to choose between particular harm-avoiding paths. It is a case of having free will because we believe we have it, and our belief that we have it, and willingness to be(lieve that we are) driven by it, has arrived through evolution.

For the most part, I find Dennett's work on the matter somewhat confusing and cloudy. Determinism still plays the most important role, and the notions of freedom are either illusory or only philosophically evident. I think that the main gist to his compatibilist arguments boil down to the apparent absurdity of determinism in practical terms necessitating some form of freedom to exist, but I think he fails to give the clear and concise explanation for exactly how this happens physically, mechanistically and to some extents, philosophically. Though he presents many good points to either deconstruct libertarian points of view, or to illustrate the power of evolution on human culture and behaviour, there is still some missing clarity on free will.

To substantiate this confusion, some critics of the compatibilist / incompatibilist arguments, such as Ted Honderich, also claim that the argument itself is invalid. This is because the problem revolves around the definition of what, exactly, freedom entails, what it means. Of the two schools of thought, Honderich (2002) says:

> *One or other has to be true. You may say there is a law of logic about that. But the either-or statement states, or anyway presupposes, something else – that there is one thing in question with respect to*

> *what is called our ordinary idea of freedom. If there isn't one thing then saying that our ordinary idea of freedom either is or is not compatible with determinism may be perfectly pointless and in fact as good as false.*
>
> *(Honderich 2002, p.110-111)*

Honderich, here, is implying that determinism effectively means 'no free will', and so by saying that free will and determinism are compatible is like saying free will and 'no free will' are compatible, which is logically incoherent.

It appears to me that compatibilism is a hard thing to sell – on the one hand you have to espouse the prevalence of deterministic qualities, and on the other hand, you have to satisfactorily explain how they can interact with the idea of free will. To conclude, critics will often level at the compatibilist camp, that it involves bending the rules; redefining the terms to a point of them meaning something different to what they clearly are; or special pleading from a position of starting out with the intuitive belief in free will, so there must be an explanation that fits with the known aspects of determinism. Having said this, compatibilism is a surprisingly popular choice among philosophers[1]. Bearing in mind these approaches to compatibilism, let us now consider how religion and compatibilism get on with each other.

---

[1] The Philpapers survey indicates that 59% of philosophers adhere to compatibilism in one form or another: http://philpapers.org/surveys/results.pl (04/2010)

Is God compatible with compatibilism?

> *That God predestines, and that man is responsible,*
> *are two things that few can see. They are believed to*
> *be inconsistent and contradictory; but they are not. It*
> *is just the fault of our weak judgment. Two truths*
> *cannot be contradictory to each other. If, then, I find*
> *taught in one place that everything is fore-ordained,*
> *that is true; and if I find in another place that man is*
> *responsible for all his actions, that is true; and it is*
> *my folly that leads me to imagine that two truths can*
> *ever contradict each other. These two truths, I do not*
> *believe, can ever be welded into one upon any human*
> *anvil, but one they shall be in eternity: they are two*
> *lines that are so nearly parallel, that the mind that*
> *shall pursue them farthest, will never discover that*
> *they converge; but they do converge, and they will*
> *meet somewhere in eternity, close to the throne of*
> *God, whence all truth doth spring.*
>
> *(Charles Spurgeon 1858)[1]*

I don't want to launch into the interesting subject of theological determinism just yet, but this quote from the influential British Baptist preacher is right on the money in illustrating the issues that Christianity faces. There is a seeming contradiction between the idea that God is prescient, and knows the future (and has pre-determined it?) and the idea that humans have free will. Most counter-arguments involve the a-temporal nature of God, that he sits outside of our time system, and can thus know and affect us without meaning that our choices are already determined. This, itself, has problems, as we shall see.

The notion of compatibilism doesn't differ greatly from that of libertarian free will in the context of the bible and Christianity in general. The problem, for the more naturalist of Christians, is that quite often the answer, as Spurgeon hints, is that free will and determinism must be compatible, but no one is quite sure exactly how. Donald Carson (Carson 2000, p.51)

---

[1] **http://www.spurgeon.org/sermons/0207.htm** (08/2007)

claims of compatibilism, "It does not claim to show how they are compatible. It claims only that we can get far enough in the evidence and the arguments to show how they are not necessarily incompatible." However, Carson gets himself into trouble with the examples of compatibilism that he gives from the bible. For example, in Isaiah 10:5, when God speaks to the nation of Assyria, Carson claims they are his tools that he will use to exact punishment on the 'wicked nation of Israel'. Carson claims this is compatibilism because the Assyrians do not see it like this, they believe they are doing it by their own means, their own power. After using the Assyrians as a tool, the Lord tears them to pieces to "punish their hubris". Carson claims, "This is compatibilism. There are dozens and dozens of such passages in Scripture, scattered through both Testaments." Well, if this is compatibilism, I am Nancy Reagan. This passage implies that the Assyrians believe they have free will, but are unwittingly being used as tools. This is a very good example of the *illusion of free will*, which is very different from free will. A mirage is an illusion of an oasis. It is not an oasis. It is an illusion.

Carson uses many examples, another being the conference between Herod, Pilate and the Gentiles in Acts 4:23-29, where they decide and conspire to crucify Jesus, an act that God had pre-ordained. Carson says:

> *On the one hand, there was a terrible conspiracy that swept along Herod, Pilate, Gentile authorities, and Jewish leaders. It was a conspiracy, and they should be held accountable. On the other hand, they did what God's power and will had decided beforehand should happen.*
>
> *(Carson, 2000, p.51)*

How can something that is pre-determined by God allow for free will to happen? This seems to be a flat contradiction, and one that does not address the issue of the illusion of free will. Of course, I will be analysing concepts of predestination in Part IV, discussing how some theologians interpret omniscience, and how they believe it can be compatible with free will. Carson, though, shows his true colours by stating this, of these examples: "A moment's reflection discloses that any other account of what happened would destroy biblical Christianity."

Thus, rather than arguing for compatibilism rationally, Carson ends up arguing from necessity – without compatibilism, most of the bible is rendered incongruous. Without the idea of free will, then judgement becomes mitigated, and if we can exonerate the actions of evil-doers, then atonement is rendered impotent, and Christ's cross needless. Free will is essential to the doctrine of Christianity, that much seems to be quite clear. However, many Christians find it hard to deny many of the constraining forces that influence us, and so in reality, they adopt something that appears to be, if not compatibilism, then something that is very close. Romans 6:14-20 includes some fascinating insights to the choice humans have between good and evil, and implies that either choice results in a determined outcome:

> *For sin shall not be master over you, for you are not under law but under grace.*
> *What then? Shall we sin because we are not under law but under grace? May it never be!*
> *Do you not know that when you present yourselves to someone as slaves for obedience, you are slaves of the one whom you obey, either of sin resulting in death, or of obedience resulting in righteousness?*
> *But thanks be to God that though you were slaves of sin, you became obedient from the heart to that form of teaching to which you were committed, and having been freed from sin, you became slaves of righteousness.*
> *I am speaking in human terms because of the weakness of your flesh. For just as you presented your members as slaves to impurity and to lawlessness, resulting in further lawlessness, so now present your members as slaves to righteousness, resulting in sanctification.*
> *For when you were slaves of sin, you were free in regard to righteousness.*

All the talk of slaves is certainly not to be confused with free will. The compatibilist notion here is that ultimately, one has free will, but one's nature certainly plays a big part in whether we embrace sin, or fight against it. Theistic compatibilists usually argue that for a given situation, God

Jonathan M.S. Pearce

determines the conditions that will be sufficient to ensure that the person will want and choose to act in the manner that God has previously decreed. Yet, to me, this just sounds like a whole lot of determinism, dressed up to look like there is a part to play for free will. The idea that humans should be culpable for their sin is so ingrained in Christianity that, as I have said before, the necessity to shoehorn in free will comes at the expense of decent rational explanations.

The issue with theistic views of compatibilism that are often levelled at proponents of the theory are that, at the end of it all, if it is God that is setting up the parameters (the conditions in which 'free' choices are made) then the eventual choice is not free, and culpability for sinful actions rests with God. Moreover, there is a *circular argument* involved in saying that people are free since one's decision is in accordance with one's desires. The nature of free will means that a human must have the ability to act outside of what God has decreed, what God wants.

Thus, the argument for free will in a compatibilist sense, boils down to the argument set out in Part III, 1 – Libertarian Free Will, about people being *potentially* able to choose a different choice, which has its own problems.

So, is God responsible for our sins?

What we have discussed, then, is that compatibilism can be a necessity for the Christian if they believe 1) God has determined all things in advance but that we have free will[1], or 2) that every event is deterministically caused, such as a naturalist determinist would think. In either of these cases, how do compatibilism, God and responsibility work together? We all like the idea of free will, since it gives purpose and ownership to our lives, and moral responsibility. In spite of that, how do theologians argue that God is not culpable himself for our sinful actions, if it is he who defines the conditions which determine our decisions?

One argument that allows God to escape responsibility for our actions, is the theory that what makes man responsible is the notion that he is accountable to someone else for his thoughts, words and deeds. Since God has no one 'above' him to be accountable to, he is not accountable. He has no culpability. However, we then return to the idea of God having his own benchmark characteristics – he is maximally good and loving. God, then, is still constrained by his own nature. In that way, God is accountable to himself. The application of desire in humanity to actions and responsibility should be a standard applied to God too. God, if he wanted humans not to commit sins, to just be good, could make this so (in his omnipotence); but since there is sin, and humans are bad, it must be that God wants this to happen (it is permissive will - just letting it happen). God is decreeing that which is contrary to his nature, and that which is not what he desires for us – a little contradictory. Unless, of course, that the pain of suffering is outweighed by the benefits of something that necessitates that suffering.

A great quote that exemplifies compatibilism in the bible is in Matthew 7:15-19:

> *"Beware of the false prophets, who come to you in sheep's clothing, but inwardly are ravenous wolves.*

---

[1] This is actually the belief of a sect of Christianity called Arminianism, similar to the Calvinist that I mention later, differing in that Arminians believe in free will.

> *"You will know them by their fruits. Grapes are not gathered from thorn bushes nor figs from thistles, are they?*
> *"So every good tree bears good fruit, but the bad tree bears bad fruit.*
> *"A good tree cannot produce bad fruit, nor can a bad tree produce good fruit.*
> *"Every tree that does not bear good fruit is cut down and thrown into the fire.*

Good people are good because of their determining influences, and bad people are bad, and together with the implicit acceptance of free will throughout the bible, responsibility is meted out. The main defence that compatibilists serve to absolve God of responsibility here, is as follows. It takes its form in the 1689 Confession of Faith, a declaration of their (Baptist) faith:

> *From all eternity God decreed all that should happen in time, and this He did freely and unalterably, consulting only His own wise and holy will. Yet in so doing He does not become in any sense the author of sin, nor does He share responsibility for sin with sinners. Neither, by reason of His decree, is the will of any creature whom He has made violated; nor is the free working of second causes put aside; rather it is established.*[1]

Without quite explaining how, the Baptists have successfully produced a get-out-of-jail-free card, exonerating God from any responsibility. In consequence, it seems that compatibilism offers little in the way of an arguable defence for God's moral responsibility.

---

[1] *A Faith to Confess: The Baptist Confession of 1689 Rewritten in Modern English* (New York: Carey Publications, 1997), 3:1

Compatibilism in other religions and Eastern Philosophy

Initially, let us look a little further into the place free will takes in Hindu theology. As mentioned earlier, free will has presented a few sticky moments for the great Hindu thinkers. The previous quote from Vivekananda illustrated this, and he furthers this with his proverbial quote, "It is the coward and the fool who says this is his fate. But it is the strong man who stands up and says I will make my own fate." A person can stand up, can fight against seemingly determined constraints, and create their own, chosen future. Here, it is clear that he believes that past actions determine what you are now, and one would assume that the person you are now defines the sorts of choices you might make in the present:

We are responsible for what we are; and whatever we wish ourselves to be, we have the power to make ourselves. If what we are now has been the result of our own past actions, it certainly follows that whatever we wish to be in future can be produced by our present actions; so we have to know to act.
(Swami Vivekananda, reprinted 1977)

His teacher, Ramakrishna Paramhansa, supports this view with an analogy that he gave after listening to two groups of disciples discussing fate. He declared that karma is like a cow being tied by a rope to a pole. Free will operates in this manner – we have free will, but only so much that can take us to the limits of the rope. The grace of the Divine can make someone free by removing the rope, or in other situations, by moving the pole. Overcoming fate, overcoming karma, is possible. However, it is my (controversial) view that, as with many Eastern philosophies and religions, there is little explanation of exactly how this happens. For all the wonderful analogies, and sound-bites, there are few arguments of any real substance and explanatory power.

Within Zen Buddhism and Taoism, it is thought that the idea that when the conscious mind relaxes, stops trying to work apace to figure everything out, only then can the person become really free, in a creative sense. There is a doctrine in Buddhism called the doctrine of Dependent Origination, that is well summed up by the Buddhist story of the Net of Indra. Imagine a massive auditorium decked out with mirrors aplenty and prism-like baubles hanging from a multitude of different places on the ceiling, and each of different lengths. It only takes one light to be sent into the auditorium, to reflect off each and every bauble, bending and reflecting off every surface as it travels round the huge place. Each bauble represents one of us, as we are lit by each and every one of the other baubles in the auditorium. This represents the interdependence of all sentient beings, and their relative value to each other. Rather than our actions defining our future choices, the Buddhist in this situation would have our choices defining our actions. This is a compatible ideal of deterministic variables working with free will and volition. However, the finer details are harder to come by.

As far as Judaism is concerned, it is probably wise to assume that their belief about free will is realistically dependent upon interpretation, what with the God of the Old Testament being ostensibly the same God for Christianity as it is for Judaism. In other words, there are those that find that free will is necessitated by judgement, and emotions such as love (that love can only really be true if it is freely given), and those that interpret the Torah[1] as deterministic. God determines certain parameters (arguably all of them, if certain understandings of prophecy prevail), but man is ultimately responsible for their own actions, and they are answerable and accountable to God.

---

[1] The Hebrew bible of the Old Testament is known as the Torah.

3 – DETERMINISM

"Determinism is self-stultifying. If my mental processes are totally determined, I am totally determined either to accept or to reject determinism. But if the sole reason for my believing or not believing X is that I am causally determined to believe it, I have no ground for holding that my judgment is true or false."
(H. P. Owen)

"The initial configuration of the universe may have been chosen by God, or it may itself have been determined by the laws of science. In either case, it would seem that everything in the universe would then be determined by evolution according to the laws of science, so it is difficult to see how we can be masters of our fate."
(Stephen Hawking)

"You will say that I feel free. This is an illusion, which may be compared to that of the fly in the fable, who, upon the pole of a heavy carriage, applauded himself for directing its course. Man, who thinks himself free, is a fly who imagines he has power to move the universe, while he is himself unknowingly carried along by it."
(Baron d'Holbach)

There may seem to be an imbalance in the amount of pages devoted to determinism, but there are some good reasons for this. Firstly, we take free will for granted; we live by it, assume it as the basis for most of our actions and daily lives. And yet, there is very little credible explanation, certainly from a naturalist point of view, of how it works mechanistically. On the other hand, there is a huge wealth of evidence to support determinism from all sorts of different disciplines. In fact, as the years go by, the range of free will which most of us think we have, diminishes in the light of new scientific findings. At the same time, belief in a dualistic method for allowing for choice becomes harder to adhere to. This next section is devoted to showing that our range of free will, even to the most hard-line Free-Willer, is undoubtedly smaller than people generally think.

Some very interesting research has been done over the years by Daniel M. Wegner, and I will attempt to summarise many of his views, and much of his research in the following pages, as we delve deeper into the wonderful and mysterious world of our consciousness and factors that may determine our actions. Wegner's eminently readable 2002 book, *The Illusion of Conscious Will,* provides the backdrop to much of this discussion.

Consciousness is really quite slow

In this section, I will look at some remarkable research that has been done into reaction times, and what brain activity takes place when we carry out certain actions. I will conclude that most of the actions we do on a daily basis from driving to work and typing a letter, to playing computer games and making a cup of tea, are carried out automatically and before our conscious mind has "made the decision" to carry them out, or realised that we have carried them out.

One of the oft cited researchers in the field of neural activity and volition is Benjamin Libet. He was famous for conducting a series of experiments (which have now been carried out in other research institutes, and in slightly different manners) whereby he could measure and compare when a person consciously willed a voluntary act to take place with the neural activity associated with the physical action. His results were famous and somewhat controversial. To do this, Libet connected an electroencephalogram (EEG) to the subject's scalp to record brain activity in the cortex and an electromyograph (EMG) to record the time of the muscle movements in the arm. Using a cathode ray oscilloscope which had a moving dot on it, he managed to time when a person willed to move a finger (they recalled where the dot was when they felt the urge), and time when the brain was active, and when the muscle moved. It turned out that there was a period of some 200 milliseconds between the moment of volition and the act starting to take place in the muscles. Remarkably, though, the moment of brain activity associated with the movement started to take place some 500 milliseconds before the muscles moved, which means that 300 milliseconds before the person willed the action to take place, the brain had already decided it was to take place and started to action it. So, before we will certain actions to take place, there is a period of time, known as the readiness potential (RP) where the brain gears up to do the action, and after this period, the conscious mind 'wills' the action to take place. This hearkens back to Epiphenomenalism, which states that the conscious mind reflects what the brain has decided and the body does at the same time or after the event, but has no influence on the causality of the events themselves. Could this mean, with Libet's findings, that this theory of consciousness is true? Has Libet found out that we do not consciously will actions to happen?

Well, in a nutshell, not really. The type of actions that Libet was working with were smaller, more reflexive and automatic reactions. Although they are not necessarily confined to smaller actions. How many times have you sat in a car, driven a journey, and not really remembered it, or wondered exactly how you got there. I remember driving from the South coast of Britain to Leeds once, some 4 or 5 hours in the car, and arrived at Leeds barely remembering any of the journey. It was as if I was on autopilot, with the brain reflexively going through the automatic motions of driving, feet accelerating and decelerating, pressing the clutch down countless times and changing the gear with my hands, putting on the indicators, changing lanes and so on. All of these things can hardly be said to be consciously willed. My consciousness was swanning around elsewhere thinking of goodness knows what, whilst my brain was acting like an automaton.

This sort of automatic action is akin to playing a game of table tennis, or a computer game. The reaction time of the brain and body is so quick, by necessity; that it acts outside of being consciously willed. If you watch a table tennis player, they move and register and hit the balls so quickly that the actions bypass conscious will, and the neurons fire instinctively, relying on the proficient nature of all the sensory organs gathering data, and processing that data to make the next move. In fact, most quick sports entail a strong emphasis on subconsciously willed and rapid movements that are just too necessarily fast to be able to be controlled by the conscious will. Wegner (2002) notes:

> *These automatic processes also are often uncontrollable in that once they have been launched, they continue until they are complete (Logan and Cowan 1984). Conscious processes are more flexible and strategic but they also take more time – in the range of 500 milliseconds or beyond. Half a second doesn't seem like much, of course, but it can be an eternity when you're trying to do something fast. Consider that a skilled keyboarder might be able to type at the rate of 120 words per minute. That means two words every second, a phrase that itself would have taken me only 2 seconds to type if I were such a skilled keyboarder. So, a 500-millisecond interval would allow for the typing of an entire word. All the automatic keystrokes that go into typing that word are so fast that they are telescoped together into a sequence that takes only as long as it takes for something once to enter into a conscious response.*
>
> *(Wegner 2002, p.57)*

Some people like to dispute Libet's findings and the conclusions that were drawn from the original experiments, but as I mentioned, they have been replicated many times. One such example would be the work of C. S. Soon et al (2008)[1], at the Max Planck Institute, which differed slightly in format, using letters streaming by that triggered the press of a button. To cut a long story short, the volunteers took an average of 22 seconds to press the button, and felt that they had made the

---

[1] Available online at http://www.nature.com/neuro/journal/v11/n5/abs/nn.2112.html (10/2009).

conscious decision about 2 seconds before the movement. The frontopolar cortex and the precuneus parts of the brain showed activity that preceded the conscious choice by 7 seconds. This is a huge time lapse, and the same conclusions are being drawn as in the Libet experiments. Here, one award-winning science writer, Ed Yong[1], sums it up:

> *The study goes well beyond Libet's original work. It shows that this preliminary activity is far from a general and non-specific curiosity, but can actually predict a decision. Nor can it be explained away by inaccuracies in measurement - the timescales involved were far too long for that.*
>
> *These associations have never been seen until now because neither the frontopolar cortex not the precuneus were more active in total in the time leading up to the button press. Instead, it was the pattern of firing neurons within these areas that predicted the final decision, and it took the use of pattern recognition techniques for this effect come to light.*
>
> *The involvement of the frontopolar cortex isn't surprising. It fulfils the role of an executive manager and is involved in retrieving memories and controlling other high-level parts in the brain. Soon thinks that it is the source of the decision itself, with the precuneus simply storing the decision until it reaches a conscious level. When he changed his experiment so that volunteers were shown a cue to tell them when to make their choice, the frontopolar cortex still showed predictive activity before the signal, but the precuneus only did so in the time between signal and action.*

Thus, many of our actions are automatic, and many of these actions, as Wegner (2002) says, "involve the operation of

---

[1]http://scienceblogs.com/notrocketscience/2008/04/unconscious_brain_shapes_our_decisions.php (10/2009)

preconscious mental processes" (p.57). It would be interesting to know what proportion of our daily actions fall into the category of being automatic actions, but I would wager it is a larger proportion than one might have initially thought.

Nevertheless, one must also wonder if the previous intention to do an action is a good enough causal factor to action a later automatic response, such that the brain activity that we see as preceding the conscious will may, indeed, be preceded by a more final conscious will sometime before.

Another aspect that supports the fact that consciousness is on the tardy side of things, and lags behind our body and subconscious mind, according to Wegner, is the observation that humans cannot seem to slow down their reaction times in a gradual manner. Wegner reports Jensen (1979) as observing that people could not consciously lengthen the time they reacted and that their reactions jumped from unconscious minimum times to a much larger conscious time. The implication is that conscious and unconscious responses are two very different animals. Moreover, our conscious will seems to be less powerful, in many ways, than unconscious will, and the former struggles to control the latter effectively. In the same way that we may struggle to overcome our addictions, that Doug (from Part I) may lose the conscious battle to overcome the natural addictive tendency in his genetic heritage, our conscious will often comes out second best in a showdown with our unconscious responses.

With Libet's and other researchers' experiments[1], it seems to be clear that the consciousness that we experience as a thought in the Cartesian Theatre[2] (Dennett 2004 quoting from his previous work) is seriously lagging behind many other activities in the brain, and that that there may well be a high proportion of actions that fall into this category. Although on its

---

[1] According to Dennett (2004) and Wegner (2002) another similar experiment was carried out by Grey Walter in the 1960s who experimented with epilepsy patients who clicked to change a slide on a projector, but the button was a dummy button. The projector was actually wired up to electrodes in their brains, and their brain activity changed the slides just before they actually willed it, making them feel like the machine was reading their minds, which it kind of was. Results to this were never published, and people expect this is due to the slightly dubious ethical nature of the research.

[2] An imaginary sort of cinema in the brain where our inner self and feeling of consciousness comes together, watching ourselves – the "I" in our heads.

first reception, Libet's research was heralded by determinists as proof for determinism, I would not be so hasty, but it certainly cuts down our scope of actions that can perceivably be consciously willed to a much smaller range. The trouble being that Libet's work doesn't concern itself with long term planning and intentions.

Jonathan M.S. Pearce

Mental Causation

*"I really do think with my pen, because my head
often knows nothing about what my hand is writing"*
(Ludwig Wittgenstein)

There have been many researchers who have looked into the intricate subject of mental causation, and the confusion that can ensue therein. Wegner (2002) states that there are three different sources for the experience of conscious will – *priority, consistency* and *exclusivity*. Simply put, priority infers that the timing of an action in proximity to thinking about it is vital to having a feeling of it being consciously willed. For example, if you thought about hitting a billiard ball a second before hitting it, then you would feel as though you consciously willed it. On the other hand, if you thought about it a minute before doing it and not in the intervening period, or thought about it *after* doing it, then the feeling of having consciously willed it declines greatly.

The consistency principle infers that for conscious will to be experienced, the action and consequences have to fit into the understood nature of how the world works. For example, if you kicked a football to your friend, you would expect it to move towards the friend in the general direction of the swing of your leg. If it fired off midway through the pass at a right angle to hit an old lady in the face, then you would not connect that as being consciously willed. Furthermore, consistency refers to *thought* and action in a way that if you thought about going to the local shop to buy some milk, and ended up being there buying some milk, then there is consistency, and one would feel conscious will in action. If you thought about going to the shop for milk and ended up standing in the bus stop stuffing tissues into your mouth, then there would be an inconsistency between thought and action, causing a lack of feeling of conscious will. Quite often, one can place conscious will onto things which don't necessarily deserve it, simply because they are consistent. There have been experiments into the 'helping hands' scenario, where you have someone putting their hands through your arms that you put behind your back. The feelings of consciously willing those hands to carry out tasks were surprising, as one could imagine, even though someone else

124

was actually controlling them. This is because those hands are consistent with the body – they seem to go together. Also, one can often feel like willing a chance event that was not actually affected by any personal cause at all, and this can happen in many guises. I have often said, whilst waiting for a bus, that if a bus doesn't turn up within the next 20 seconds, then I'll walk. Upon its arrival, I feel like I was actually responsible for its advent. That said, I never walk if it doesn't turn up in 20 seconds – I just give it another 20 seconds... There are many variations for this kind of imagined will.

There are other interesting asides to dabble in here, including mental disorders such as schizophrenia, which have been known to confuse the boundaries between cause and effect, mind and action. Feelings of alien control and inconsistency in mind to action can cause a schizophrenic to feel as though an internal 'someone else' is willing their actions, or whispering voices in their ears or minds. This can be connected to language deviation, whereby their use of language often deviates in conversation from the topic at hand. The breakdown in the circuitry of their minds, leads to the inconsistency of thought and action, which leads to the schizophrenic believing that someone else has willed their actions. The normal working brain, then, can be seen to determine consistency.

In addition, it is useful to look briefly into those moments in our lives that we may see as 'Eureka!' moments or moments where thoughts just pop into our minds. We can be walking down the street, or sitting on a train thinking about something completely different when suddenly, a thought pops into our head that may answer a problem, or be something of great importance. This thought, though, is clearly not one that has been consciously willed into our heads, but seems to have unconsciously popped in. As Wegner (2002), amongst others, has pointed out, many of the greatest artists and musicians find their creative optimum when they disconnect from their conscious minds, and go into a sort of unconscious 'zone'. The nature of improvisation amongst artists is often at the exclusivity of conscious will. In fact, it is interesting to ponder exactly how our conscious minds work out things that we do labour at, such as mental mathematical calculations. We may break down 10 x 12 into (10 x 10) + (10 x 2) but when it comes down to the simple 10 x 2, it just pops into our heads. We simply don't know how the mechanisms of our brains work, and our conscious mind simply reports on the outcomes of what our unconscious computations are. It seems our conscious minds use our non-conscious minds as computers or calculators, demanding them to magically compute raw data. A great scientist can be on the cusp of working out some world-changing formula in their job, and he might be sitting on a train on holiday, looking out of the window at the lovely meadows passing by, when the formula pops into his head, worked out. Has he willed this? The subconscious computations of the brain have (though not willed by the conscious brain) been working away in holiday time, unbeknownst to the scientist, and have correctly come up with the answer to his conundrum. And yet he may, or may not, feel like he has willed that answer.

The third source of the experience of conscious will is the exclusivity principle. This suggests that if there is another plausible explanation that can account for an effect, then it can render a possible perception of mental causation impotent. For a very obvious example, if the football that was kicked to a friend suddenly veered off at a right angle half way through its path, and there was, at the point of veering, someone else who ran up and kicked it, then this would lead one to believe that there is another cause to the action taking place, other than their own mental processes. Wind, people, other animals, the supernatural (often in the guise of God): all these offer external influences that can act as causal agents to making an effect happen.

Often, when taking direct orders, or being in a situation where one is highly influenced by another person in a situation, one can act with the feeling that they have no control over their will, that their actions are really the intent of an external will from the person or people commanding or influencing them. A topical example may be the case of Lynddie England in the Abu Ghraib prison debacle in Iraq. The horrific photographs and events that took place involved the young female private, and she seemed 'happily' involved, and complicit in the procedures and happenings. However, after the fallout from the public awareness from these events, she has been shifting much of the (moral) responsibility onto those around her, above her (one of the main ringleaders was a superior soldier with whom she was involved) and onto the military as a whole. In fact, National Security seemed to somehow play more of a role in her actions than her own conscious will. Situations such as these, no matter how you take them, can certainly show that conscious will is not as clear cut as one might think.

Group psychology can also present some grey ground for working out whether you have willed something or not, and may cloud the previous three sources of experience of conscious willing. People can often feel themselves acting as part of a group, where decisions and actions are carried out collectively, and conscious will seems to be depreciated somewhat by the effect of the group. The agency of self becomes clouded, and one is not quite sure, often, of who wills what. The 'I' becomes a 'we' (known as deindividualisation) and responsibility is apportioned differently. The number of people in a group can often influence their behaviour, such as a group of youths walking down the road being more likely to break a bus shelter than two youths, and far more likely than a solitary youth. Quite often, one exonerates themselves of responsibility in a group situation by attributing the action or determining influence to the other person(s) in the group. Causality gets frequently confused when there is a circular characteristic to arguments or other interactions. Because less people are attending matches, the price goes up at the local football ground. Because the price goes up, less people go. Less people go, the higher the price is pushed, and so on. What is the cause of this circular issue? Mr. Scelta always takes the mickey out of his wife for being miserable, but she says she is miserable because her husband always takes the mickey out of her. This circular characteristic to their interactions can devolve a sense of causal responsibility.

Other causal influences that cloud the issue of whether something is consciously willed by an individual can be internal, such as "emotions, habits, reflexes, traits or other unconscious action tendencies" (Wegner 2002, p.20). To return to Doug, this internal agency can be exemplified in Doug's mental addiction to a drug, whereby his taking the drug seems to be the 'involuntary' demands of his addiction overcoming, or seriously lessening, his conscious will. In the legal system, people often have their actions mitigated, their 'normal', 'conscious' wills outmanoeuvred by fits of passion, irrational rage, mental disorders, profound depressions etc. The term 'crime of passion' immediately summons images of someone committing a crime against their rational will, pushed along involuntarily by their powerful passions. Their responsibility for their crimes is abrogated to this third party, this passion, that seems to have a 'mind of its own'.

Impulsive behaviour also falls into this category, both physical and mental, such as tics and motor disorders, which again depreciate the value of conscious will. Thus, internally, there are still many occasions, many varying situations, whereby our conscious will is competing with unconscious influences and causal mechanisms for command over our actions.

So what we have looked into here is how will works with our reasoning and the fact that a good deal of what we think a person has willed can be open to debate. Was their will to do something actually willed by the group, was it an addiction, or an internal mental disorder? Can our brains be confused over who willed an action, or over whether we ourselves have actually willed an action?

Isn't that spooky!

Daniel Wegner has spent a good deal of time researching the strange and intricate world of automatisms, which themselves can take on many different forms and have been of public interest for some time (but particularly in Victorian times) inspiring quite a plethora of literature and analysis. "What are automatisms?" I hear you cry. Well, an automatism is an act that is carried out in the absence of conscious will or awareness of the part of the performer. Such examples might be automatic writing, dowsing (for water), using a Ouija board, table turning or using a Chevreul Pendulum. In the Victorian period there was a heyday of spiritual mediums, of going to parties and having séances, of believing that the spirit world could contact you through different media, and control your actions, collective or individual, to communicate some kind of message. And who said the Victorians were restrained? That sounds like fun!

Since these sorts of behaviours deal very much with factors of will, or lack thereof, then they have been of great interest to those studying the mechanisms of conscious will, and the relationship of intention to action and vice versa.

The Ouija board and automatic writing work on such a principle, whereby a person or persons have their hands resting lightly, but exerting no conscious force, on a planchette (often a small, spade-shaped, wooden board, sometimes on rollers). After some time, the planchette might start moving, seemingly of its own volition, from letter to letter in the case of the Ouija board, or in the shape of words if one is partaking in automatic writing (the planchette has a hole at the front in which a pen is inserted, so the boards can write).

Words, sentences or answers are often formed or pointed to in a 'sensible' fashion, but the feeling of lack of conscious will on the parts of those involved is famous. The same applies to 'genuine' dowsers (not those who used to con others by knowing where water was using other clues, and moved their dowsers consciously to 'wow' their colleagues) who found their dowsers moving in their hands without consciously willing it, and the pendulums, that swung around in patterns without the performer seemingly willing them. Wegner (2002, p.100) states that not only do people claim that they do not will these actions and outcomes, but that the source of agency comes from elsewhere entirely.

A representation of automatic writing, though this can be done individually, and with blindfolds attached.

In 1888, a chap called William Carpenter took a great interest in these 'spiritual' practices and sought to explain them in more naturalist terms. He developed a theory, which is still prevalent today, that explained how all of these automatisms manifested themselves, how people carried out actions that they did not will. His ideometer action theory declared that the mere thought of the actions was enough to cause the action to happen itself. As Wegner (2002, p.121) says:

> *This ideometer action theory depended on the possibility that ideas of action could cause action but this causal relation might not surface in the individual's experience of will. Thoughts of action that precede action could prompt the action without being intentions.*

This seems to make quite some sense in the context, and I think the mere thought of something can often make us want to do it, without us consciously reasoning why. When I 'order' a child not to do something at school, quite often their immediate reaction is to try to do it, and you can almost see the internal battle of automatic response and will. Rules are there to be broken. The trick is making a command seem like something that they want to do. This is perhaps the source of the power of subliminal advertising. A trick I teach my children at school, occasionally, is to go home and talk to their parents, but before doing so, they must pick up a piece of rubbish (an empty crisp packet). Whilst engaging the parent in serious conversation, they should hold out their hand with the crisp packet in, at waist level, and keep eye contact with the parents. The parent, more often than not, will automatically take whatever is being handed to them without consciously willing it, and will quizzically wonder why they are holding an empty crisp packet after a few seconds.

I would posit that there are multitudinous occasions throughout the day when we are influenced by things and we do not realise it. Subliminal messages have been shown to have good effect, both audio and visual, particularly when they are in tune with the goal of the mind. For example, if you are thirsty, and there are pictures flashed up of a particular brand of drink, the thirsty people are more likely to choose that brand. However, people who are not thirsty will be less affected by the subliminal pictures. I would take subliminal messages much further, and say there are far more occasions of influence that are not cynical or contrived. When you see someone smiling, it will influence you to smile (pass the smile! Pay it forward!), and, as I know from experience, if one child starts coughing in assembly, they all do! Passing lots of For Sale signs on the way back from work may influence you to think about moving house, and watching a drama on TV about marital break-up may cause you to start questioning, or appreciating more, the relationship that you have. Our five senses are receptacles for influence, for determining variables, and our brains sort through all the sensory data and it can latch on to certain things. We are starting, here, to build up an idea of how influence-able our will really is.

So if the idea of something can force an action, then why does this not happen all the time? Why, if I think of stuffing a doughnut in my mouth and jumping, arms flapping, around the staffroom shouting "I love milking cows!" do I not automatically do so? It is theorised that whenever a thought of action pops into our minds, our conscious will acts as a counterforce *not* to do the action. Our will, then, is *not to do*, rather than *to do*. With the reception of the crisp packet, there is no will not to do it, so it is carried out – the process is not vetted. As Wegner says, it is why we can lie around in bed all morning thinking of all the things we could do, but still remain lying there without actioning those thoughts – they are overruled by our conscious will, willing us not to do it[1]. Where we can see some good scientific evidence of these theories is, again, in the field of brain damage, particularly frontal lobe damage. The damage seems to interfere with the processes that the brain usually performs to stop acting on things from just the simple idea; it stops the conscious will from vetting the processes which stop the actions from taking place. Wegner (2002, p.122) describes how patients with such brain damage have sat with an examiner, and with no other prompting, the examiner has touched their hands with a carafe of water and glass, and the patient has poured out a glass of water with no reasoning for it (and, likewise, with a packet of cigarettes and a lighter). More stunningly, a patient was touched with three pairs of spectacles, one after the other, and he promptly placed all the spectacles on his face, wearing three pairs of glasses at once, none of which were consciously willed[2]. The brain did not have the ability, due to the damage, to vet the ideas from being actioned at the mere (almost subliminal) suggestion of the examiner.

Anecdotally, I am positive that I have observed this in children that I have taught who suffer from particular types of autism. Such children have exhibited impulsive behaviour and on close questioning, they have no idea why they committed the actions that they did. It just came into their heads. This supports the notion that they had no vetting system to stop them carrying out actions in when the thought of those actions popped into their heads. As a result, their impulsive behaviour was also very difficult to control, because the children

---

[1] Wegner (2002), p.122
[2] Wegner (2002) sites the work of Lhermite (1983, 1986) here.

themselves were unable to control their own behaviour, since it incurred no forethought. The pencils flew across the room, or the ridiculous comments came out of their mouths before they even had time to register consciously that which they were doing, and in the absence of any mechanism in their brains that counteracted the idea of the actions in the first place.

The power of suggestion in humans is palpable, and many other instances have been researched, such as connecting people up to EMGs to measure muscular activity, and meanwhile the simple suggestion of doing an action causes the appropriate muscles to begin to act (with our conscious minds then willing them *not* to act). The suggestion by an examiner to relax the right arm will make the patient relax their right arm without consciously willing it to do so[1]. Thus, thinking *about* an action can cause that action, rather than the action being caused by conscious will.

Wegner produces a plethora of other observations and scientific experiments to show how behaviour can be unconsciously influenced: participants made to think about professors answering *Trivial Pursuit* questions more accurately than those who didn't, and ones prepped with thinking about less intelligent football hooligans scored much less[2]. Furthermore, in another study, participants made to unscramble sentences about old people and their characteristics were seen to shuffle out slowly of the hall in the unconscious manner of an old person, as opposed to those who hadn't who walked out normally[3]. Unscrambling sentences about the characteristics of helpfulness unconsciously influenced participants to do helpful acts towards their examiners, such as picking up dropped pens[4].

The vital claim that Wegner makes, in reference to these findings, is that these ideometer actions do not need to be explained by a separate theory, but that they adhere to a similar mechanism as consciously willed actions.

> *Automatisms could flow from the same sources as voluntary action and yet have achieved renown as oddities because each one has some special quirk*

---

[1] Jacobsen (1932)
[2] In Wegner (2002), Dijksterhuis and van Knippenberg (1998).
[3] In Wegner (2002), Bargh, Chen and Burrows (1996).
[4] In Wegner (2002), Macrae and Johnston (1998)

> *that makes it difficult to imbue with the usual illusion of conscious will. Automatism and ideometer action may be windows on true mental causation as it occurs without apparent mental causation.*
>
> *(Wegner 2002, p.130)*

So Wegner implies that the automatisms and ideometer actions are the 'real thing' and that this is generally the rule of how actions are performed, and that when we consciously will things, these are the anomalous occurrences, the exceptions to the rule. Thus, by starting with the premise that "voluntary behaviour can occur without conscious will", it is explicable that humans create an experience of will, that there is an *apparent* conscious will that is applied to the action. We would then have to explain why intention so comfortably often precedes and predicts action. On the other hand, if we assume that all voluntary action is willed consciously, then it is necessary to explain the exceptions to the rule, the myriad of examples (of which I have only given a few) of automatic and ideometer actions that exist without a clearly evident conscious will. Each path has its own issues.

There must be a reason! There must!

Just think of all the actions your body does in a day. There are simply too many to even conceive, from pumping blood, digesting and breathing to scratching you leg, driving to work, arguing with your boss, making a sandwich and playing a game of tennis. Every second you are moving, doing and thinking. Our brains are amazing things that can regulate, operate and coordinate all of these things, every second of our lives, until at last they give up, knackered. I find this monumental task quite breathtaking. Many of these incredible duties may well be misinterpreted as being consciously willed. Is it the case, then, that we actually ascribe conscious will to actions that are not consciously willed? Is there a prevalence for humans to find a reason for doing things?

There are certainly cases where we can observe this sort of thing happening. For example, our good friend Daniel Wegner (2002) talks of posthypnotic suggestions, whereby a hypnotist will ask the hypnotised person to do a particular action upon the end of the hypnosis (along the lines of "When I click my fingers three times, you will wake up and..."). There are some varying reactions to people finding themselves doing certain actions while newly back in the world of conscious will and reality. The interesting observations made by Albert Moll, a late 18th century German expert in hypnotism and, er... sexology[1], show how these people can, post facto, overlay conscious will onto unconsciously willed actions. One of the more exuberant explanations given to Moll is reported in Wegner (2002, p.150):

> *I tell a hypnotised subject that when he wakes he is to take a flower-pot from the window, wrap it in cloth, put it on the sofa, and bow to it three times. All which he does. When he is asked for his reasons he answers, "You know, when I woke and saw the flower-pot there I thought that it was rather cold the flower-pot had better be warmed a little, or else the plant would die [sic]. So I wrapped it in the cloth, and then I thought that as the sofa was near the fire I would put the flower-pot on it; and I bowed because I was pleased with myself for having such a bright*

---

[1] I wonder what form practical experiments take in this discipline...

> *idea."   He added that he did not consider the proceeding foolish, [because] he had told me his reasons for so acting.*
>
> *(Moll 1889, p.153-154)*

This is a fascinating example of someone creating a reason for completing an action after they had completed the action so as to make the whole process make sense – the ascribing of intention to an action after the action has been started or completed.

Reason, in and of itself, is an obviously vital component of causality. When considering human behaviour, we almost always give a reason (good reason) for completing an action. A voluntary action is accompanied by reason. If we take the reason out of the equation for why an action takes place, we are invariably left with a random, or involuntary, action, and these are not the sorts of actions we are concerning ourselves with. Accepting that reason is a cornerstone here to understanding causality, we have to discuss what caused this reason. This is a topic I will return to later in the book, in the final section on moral responsibility, but I will say one or two things before continuing, starting with the idea that reason doesn't just pop out of nowhere, and reason is a changing animal. To expand a touch, reason is created by inputted variables, and the ability to reason is one of humanity's great evolved characteristics. Other animals can reason in more simplistic terms, but we can add so much more nuance with our superior ability to communicate through language. However, reason is still defined by real cognitive abilities and tangible neural networks. Reason is an effect from an earlier cause in the chain of cause and effect. For example, Mr. Scelta reasoning that it would be a better choice not to drink at the meal with his wife is born out of previous experiences with alcohol at meals where he has become argumentative. Together with the extortionate prices that Mr. Fato charges for a Peroni, we have a set of determining influences that make up his reasoning. His reason is the effect of previous experiences and variables.

If one disagrees with this, then one has to answer the fact that our reasoning clearly changes throughout our lives, and is dependent on different circumstances. If Mr. Scelta is out at a pub with his friends, the variables are different, and he uses his reasoning to order his fourth pint of beer – the fact that he loves

Old Mottled Rat's Arse beer, the fact that it is his first night out with the lads in two months, the fact that he doesn't have work tomorrow etc.

Let us look at another example of a lad passing a bin in the street. He decides to kick it over. His reasoning, though perhaps minimal for this behaviour, is based on his disaffection with society, the relationship he has with authority, and his hormonal imbalance of high testosterone from the back end of puberty causing him anxiety and anger. Now five years ago, that lad, at the age of ten, would have reasoned differently not to do that due to not having had those experiences. And ten years on, after two stints in prison, and with a child now and a long-term girlfriend, his reasoning is different again. Now, he remembers the trouble he got into last time, and the downhill path he took that made him end up in prison, and thinks about his son, and the kind of neighbourhood he wants his son to grow up in. Reason is malleable, and is informed by our personal development, our experiences, and our raw circuitry in our brain (reasoning with an anxious Asperger's Syndrome child will enlighten you here!). The difference between humans and other animals in the context of reasoning is huge, with animals often only being able to be entirely 'logical', or digital (remember the situation-action machines). Some animals can carry out associative thinking, meaning that a cow that has walked over a cattle grid before and been injured, can reason to stay away from something that looks like one in the future. Humanity's ability to reason is far more specific, and can be far more nuanced, resulting a great deal from our gift of language.

What I am saying here, then, is that when one reasons when making a decision, and thinks they are freely choosing to decide one action over another, they are using variables that have already been defined. Their reasoning is out of their control, if you will. The agent is being determined by their reasoning. This is another powerful, and often taken-for-granted ingredient of the determinist recipe.

Let us now return to looking into the research of Wegner, and his view on intention.

Jonathan M.S. Pearce

The development of intention

As discussed in Part II, intention is the conscious thought preceding an action that seemingly directs the action to take place. But how does this feeling of intention develop in humans over time? Are we born with the ability to intend?

These can be hard questions to answer, since it is impossible to get inside the brain of an infant who cannot yet speak, in order to work out whether it can intend any of the actions it does, or whether they are unconscious, automatic or situation actions. Actually, the idea of speech is key here to intention. It possibly seems a little far-fetched to believe that babies have any semblance to anything resembling conscious will. Children learn, through their developmental stages, the abilities to not only carry out different actions, but to think about those actions, both beforehand, and after carrying them out. To preview them as well as to review them. This *theory of mind* has been the work of many a psychologist, and it is clear that the ability to reason is wrapped up with the ability to create intention and analyse the experience of preceding thoughts and resulting actions.

Things get interesting when children start grasping the rudimentary skills of speech. Wegner (2002) explains that children who start to use non-social speech report on what they are doing, rather than what they intend to do in the future, such that a child might say "I throw bunny" just after throwing the toy across the room[1]. At a later developmental stage, the child might say "throw bunny" whilst doing so, and later still "I've a good mind to throw this bunny" showing that children develop the means to explain intention, but more importantly, that intention itself seems to be created and blossoms in childhood. This previewing of our actions does seem to increase in frequency and in complexity as we get older, as we learn more about ourselves, and the world around us. Children struggle to understand how intention is something that occurs before action. This idea was reported in a study[2] that when very young children were told a story of how a particular child likes going to a friend's house, and not the ice skating rink. His mum, though, tells him to go to the ice rink, and so the child

---

[1] Vygotsky (1934) and Luria (1961), as cited in Wegner (2002)
[2] Abbott and Flavell (1996) as cited in Wegner (2002)

138

obeys and gets on the bus to the rink. The bus driver gets lost (they're not as good as they used to be) and the child ends up at the friend's house anyway. The younger the child (around three, it seems), the more the child does not understand intention, and sees the boys as intending to go to the friend's house. The intention is aligned with his desire. Older children start understanding that, though he desired to go to his friend's house, he *intended* to go to the rink.

In my teaching job with eight to ten year-olds, and this is backed up by this such research, I have anecdotally witnessed that children invent intention after the event of an action if it is in line with their desires. In blindfolded problem-solving games, I have set up a netball court with obstacles that, if they tread on, they are blown up[1]. They have to negotiate the fields by remembering the fields, and then walking through them with a blindfold on. If I move some of the obstacles unbeknownst to their blindfolded selves, and they 'accidentally' still succeed by seemingly randomly avoiding a cone or mat, they sometimes still claim that they intended to do this, even though they are not aware that the court is different to when they put the blindfold on. Similar such reports from more official research comes to the same conclusion, but with more consistency since the children are younger.

It seems that young children cannot often remember their own thoughts or knowledge, such that newly learnt information is often assumed to have been always known. Examples showing this include three-year-olds being shown a sweet box with pictures of sweets on it, only to find out that when opened, it contained pencils. When asked what other people might think it contained, they answered that they would think it had pencils in[2]. This seems to show that they had forgotten their own initial mental state. Moreover, in another experiment, the same children were asked what they initially thought was in the box, and over half thought that pencils were initially in there[3].

It is with this theory that the mind, certainly in its infancy, can retrospectively edit previous thoughts and intentions at a later stage, that Wegner looks to explain much of our conscious intention. Because we were all children once, we already have

---

[1] Of course, not literally. That is against health and safety regulations.
[2] Perner, Leekam and Wimmer (1987), as cited in Wegner (2002)
[3] Gopnik and Astington (1988), as cited in Wegner (2002)

the ability to do this, and we, he claims, do this more often than we think in our adult world of conscious will.

It's all just an illusion

But it's just an illusion

Saw the world for you one day
With all the curtains pulled away
Every mirror was a wall
Every eye a crystal ball
(Just Another Illusion – Hurricane #1)

We have looked already at unconscious and automatic actions that are not intended, the sort of actions that you don't really consciously intend doing, such as driving, making tea, carrying out a rally in tennis and scratching your leg whilst talking to someone. In fact, it is certainly the case that unconscious actions make up a far greater proportion of our total actions than consciously intended actions. We have seen how posthypnotic suggestion can be retrospectively willed by the agent, and how people can retrospectively invent intention and reason for actions already carried out (by their non-conscious minds).

However, when talking about an action itself, the idea of the action can be different depending on who you talk to and when you talk to the person about it. 'Going to work' can be 'paying the bills' can be 'doing what you love' can be 'pleasing the parents / wife' and so on. The idea of marriage is often one that metamorphoses throughout its duration from 'tying the knot' and 'confirming our love', 'being walked down the aisle' or becoming 'legally bound' to 'doing the deed', 'getting tied down', 'losing your independence' and 'going through the motions' depending on when, where and by whom you are asked about it. Along with a change in opinion of an action, humans can certainly experience a change in perceived intention of the action. Imagine the different ways that shooting an enemy soldier can be described, or torturing a prisoner in Abu Ghraib.

Within the sphere of unconscious mental causation, we have some interesting theories to look at. We have already talked about how unconscious stimuli and thoughts can influence and determine certain behaviours (the Trivial Pursuit experiments, and sentence unscrambling). This is perhaps understood a little better in light of the theory of unconscious mental causation explained by Wegner[1] who posits that there is a level of consciousness that allows thoughts to have a sort of *readiness*. These ready thoughts, have a property of being *accessible*:

> *An accessible thought is one that the person may or may not be able to report as conscious but that has some measurable influence on the person's conscious thoughts or observable actions.*
>
> *(Wegner 2002, p.162)*

I don't know about you, but I have this feeling very often, that there is a murky level of consciousness where things are almost in my Cartesian Theatre of consciousness, but are not quite there, and yet seem to pop into my head of their own accord (remember the 'Eureka!' examples), or influence my actions without me willing them to do so. I think this is also prevalent in the world of advertising. I have the feeling, when I am buying my groceries at the supermarket, that when selecting one brand over another, subconsciously, my brain is rifling through my files to compare the two brands, presenting me with the idea that I would prefer product A over B, without consciously weighing it up. I may be weighing up local over organic over seasonal, all in a millisecond. Subliminal advertising also unconsciously influences, perhaps, the accessible consciousness. These accessible thoughts can be exemplified with you reading this book. If you are sort of absent-mindedly reading this, but are really quite bored, then although you have the thoughts of this book in your conscious mind, accessible thoughts might keep popping in like "I can't wait to watch Police Academy 7 tonight" or "I must finish my embroidery pattern of that naked sailor". These unconscious, but accessible, thoughts may even tempt you enough to be overcome and set about actioning them. The popping into your head of one of these ideas might well cause you to close the book, all of a sudden, stand up, and walk over to get your needles. These actions might have completely bypassed your conscious will, being entirely influenced by your accessible thoughts. An example that has been born out by similar tests, might be asking a disfigured man to complete the word "U_ _ _".

---

[1] Jerome Brumer (1957) as cited in Wegner (2002)

Due to recent experiences, he might well write "UGLY", since this thought might be more accessible than any other 4 letter U-word, based on experiences he had had at the shopping centre that day, or that are simmering away behind his consciousness.[1]

Wegner sees this as helping to show that we have three ways that thoughts can be activated before action. The *surface activation* is the top level of conscious thought, such as the thought of this book when reading this book (but not the accessible thoughts that might jump in). *Full activation* implies a surface and accessible thought confluence, where you might be so engrossed in this book, or a favourite memory, that it brings in other similar accessible thoughts of the same type, and lines yet more up to come next. The Hollywood sounding *Deep Activation* is the accessible thought that is not conscious, and occurs when we want to think of something, when something is on the tip of our tongue, but it is not yet quite in our consciousness. These deep activation thoughts influence us all the time, such as in the simple area of our choice of words. I know for sure that when I hear particular words from any given source, they usually end up in my own vocabulary for a period of time. The other day, I heard the word 'dilapidated', which I had not used or heard for some time. I ended up using it four times over the next two days, as it was thrown up by my deep activation processes. Deep activation thoughts, when they happen, can influence people's actions, and they feel as though they have not consciously willed those actions. The previous talk of "nonconscious behaviour priming" (people shuffling out like old people, answering Trivial Pursuit questions in a particular way) and automatisms would exemplify this. This, then, can lead to the invention of intention.

In order for our intention to work, we must have memory, and memory of our intentions which can be split into three different temporal types – *prospective memory, synchronous memory* and *retrospective memory*. Or in common parlance, remembering what you are going to do, what you are doing now, and, after the action, what you thought you would do. These can be influenced by disorders such as Schizophrenia (or, indeed, vice versa) but can also be exemplified by such

---

[1] Steele and Aronson (1995) did this with African Americans and "LA_ _", when asked to do an intelligence diagnostic test. They were more likely to complete the word as LAZY (Wegner 2002, p.163).

things as knowing the amount of times you have walked into a room to say something, and forgotten what it was you were going to say, or not remembering what you opened the cupboard for, or forgetting what you were going to do next.

What Wegner is doing by posing all these theories is building up the argument that we, as humans, cannot be seen as *ideal* agents, that is, ideally in control of our intentions and thus actions, if we didn't "consciously intend *each and every action we come to understand we have performed*" (Wegner 2002, p.171, his emphasis). With all these examples, it is clear that how we come by our intentions is not only under the microscope, but whether they are consciously willed intentions at all.

One way we like to invent intention is when we do something that is at loggerheads with our own desires or beliefs. Just like in Aesop's Fables when the fox cannot reach the grapes, so decides they are sour and not worth having, so we do the same thing (known as *cognitive dissonance*). I remember buying my first campervan, 'The Beast', for what to me was a fortune (£2300), and using many different mechanisms to convince myself that it was a better buy than I thought it was; that it was a good thing it didn't have a table, because then I could comfortably eat my food on the bed etc. People do this relatively frequently, in such situations as buying a house that has certain issues, or following the Nazi party in the Second World War. Jason Long, in his tirade against the bible in his 2005 book *"Biblical Nonsense"* claims that cognitive dissonance is at play with the majority of Christians as a way to deal with evidence against their belief such as the non-answering of prayer. In reasoning why Christians, in his opinion, give unusually implausible explanations to such issues as the problem of evil (and natural disasters), the amount of deaths in the bible caused by God, and apparent contradictions, Long claims, "Because the evidence contradicts their deepest convictions, Christians provide nonsensical solutions to the perplexity and ignore valid rebuttals when they can't answer them" (Long 2005, p.17). As you will see, cognitive dissonance can drive our minds to create intentions for our actions or beliefs. Could it also be, that with the evidence that seems to be undermining aspects of free will, that by defending free will we are showing cognitive dissonance ourselves?

As debating groups will concur, experiments have been done to show this, asking people to debate or make speeches about certain issues that the speaker is not in agreement with. After making the speeches, the person is quite often more aligned to, or understanding of, the position they were asked to argue. In one piece of research[1] a group of students were asked to write an essay on something they all disagreed on. The students were told that they did not have to write it (i.e. given a choice) but they ended up writing it anyway; some were paid 50 cents and the others were paid the then sizeable payment of $2.50 for their efforts. The people who wrote it for 50 cents actually became more positive toward the topic (even though they had less reward). The students that wrote it for only 50 cents not only changed their attitude to the topic, but their perceived intention changed, such that their new attitude led them to believe that they must have had a prior intention of having wanted to do it.

Interestingly, it was only while writing this that the film director Roman Polanski was arrested in Switzerland to be possibly extradited back to the States for a crime of sex with a thirteen-year-old girl that he committed some thirty years ago. What struck me as strange were the lines of people on the streets at a film festival in Switzerland, and similar protests in France, to object to his arrest, as well as the objections of many famous people in the film industry (fans of Polanski's work). I found this bizarre, since I can hardly imagine that they would have protested that a suspected paedophile *not* be arrested for having sex with a minor, especially one whom they didn't know, or had not heard of. It appears that this is a result of cognitive dissonance as their [desires] approval of his work, their being Polanski fans, is trying to be reconciled with the fact that he is a fugitive and suspected paedophile. The outcome is the strange behaviour of *supporting* his not being extradited and not being convicted. The shock of knowing this about Polanski was outweighed by their mental investment of admiration for him as a person and artist. Surely, in the eyes of justice, it matters not a jot that you murder, rape of have underage sex yesterday, or thirty years ago! A crime is a crime, no matter the temporality...

---

[1] Linder, Cooper and Jones (1967)

Wegner claims that there are three ways that we may invent intention, one being the previously discussed cognitive dissonance. In addition, there are two other ways – self-perception and the way our hemispheres, left and right, interact. Self-perception seems to happen when there is less of a conflict between two psychological emotions in the consciousness, such as with Mr. Scelta choosing his restaurant. Even though the Indian restaurant may be closer, and may have better food, there may be subtle things at play in the mind of Mr. Scelta, such as the last time he was at an Italian restaurant, he flirted outrageously with a beautiful waitress. However, in his mind, he might self-perceive that he prefers pizza to korma. This reason may not be the real reason, and thus an invented one, that causes his actions.

The third conception about the invention of will can be seen in how the left and right hemispheres work in our brains. Our different hemispheres control different things in everything we do, see and perceive. This would be, for example, the left hand side controlling the right visual field and vice versa. Some research has been done into people who, for medical reasons, have had the left and right hemispheres fully or partially severed from each other (ouch). Most verbal responses are produced in the left brain, and the right brain does not normally produce speech. In this area, there is research that reports[1] that a patient was shown in the left visual field, thus right brain, the word "laugh" and he would often laugh. When asked why, his left brain would kick in and 'make-up' a reason as to why the right brain had made him laugh – "You guys come up and test us every month. What a way to make a living". The word "walk" shown to the right brain would make the patient get up and leave. Upon being asked why, he answered, "I'm going into the house [from the testing van] to get a Coke". This is one of several such examples of left to right brain interaction that leads to the invention of intention.

So what does this tell us? This shows us quite clearly that, as Wegner so eloquently says:

> *The person who views actions as plausibly caused*
> *by the conscious will must necessarily complete the*
> *puzzle whenever parts are missing. Imagining oneself*

---

[1] Wegner cites Gazzaniga (1983)

as a conscious agent means that conscious intention, action, and will must each be in place for every action. Intention and action imply will; intention and will imply action; and action and will imply intention. An ideal agent has all three. Putting these parts in place, it seems, involves constructing all the distortion of reality to accommodate the birth of the ego.

(Wegner 2002, p.186)

So whenever we are lacking one of the pieces of the jigsaw, then our brains seem to necessarily fill it in with a constructed piece, or distorted piece. Even actions can be distorted, as discussed through memory, but also through bias. The last time I went to a football match, my shouting at the referee for awarding a free kick against my team was not an identical interpretation of the action to what an opposing fan thought of it. The game I watched was, indeed, a different game, in many senses, to the game seen by a fan of the other team. Two people have their brains inventing different aspects of the same visual phenomena.

Jonathan M.S. Pearce

We're all control freaks

Looking at all of the evidence that Wegner gives us for the fact that much or all of our conscious will may well be illusory (and there is much more in his book than I have summarised), the crux of what he has to say involves the idea that conscious will is "emotion of authorship". Much like we feel angry or sad, annoyed or contemplative, we can also feel will, from feeling that we have no will over an event or action, right up to feeling solely responsible for a will.

As a concept, and as I have mentioned before, free will does not make sense. Free will without any determining influences is simply random. I could walk into a bar and, if I had no determining factors to my behaviour, I would simply do anything that came into my head. This randomness makes my behaviour completely meaningless. Therefore, I absolutely need determining influences to give my decisions any kind of meaning. I would need to be determined by my knowledge of social conformity not to take my clothes off and run round the bar naked. I would need my learnt behaviours that have embedded themselves in me to influence me not to punch the nearest person full in the face. I would welcome the kindness influenced by my genes, and my upbringing, and my learnt socialisation, to buy my mate a drink at the bar. This is what makes behaviour meaningful. To have complete libertarian free will, in its extreme sense, is no help at all.

It is no help at all because we are a social animal that relies on reciprocity of behaviour. If I scratch your back, then there is a good chance that you will scratch mine. This is how we learnt to co-operate, and this is a good part of the reason why we have been successful as a species. We have learnt to work together in communities, we have learnt to farm, and to organise ourselves into specialised groups in a very complex society. Absolutely none of this would have been possible if we were unable to decipher ownership over our actions. In order for us to be human, to act in all the ways that make us human, and thus seemingly far more advanced than all the other species, we need to understand ownership and control of our actions and those of others.

To attach causality to our own actions, and to the actions of those around us enables us to create a highly socialised society. Establishing this ownership allows us to "appreciate and remember what we are doing" (Wegner 2002, p.325) and marks our actions with the all important ownership. This may sound obvious to us now, but if I did not attach ownership to the farmer, by seeing will in his actions, for giving me a bushel of hay, then I am unlikely to put a horseshoe on his horse in return for his evidently willed action. This is the basis of co-operation, but actually will is useful in understanding our own more basic behaviours. People who have been brain damaged and cannot understand emotions in the same way as "normal" people struggle to operate in society as effectively, and rely a good deal on the understanding and compassion of those around them. As Wegner says:

> *The experience of will then serves to mark in the moment and in memory the actions that have been singled out in this way. We know them as ours, as authored by us, because we have felt ourselves doing them...*
>
> *Conscious will can be understood as part of an accounting system...[it] serves as an aid to remembering what we are doing and what we have done. This, in turn, allows us to deserve things...We must remember what we have done if we are going to want to claim our actions have earned us anything (or have prevented us from deserving something nasty).*
>
> *(Wegner 2002, p.327-328)*

To back this up, there has been research into the field of *perceived control*. It is apparent that people who feel that they have more control over their actions, and thus their life, are invariably: more optimistic; feel they are in better control of their behaviour; and amongst other things, are more inclined to seek information about their own situation.

People that believe they have control over situations are much more likely to be optimistic about them. Take climate change, for example. Imagine that I explain climate change to my class, and then say that most of the actions that can affect the problem positively can be carried out by the decisions of the governments of the US, India and China. The children in my class will likely give up trying to do something about it, because of their perceived lack of control. However, if I break it down to them, and explain that we can do our bit by planting some trees in the school, and planting some flowers that might encourage more bees and biodiversity, and so on and so forth, they are more likely to feel enthused and optimistic about our environmental problems. Their perceived control over the situation and actions led them to be much more optimistic. Give an old person in a care home the ownership of a plant to water, and see their spirits rise from having no control over their actions or lives.

People who have a low internal feeling of control are far more likely to attribute actions and will to fate, chance and others (people or divine agents). To be a successful species, and a successful member of that species, and thus have more chance of out-competing other members, a strong feeling of control and will of our actions is necessary; we are then much more likely to see ourselves as achieving highly, and thus more attractive to a mate. A perennial underachiever, who pessimistically sees things out of his control, who thinks anything he does is useless, ends up on the road to depression, which is not generally seen as a benefit or attractive characteristic to a prospective mate. In evolutionary terms, we are more likely to evolve characteristics of control and will into our species. As Wegner (2002) says, it might be "better to err on the side of too much perceived control".

All in all, with these points in mind, it seems to Wegner that authorship of will, and thus, the feeling of control, make us what we are. This gives a sense of self and, whether we have actually willed an action or not, the apparent will of that action is the important thing. The illusion may or may not be correct, but it is all we have. He expounds the feeling that "how things seem is how things are".

For me, Wegner, at the very least, confines the range of actual actions that we really, truly will, to a much smaller range than at first one might think. At the extreme, one could posit that all our wills that precede our actions are illusions, and that effectively we are automatons, enslaved to our subconscious minds and all the influences around us. Like Kane, it may be that Wegner sees the rarer SFAs as moments when we can really will things in our lives. These moments may be when we set out our plans, our overarching decisions that may underpin the direction of our lives. The long-term planning that we make for our lives is not something that Wegner looks into much in his book, concerning himself with the smaller, more immediate actions and their wills and intents. But then, surely the same sort of determined variables apply to the bigger actions and intentions as to the smaller, more obviously influenced actions?

Jonathan M.S. Pearce

Can our beliefs be biologically determined?

Research is taking place apace in the world of science that is helping to illuminate the dark passages of our minds, the murky channels of our bodies.

One example of how we, and particularly our beliefs, can be influenced beyond our control, is the theory that our political beliefs are influenced by biology. Rice University Professor of Political Science, John Alford, has done several experiments to look into this area. His research has included work with identical and fraternal twins, as well as assessing people's sensitivities to threatening images in connection to their political beliefs. This is how Newsweek reported the sensitivity research:

> *The results seem to suggest that our ideas about the world are shaped by deep, involuntary reactions to the things we see. As evidence, the study found that greater sensitivity to the images was linked to more fervent support for a conservative agenda—including opposition to immigration, gun control, gay marriage, abortion rights and pacifism, and support for military spending, warrantless searches, the Iraq War, school prayer and the truth of the Bible. In other words, on the level of physiological reactions in the conservative mind, illegal immigrants may = spiders = gay marriages = maggot-filled wounds = abortion rights = bloodied faces. Before liberals start cheering, however, they don't come off much more noble or nuanced. They were less sensitive to the threatening images, and more likely to support open immigration policies, pacifism and gun control. But according to the research, that's hardly desirable, since it suggests that liberals may display mammal-on-a-hot-rock languor in the face of legitimate threats. "They actually don't show any difference in physical response between a picture of a spider on someone's face and a picture of a bunny,"[1]*

---

[1] http://www.newsweek.com/id/159540 (11/2009)

In addition, the twins research threw up powerful hints at our beliefs being determined:

> *Alford, who has researched this topic for a number of years, and his team analyzed data from political opinions of more than 12,000 twins in the United States and supplemented it with findings from twins in Australia. Alford found that identical twins were more likely to agree on political issues than were fraternal twins.*
>
> *On the issue of property taxes, for example, an astounding four-fifths of identical twins shared the same opinion, while only two-thirds of fraternal twins agreed.*
>
> *"What we found was that it probably is going to take more than a persuasive television ad to change someone's mind on a certain political position or attitude," said Alford. "Individual genes for behaviors do not exist and no one denies that humans have the capacity to act against genetic predispositions. But predictably dissimilar correlations of social and political attitudes among people with greater and lesser shared genotypes suggest that behaviors are often shaped by forces of which the person themselves are not consciously aware."*
>
> *Alford believes that political scientists are too quick to dismiss genetics; rather, he believes genetics should be studied and taught along with social-environment influences.[1]*

John Hibbing, a University of Nebraska political scientist, interpreted the results in this way:

---

[1] Rice University (2008, February 6). Political Views May Be Genetically Influenced, Twin Study Shows. ScienceDaily. (Retrieved 11/2009 from http://www.sciencedaily.com /releases/2008/02/080206091437.htm)

> *"Forty, perhaps 50 percent of our political beliefs seem to have a basis in genetics," said Hibbing... While genetics are unlikely to "hardwire" people into being liberal or conservative, Hibbing said that genes could make people more or less likely to have certain values or react to situations in a particular way.[1]*

Hibbing thus implies that although there may not be a magic gene that defines your political beliefs, a set of genes will determine the sort of values you have that, depending upon the rest of your genetic makeup that may interfere, will determine your political leanings.

These determinist ideas are also employed in investigating whether we, as humans, are determined, or at the very least have more propensity, to believe in God. Much research has been initiated to investigate this theory, notably including a £2 million research project into finding whether there is an evolutionary basis for religion. Geneticist Dean Hamer has posited the God Gene hypothesis, claiming that there are 5 basic genetic reasons why one is predisposed to believing in God:

> *Dr Dean Hamer, the director of the Gene Structure and Regulation Unit at the National Cancer Institute in America, asked volunteers 226 questions in order to determine how spiritually connected they felt to the universe. The higher their score, the greater a person's ability to believe in a greater spiritual force and, Dr Hamer found, the more likely they were to share the gene, VMAT2.*
>
> *Studies on twins showed that those with this gene, a vesicular monoamine transporter that regulates the flow of mood-altering chemicals in the brain, were more likely to develop a spiritual belief.[2]*

---

[1] http://www.livescience.com/strangenews/070524_ideological_leaning.html (112/2009)

[2] http://www.telegraph.co.uk/news/uknews/1476575/God-gene-discovered-by-scientist-behind-gay-DNA-theory.html (11/2009)

Although religious people love to hate this theory, and try to criticise it from all angles, it does seem fairly common-sensical. If we can find genes that influence our other behaviours from anger to depression, from a love of sport to willpower, then it would be totally illogical to claim that behaviours underpinning political and religious belief are not regulated by genes. Furthermore, research into the brain has shown that there are several areas of the brain that are seen as responsible for the foundations of religious belief. This perhaps endorses the belief that the brain has evolved to be sensitive to any kind of belief that improves the chances of survival for the species.

Professor Jordan Grafman, from the US National Institute of Neurological Disorders and Stroke in Bethesda, near Washington has stated of the research he has done: "Our results are unique in demonstrating that specific components of religious belief are mediated by well-known brain networks, and they support contemporary psychological theories that ground religious belief within evolutionary-adaptive cognitive functions."[1] As mentioned later in the book in more detail, this could also be a mis-firing of genes that would normally be used for something slightly different, such as the understanding of purpose and coherence in the world around us. There are some different findings published in the Proceedings of the National Academy of Sciences[2] by Kapogiannis et al (2009). They found that all people, irrespective of religion, used the same area of the brain to solve moral conundrums, but that religiously inclined people used these same areas when dealing with issues of God. Some of these areas of circuitry are unique to human brains, and yet others are part of the older structures used in other primate brains. As the report's authors declare:

> *Our results are unique in demonstrating that specific components of religious belief are mediated by well-known brain networks, and support contemporary psychological theories that ground religious belief within evolutionary adaptive cognitive functions.*
>
> *(Kapogiannis et al 2009, p.1)*

---

[1] http://www.independent.co.uk/news/science/belief-and-the-brains-god-spot-1641022.html (11/2009)

[2] http://www.pnas.org/content/early/2009/03/06/0811717106.abstract (11/2009)

The theories abound that anchor our religious beliefs into the neurological framework of our biological brains. Of course, for me, this is not an argument over whether or not God exists, since one can argue, like with religion, that God has designed these mechanisms into us. No, this is more a case of illustrating that many of our 'conscious' beliefs, of our core values, are reliant, determined even, by the mechanisms that mediate them, or by external processes (such as evolution). In The article 'Natural Born Believers' by Michael Brooks in the New Scientist[1], we are given a great synopsis of the current theories, some of which I have already touched upon:

> *It turns out that human beings have a natural inclination for religious belief, especially during hard times. Our brains effortlessly conjure up an imaginary world of spirits, gods and monsters, and the more insecure we feel, the harder it is to resist the pull of the supernatural world. It seems that our minds are finely tuned to believe in gods.*
>
> *(New Scientist, No 2694, p.31)*

Many experiments show that children are far more receptive to believing in Gods because of the way their brains are hard-wired. This is partly due to the fact that our brains have different cognitive systems for living and inanimate objects. As humans, although dualism may not, as discussed, be a real and tangible thing, we develop what some call a common-sense dualism. That means that we disembody minds from the physical body. "Without it we would be unable to maintain large hierarchies or alliances or anticipate what an unseen enemy might be planning" (p.32) and Paul Bloom, a Yale psychologist adds, "Requiring a body around to think about its mind would be a great liability" (p.32). This promotes the faculty of believing in life after death, a mis-firing of the ability. Children have the increased ability to conceive of gods, which usually diminishes with education.

Humans combine these abilities with the strong characteristic that we have of the over-attribution of cause and effect. This basically acts as a survival mechanism that has to

---

[1] New Scientist, 7th February2009, No2694

be over-emphasised for reasons of continued existence. For example, if I heard the bushes rustle over there, I would be better off in attributing that effect to the cause of a predator waiting to get me (even if it was only the wind), causing me to run away as a result. If I had an under-emphasis on cause and effect, I might not attribute that cause to the effect, and could well end up being tiger lunch. This is apparent when looking at children again, who are very likely to attribute purpose and design to inanimate objects. A river exists *so that* a boat can float, and a pointy rock exists *so that* an animal can scratch themselves on it.

The New Scientist continues by reporting that Olivera Petrovich of the University of Oxford found out that pre-school children are seven times more likely to answer that plants and animals were made by God and not people. The children invent the concept of God based on their experiences of the everyday world around them. When they are then introduced to the notions of religion, they seem to make perfect sense, and these predispositions remain with us as we grow older. The attribution of design and intention to areas where there may not be any is exactly what this last chapter has been dealing with.

To add to this, some similar experiments were done at the University of Texas and the University of Evanston[1]. Here, half of the participants were made to feel a sense of lack of control, either by giving them unrelated feedback to their performance, or by having them remember occasions and experiences when they had lost control of a situation. The participants were then asked what patterns they could see in different arrangements of dots or stock market information. The people who had been given a sense of loss of control were far more likely to find patterns where there weren't any. This goes a long way to explaining why, in hard times, religions do fairly well, which is a generally accepted observation. When you suffer a disaster, such as a death in the family, one often looks for purpose, or to blame, question or seek comfort in a god. The interesting, though somewhat unethical, experiment would be to leave a group of children unattended on an island. In the same way that children are hard-wired to create language (and evidence shows that they create their own 'creole' style languages if left

---

[1] Whitson and Galinsky (2008)

to their own devices), it is assumed that children would create their own religion too, much as has every society over the course of history, irrespective of evidence.

These sorts of findings show that while it is difficult to prove or disprove the existence of God, it is evident that atheism is a hard-sell – one has to fight hard to accept atheism over a more hard-wired belief in God. From my point of view, it shows how determined we are, as a species, to believe or behave in certain ways. Our genes and our brains really do have an incredible power in deciding the outcome of our lives, in deciding every outcome.

It would be a great time to bring in the biology of willpower here, since willpower is a key to why we do, or don't do, certain actions. However, I have decided to include this subject in the section on moral responsibility, so you have something to look forward to later in the book. But to whet the appetite, let me mention the research that has been carried out into genetic determinism and kindness. It is usually assumed that kindness is something that we choose of ourselves. Not so, according to Masahiko Haruno of Tamagawa University in Tokyo, along with Christopher Frith of University College London[1]. They have found that generosity (also seen as the desire for fairness) appears to be automatic – activated by the area of the brain that controls intuition and emotion. The findings are in line with current neuropsychological understanding, that humans are on a scale of being 'prosocial' or 'individualist', with prosocial people being more inclined to share with others. The new research has found that experimenting on two groups of people (a pre-sorted group of prosocial people and one of individualists, sorted by standardised behavioural tests) has produced results that show activity in the amygdala region of the brain increased significantly in prosocial people when dealing with unfair distributions of money. The amygdala did not show such activity in individualists. The more that the prosocial people disliked the distribution of money, the more the activity fired in the amygdala. There are two crucial parts to these findings. Firstly, it was originally theorised that generous people used their prefrontal cortex to suppress selfish feelings, and thus people were thought to control their kindness in the active suppression of selfishness. This experiment showed no

---

[1] Haruno et al (2009)

activity of the prefrontal cortex, and no difference between the groups in this area. Secondly, the region that was activated (the amygdala) is an area that responds automatically, without thought or awareness.

The researchers consolidated their findings by creating extensions to the experiments, whereby they gave the participants memory tasks to carry out whilst rating the splits. The parts of the brain usually responsible for deliberation over things were being used, and yet the prosocial participants still had the same brain activity, showing that they were not suppressing selfish desires, but responding automatically. Whether the automatic response is in-built or as a result of learned behaviour is not important to the determinist, since at the point of making the moral decision of kindness, those automatic reactions are out of one's control, regardless of how and why.

Carolyn Declerck, a neuroeconomist at the University of Antwerp, Belgium, claims that this evidence backs up her own as yet unpublished research that shows that prosocial people are driven by an automatic sense of morality: "So far, all our behavioural and fMRI experiments confirm that prosocials are intrinsically motivated to cooperate.[1]"

> *Haruno will next try to figure out how this difference in the activity of the amygdala arises. It's partly genetic, but also likely influenced by a person's environment, he says, particularly the social interactions during childhood. He says it is interesting to think there might be ways to promote this activity to "realise a more prosocial society."*[2]

This is a massive piece of evidence to support determinists' worldviews. Kindness, generosity, nay morality is seemingly the outcome of genotype, with a healthy dollop of determined environment. If this wasn't enough then just open any science journal and you will find supporting evidence. Take Reuter et al (2010) who have discovered a gene variant of the COMT gene influences altruism in the form of willingness to donate. This

---

[1] http://www.thaindian.com/newsportal/health/generosity-comes-naturally-to-kind-hearted-people_100292882.html (01/2010)
[2] http://www.visembryo.com/baby/NewsArchive143.html (01/2010)

activity of kindness was twice as evident in people with a certain variant as with others. As ScienceDaily reported:

> *This mini-mutation also has effects on behavior: "Students with the COMT-Val gene donated twice as much money on average as did fellow students with the COMT-Met variant," explains Reuter. This is the first time that researchers have been able to establish a connection between a particular gene and altruistic deeds.*[1]

To be honest, the plethora of human behaviours and emotions are being mapped out more and more by the work of neuroscientists and geneticists, that at some point, I wager, little mystery of the human persona will remain, if any. Just as cartographers' satellites have mapped out every inch of the world, so too might scientists map out every defining atom of our human existence.

---

[1] University of Bonn (2010, November 8). 'Altruism gene' associated with higher willingness to donate, researchers find. ScienceDaily. Retrieved November 14, 2010, from http://www.sciencedaily.com /releases/2010/11/101108072309.htm

My conclusions to the debate

Personally, I feel that the case for determinism is very convincing. I am constantly aware of the power, internally, of my genes, and often feel that I am fighting, or conceding to, the nature of who I am, of what my genes dictate. I am also aware of how important the role of my environment has been. There is a simple and highly effective poem that sums up the environmental influences that frame a child's life:

Children Learn What They Live

If a child lives with criticism,
he learns to condemn.
If a child lives with hostility,
he learns to fight.
If a child lives with ridicule,
he learns to be shy.
If a child lives with shame,
he learns to feel guilty.
If a child lives with tolerance,
he learns to be patient.
If a child lives with encouragement,
he learns confidence.
If a child lives with praise,
he learns to appreciate.
If a child lives with fairness,
he learns justice.
If a child lives with security,
he learns to have faith.
If a child lives with approval,
he learns to like himself
If a child lives with acceptance and friendship,
he learns to find love in the world.

(Dorothy Law Holtz)

It has been my experience that everything that happens in my life, or in the world, happens for a reason, and I don't mean a pre-ordained reason such that "I caught the bus for a reason, so that I would meet Brian" as if someone (God?) was sitting there dictating that I caught a particular bus so that I would

161

meet Brian. I mean that life is just one big causal circumstance: I met Brian because I caught the bus, and I caught that bus because I felt the urge to go to the bookshop, and I felt the urge to go to the bookshop because I have a thirst for knowledge, and I have a thirst for knowledge because of my brain circuitry and the nature of my education, and so on and so forth. My actions and decisions are clearly dictated by who I am and what I have experienced, and if I was anyone different, then I might well have chosen differently. But at the point of choosing anything, I am who I am, and that dictates my decision. If, yesterday, I had seen two seagulls flying across my path, then that would make me a different person than if I hadn't, and I mean a *physically different person*. The fact that I saw those seagulls means the memory is physically imprinted in my neurons, making me a very slightly different person. It may have even sparked me off to thinking of *Jonathan Livingston Seagull* and thinking about the joy of being as free as a bird, flying through the air, or even thinking about Neil Diamond and his musical creations thereof. These thoughts might, in turn, influence further thoughts and actions, and before you know it, the butterfly has flapped its wings, and there's a tornado in Tokyo.

Even if I was to concede to Kane his moments of true free will, his Self Forming Actions, they are, by anyone's admissions, few and far between. So, in my most generous of states, free will could only influence our actions on an infrequent basis so as to make it something that is entirely different to what we normally believe it to be. If, then, most of our actions are not freely willed, then it would be only a little step further to argue that the same theories of determinism that are given to most of our actions should be given to the SFAs themselves. How are they different, and what are the mechanisms that allow them to be freely willed?

The world of neuroscience is a world that holds great fascination for me, and is a world that is still full of many unknowns, but it is where so much is being discovered month by month. A greater understanding of how we work, how our brains, our consciousnesses and our rationality work, will be the key to understanding how we truly fit into this seemingly chaotic world.

And importantly, as I will return to later, there does not seem to be any real threat to this theory: the fact that remains is that determinism is not contradicted or proved false by anything we empirically know. The main threat to the theory comes from what we would prefer the world to be like, from the notion that the world would seem to, intuitively, be a better place with more purpose. It would be a better place if we had control of our reins, if free will existed as a rational entity. But truth and preference are two very different animals.

An ever-present hurdle requiring evasion when discussing the concept of free will, is that people muddy the waters by starting with worldviews or belief systems, philosophy and theology. People have views on free will that are necessitated or biased by their pre-existing ideals (and I am no different a victim here), and they interfere with interpretations of will in the world around them. What is important, is that we look at the actual mechanisms and evidence in our environment; at how and why actions are carried out; and how our actions interact with our neurology. Thus, starting with the premise that "I believe in moral responsibility and the fact that people are responsible for their actions, and believe that God judges us for our freely willed decisions" means that, in my opinion, a correct interpretation of the biology and psychology around us is excluded. Rather, I prefer the idea of looking at the evidence from the sciences around us, and using that to create and inform my interpretation of the world. I am more sure, for example, of the feelings I have in my decision making, and in my understanding of the biology in humans, than I am, say, in the veracity of the bible or other worldviews that exist in order to validate free will. It seems to me to be the case that, in my job and in my other life experiences, man, woman and child alike, are defined, constrained, and generally determined.

Overleaf I have created a simple flow chart that you can use to find out whether you believe you are determined, or have the Holy Grail of free will at your finger tips (or buzzing around in your neurons). This makes the book a truly interactive experience! When looking at the questions involved, I find it more useful to think of real contextual examples of what the questions mean, of what they are asking. This then means you are not answering the questions in terms of what you would prefer, or in terms of what might make sense for you in philosophical or worldview terms, but actually what you experience on a day-to-day basis.

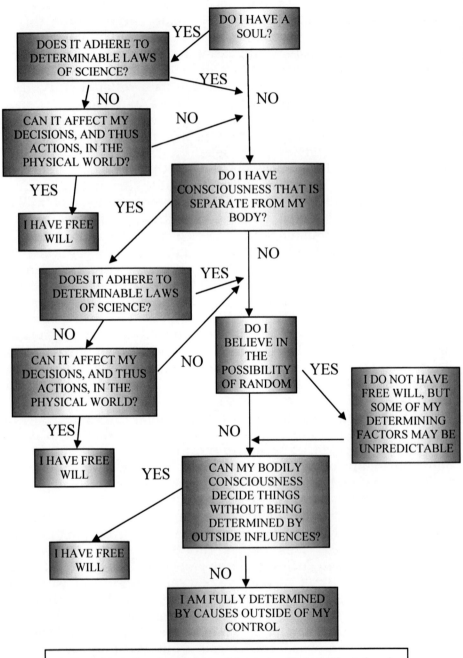

A flow chart showing the possible routes that can be taken in analysing whether you believe you have free will or not.

What has God determined?

Be warned, as things start to get a little theological now, so bear with me! It would be fairly safe to assume that, in the eyes of Christianity, determinism is generally not too popular a conversation topic at baptisms. The denial of free will in any sense of the term commonly accepted would mean many repercussions for the content and meaning of much of the bible. As I have discussed earlier in the book, choice is an inherent prerequisite for humans in much of the Old and New Testaments. What is interesting, though, is it seems that the concept of free will, in philosophical terms, was something that was developed after much of the bible was written. In fact, one of the central tenets of Christianity – the Lords Prayer (Our Father) – actually lends itself to predestination[1] to a certain degree. The lines "Thy Kingdom come, thy will be done, on earth, as it is in heaven" and "And lead us not into temptation, but deliver us from evil" hint at a notion of God willing things to happen, and delivering us from temptation, and not us doing these things ourselves. This may just be literary technique, but nevertheless, a sense of God determining actions is definitely present.

Socrates, Plato and Aristotle did their best to ruminate on the ideas and concepts of free will, linking it to morality. Free will, from the point of view of church tinkers, was not particularly considered until after the Council of Nicea in 325 CE, after which the church was formed. It was Augustine some 400 years after Jesus who first really grappled with the concept of free will from a church standpoint, and, unfortunately, it was too late to edit the bible (essentially done at Nicea, and over the centuries before that) for any contradictions that might have occurred over the notion of free will. The Catholic Encyclopaedia states the following:

The question of free will, moral liberty, or the liberum arbitrium of the Schoolmen, ranks amongst the three or four most important philosophical problems of all time. It ramifies into ethics, theology, metaphysics,

---

[1] The notion that God foreordains, decodes and facilitates, whatever comes to pass in the world.

and psychology. The view adopted in response to it will determine a man's position in regard to the most momentous issues that present themselves to the human mind. On the one hand, does man possess genuine moral freedom, power of real choice, true ability to determine the course of his thoughts and volitions, to decide which motives shall prevail within his mind, to modify and mould his own character? Or, on the other, are man's thoughts and volitions, his character and external actions, all merely the inevitable outcome of his circumstances? Are they all inexorably predetermined in every detail along rigid lines by events of the past, over which he himself has had no sort of control? This is the real import of the free-will problem.[1]

The idea of determinism was to be found everywhere in one form or another in the ancient world, and so it is unsurprising that it finds its way into the bible in many places. It is St. Augustine[2] that grappled with these ideas of a predetermined outcome to humanity, and his theology formed the basis of much of modern Christian theology and doctrine, especially with regards to this matter. The problem with St. Augustine is that he has been interpreted in such a variety of ways to the point that some people have understood him to condone a sort of determinism, whilst others have read into his theology an understanding of human free will. This is partly due to the evolution of his own ideas throughout his own life. The key to understanding what Saint Augustine proposed is to understand how he saw grace, God's character as shown through his gifts to humanity. Essentially, every good deed, even for non-believers, should be seen as a gift from God. God's providence (his sovereignty over earthly events throughout time) allows the will of man to operate benevolently. Without this providence and grace, man would not decide to do the good deed, though importantly, it does not mean that he *cannot*, but simply *would not*. Augustine asserts that man remains free, despite the reliance on God's grace – a sort of compatibilism, maybe. The

---

[1] http://www.newadvent.org/cathen/06259a.htm (08/2009)
[2] Living from 354 – 430, he was an early bishop, philosopher and theologian in the early church and had huge influence on church doctrine.

problem here is that God seems to have power over the choice of our will, but also, as the Catholic Encyclopaedia states, "that the rejection or acceptance of grace or of temptation depends on our free will". Here, we seem to have a contradiction. Without the grace of God, temptation will always overcome human will, so we are dependent on the irresistible grace of God. Augustine sees the source of sin in this world as the result of human free will, and that sin is the lack of good (and so cannot be traced directly back to God). God intended that free will be used for good, and it is humans that decide for it to be used for evil (or lack of good).

Part IV of this book deals with the idea that if you believe that God has foreknowledge of your decision, then how can that decision be free? Augustine, though, appeals to the concept that foreknowledge does not mean causality. By God knowing a decision in the future does not actually *cause* the decision to be made in that way, but simply allows him to know the future decisions of all his subjects.

Augustine continues his theories by declaring that since evil is not a thing or a being, then there is no 'cause' for an evil decision (remember, God is the source of good, but since God cannot be evil, evil cannot come from God, but it is seen as a privation, or lack, of good). Participating in a 'good' decision is participating in what goodness is – goodness comes from God, is God. God is thus the source of a good choice. The good willing of man is done with the fuel of God's being, God's own grace, but bad willing is done without the grace of God. For example, oil in an engine is responsible for the engine running well, but a lack of oil causes the engine to break down. Therefore, it is not oil that is responsible for the breakdown, but a lack of oil, and it is the driver that chooses not to put the oil in the engine. Those that choose to do ill have a will so weak that they are unable even to *choose* to repent without the help of God. So, as mentioned before, it seems (according to Augustine) that God chooses upon whom to bestow his grace in order to do good will, and thus also chooses upon whom not to bestow grace so that they decide to do evil. These predestinarian[1] concepts hint at an arbitrary God who decides who to save and who not to, seemingly on a whim. In order to

---

[1] Meaning that God has pre-calculated and willed all the events in the history of the universe. I will use this word a lot, so beware!

justify this approach, Augustine evokes the original sin[1] that Adam was responsible for, and says that God, when he changes the will of men does it out of mercy, and when he doesn't, he has that right as he is doing justice, punishing man for original sin. However, this begs the question about the historicity of Adam, or whether it was a symbolic Fall. We know, from anthropology and the like, that humans derived from a history very different from an Adam and Eve beginning. But, if we generously assume that Adam and Eve existed as the first humans[2], then it is apparent that Adam and Eve could make free will decisions without the need of grace from God, or from him allowing them to do evil as a result of justice from the Fall, since the Fall had not yet happened! In fact, their big evil decision caused the Fall, so one can safely assume that evil can be done without the necessity of bringing in the theology of the Fall!

Critics could then say that, if God (as St. Paul says) wants to save all of mankind, God would bestow his grace upon everyone. The answer is that God wants this, but it is man's will that doesn't want the salvation. This gives a weak willed man quite some strength over the will of God which is rather incoherent! It seems there is a slightly confusing idea of what

---

[1] Original sin is the concept, now not *so* adhered to throughout Christianity that humanity has an inherent sinfulness that is as a result of the Fall of Man, when Adam and Eve decided to eat of the forbidden fruit. Humanity can only be saved by the grace of God.

[2] Which is refuted by the text of Genesis (4:16-20) itself that states:
Then Cain went out from the presence of the LORD, and settled in the land of Nod, east of Eden.
Cain had relations with his wife and she conceived, and gave birth to Enoch; and he built a city, and called the name of the city Enoch, after the name of his son.
Now to Enoch was born Irad, and Irad became the father of Mehujael, and Mehujael became the father of Methushael, and Methushael became the father of Lamech.
Lamech took to himself two wives: the name of the one was Adah, and the name of the other, Zillah.
Adah gave birth to Jabal; he was the father of those who dwell in tents and have livestock.
We have Cain marrying someone in the land of Nod, and building a city, meaning there were a good many people around, and within just a couple of generations, farming had developed. It is interesting to wonder how Cain left God's presence when he is supposedly omnipresent. Since the twelve tribes of Israel derived from the descendents, it is highly likely (to me) that the account is symbolic in a tribal heritage sense.

free will is to Augustine, and his later writing sees him moving further towards a predestinarian view, though one must realise that he often wrote for different audiences, and his seemingly different theologies were just, arguably, parts of a mechanism with the same core.

Let us put this into context. According to the Good Doctor[1] (Augustine), God effectively has two lists – one of the elect (good deciders) and of the reprobate (bad deciders). I now know why my old teachers called me a reprobate. God knows what decisions these people will freely make, since he has infallible foreknowledge. So you can't say that one person can move from one list to the other. God knows beforehand that Harry is going to choose (badly) X. Harry could choose Y, but God knows his (free) will, and so he chooses, as God predicts, X. Harry is a reprobate. Does this mean that we cannot sin except of our own fault, yet we cannot be righteous without the intervention of god? Here, St. Paul, who wrote the earliest guidebook on Christianity some 25-30 years after the death of Jesus (by writing long letters to early churches around the Mediterranean), writes with predeterministic tendencies:

> *And we know that God causes all things to work together for good to those who love God, to those who are called according to His purpose.*
> *For those whom He foreknew, He also **predestined** to become conformed to the image of His Son, so that He would be the firstborn among many brethren; and these whom He **predestined**, He also called; and these whom He called, He also justified; and these whom He justified, He also glorified.*
> *(Roman 8:28-30, my emphasis)*

It is passages in the bible such as this that predeterminists, or theologians such as Augustine, use as their sources to try and work out exactly who God is, and what he is purported to know.

So, is Augustine a determinist, a predeterminist? Neither? Well, after all that, I'm not sure I'm any the wiser. I think the problem that he has is that he is dealing with these issues from a very theological standpoint, and not thinking about the actual

---

[1] He was recognised as Doctor of the Church in 1298 by the then pope.

physical mechanisms (understandably, given the medical knowledge of the time) that underpin decision-making and will. How does grace really work? I mean, it sounds a lovely idea – like the soul – but really, what is it and how do we prove it exists (other than arguing from the bible)? Aside from the issues surrounding what grace actually is (and there are many different types of grace, such as divine grace, prevenient grace, irresistible grace and actual grace), there are other problems with Augustine's thinking. His particularly theological and philosophical standpoint precludes the practical view of what happens in real life. A person, by Augustine's theory, is someone who is either good, or bad; who is either on the elect list, or the reprobate list.

And yet, individual decisions are not simply good or bad decisions, but exist along a continuum. There are so many variables in life, so many influences that impact upon each individual decision, that it seems crazy to suggest that they can be simplified down to simple dichotomous appraisals – good or bad. Life is full of decisions from each person that can be seen as both good and bad, depending on the subjective viewpoint. People change throughout life, as the moral zeitgeist shifts, and as they learn new things. As such, they appreciate life in a different way. Life simply isn't good or bad, black or white, but more realistically, shades of grey. I simply cannot practically apply Augustine's theology to life as we know it. Doug's choices in where his life goes may be seen as 'bad' choices that would instinctively place him on the reprobate list, but he has a plethora of mitigating circumstances that influence his decisions. Likewise, someone (let's call her Millie) who is born into a privileged position of having stable parents, a sound socio-economic background and future, strong ethics and morals instilled from an early age, is going to be more likely to have the tools with which to make the 'right' decisions, and be a 'good' person. Does that mean that all grace really is, are the positive variables that lead people towards making positive choices? Both Millie and Doug can be believers, but Millie, outside of her control, has been handed some very favourable circumstances on a plate, whilst Doug has been dealt a really bad hand, and yet an Augustinian view would have Millie on one list and Doug on another without taking into account all the things in their lives over which they have no control.

Of course, St Augustine isn't the only Christian to have explored the world of determinism. Thomas Aquinas, a very influential Italian Christian theologian of the 1200s, believed (as many Christians do) that the mission of humanity is to live in eternal union with God after death, which is causally linked to experiencing redemption and salvation, through Christ, on earth. Thus, on earth, a human must act towards this goal by living charitably, peacefully and with holiness. This is also the route to earthly happiness. Essentially, humanity exhibits morality that is aligned to God's own nature by choosing wisely, and by actively seeking to understand and see God. Free will is the order of the day, and if used correctly, will lead to an everlasting union with God in the afterlife. None of this approaches any kind of understanding of how we come by decisions, over whether things can mitigate against decisions made, and what influences our rationality, that in turn influences our decisions. The simplistic nature of theological ideologies is something that I often find frustrating. Anyone can sit in a pub and say, "Did you hear what Doug did the other day? What a bad choice that was! I mean, I would never have done that." It is so easy to judge people on simple 'good' and 'bad' bases. But life is not like that. Sitting in the pub and judging someone is easy, but never accurate. At Tippling Philosophers, we would never discuss what has happened over the last week in the tabloid newspapers (we spend that time arguing who will buy the first round), but many people *do* take heed of the snap moral judgements made by such institutions. To appreciate someone's actions, you really have to *be* them, and to judge them, you really need to know their causal circumstance, down to the finest detail. This harks back to Schlink's comment in *The Reader* – understanding motivations is key to whether we condemn the actions or come to a realisation of why they happened.

Jonathan M.S. Pearce

What about Calvinism?

In the 1500s, at the birth of Protestantism, there was a Christian movement inspired by John Calvin that had a very distinct flavour. Under their system of belief, the Calvinists think that God has utter sovereignty over humanity and he would be just in condemning all of humanity, since we are culpable due to original sin. Much in line with aspects of what Augustine was saying (although there are some differences in some of their other theologies), God is at liberty to save who he wants and condemn who he wants. Those who are fallen are morally unable to escape the path that God has set out for them: they are unable to sidestep condemnation. Unless God wants to, in which case the subject will live in willing obedience. This approach illustrates the complete dependence that Calvinists have on the grace of God, since all humans are born into total depravity – every part of man is inclined to sin, to think of their own selfish needs before those of others.

The importance of mentioning Calvinism in the debate about determinism is if there was clear, concise and unproblematic scripture in the bible, then movements like Calvinism would never have materialised. Movements such as these were born out of theologians creating theories that were inspired by specific interpretations of the bible. Thus, we can understand (to a degree) why these movements exist as they do. With the existence of some 32,000 different Christian sects, it can be said with some conviction that the revelations of God, through the biblical scriptures, are not clear enough, and confusion within the ranks of Christianity is apparent to outsiders and non-Christians.

Calvinists come under much criticism from all sides, Christian and non-Christian alike, because their views have so many far-reaching implications. The main objection to predestinarian Calvinism is the obvious denial it gives to free will. A further objection to Calvinism often brought up is if God has predestined who will be damned and who will be saved, it doesn't offer the Average Joe any motivation to find salvation, and it implies that a goodly portion of the world will be destined for damnation – something that an all powerful, all loving God would surely not want. This kind of theological fatalism is perhaps the most depressing of all theories, since if you are damned, well, you're damned – and there ain't a lot you can do about it.

Determinism in other religions and Eastern Philosophy

The common labels used by most religions to describe determinism are *fate* and *destiny*. These are common notions that have existed the world over, throughout history.

In Islam, there are verses in the Qu'ran that support the idea of God knowing all that has, is and will come to pass:

> *"With Him are the keys of the invisible. None but He knows them. And He knows what is in the land and the sea. Not a leaf falls, but he knows it, not a grain amid the darkness of the earth, nor anything green or withered but is recorded in a clear Book[1]."*
>
> *(Surah al-An'am, 6:59)*

The knowledge of the divine is implied as all-encompassing. As we can see, any notion that everything is pre-ordained goes against what was mentioned earlier about people having free will. It is this confusion that seems to be evident in most religions: the jostling over whether destiny and fate can interfere with a human's 'right' to ownership over his or her own future. That said, these following words are fairly explicit in their opinion that Allah has easily scripted all that is to come to pass:

> *"Every affliction that falls on the earth or yourselves, already exists in a Book before it is brought into being by us. No doubt that is easy for Allah to accomplish."*
>
> *(Surah al-Hadid, 57:22)*

These verses are seen by many to be at loggerheads with the early verses quoted in the Libertarian free will section, and this obviously has not gone unnoticed to Muslims themselves. In fact, in early Islam, the proponents of free will, the movement that believed that free will was endowed upon man by God, was the Qadarite (derived from the Arabic word for *fate*) movement. As Karen Armstrong says of Qadarite belief:

---

[1] The 'Book' mentioned here does not necessarily refer to the Qu'ran, as some might think.

Human beings had free will and were responsible for their actions; they were not predestined to act in a certain way, since God was just and would not command them to live virtuously if it was not in their power.

(Armstrong 2002, p. 40)

But does this not illustrate a possible contradiction, and does it not employ *special pleading*? On the one hand, there are verses that imply predeterminism, but on the other hand Allah cannot command them to live good lives without giving them the ability to choose to do so? Free will *has* to exist since God has said we should be virtuous, irrespective of the other verses.

These Qadarites debated with the Jabarites, who believed in a fatalistic view of the world that was pre-ordained by Allah. In order for there to be two distinct and opposing views on what the Qu'ran illustrated about free will, meant that it was certainly up for debate – there was obviously something that was not clear enough, not explicit enough, or certainly there was evidence to them of contradiction that led to two such opposing views. Eventually larger scholastic groups swallowed up these smaller ones, so that the Ash'arite movement believed in predestination, whilst the Mu'tazailites believed in free will.

The problem that many Muslims have with predestination is the fact that it can be misused to the advantage of unscrupulous so-and-sos. Someone that acquires wealth or power wrongfully and unlawfully, can just say, "Well, it's how Allah has ordained it – you need to take it up with Him." Likewise, one who is under-privileged and in a position of desperation and poverty, cannot argue with where he or she is, because it is surely the will of Allah. Someone who believes in predestination, it is argued, might have no desire to reform his immoral character, to control his actions in such a way that they do not cause undue harm, because, well, everything is 'due'.

Thus, the way forward was to declare that the doctrine of destiny was misunderstood, and that free will and destiny could, in fact, be reconciled. Two ideas help to make it possible to do this. Firstly, a person's action is written in the 'Preserved Tablet', but this does not cause the action, because God is not restricted by time, and so God can know all events by existing a-temporally. This is definitely something I will return to in future chapters. Secondly, that God, in his omniscience, has foreknowledge of all possible futures, of which some he allows (rather like the later explained Middle Knowledge), and some he does not. Essentially, when it boils down to it, the issues that Islam suffers are remarkably similar to Christianity, even though Christians poured disdain on Islam historically for their 'belief' in predestination.

At the time of early Buddhists and Jains in the Indian subcontinent were a group of people known as the Ājīvika movement. The Ājīvikas were thought to have been strict fatalists, meaning that they believed in a full form of determinism, where there was no notion of free will. They seemed to have followed a very sparse existence of fasting and being exposed to the elements amongst other things. They might well have been an atheistic movement, and were even thought to have worn clothes sparingly. Unfortunately, not an awful lot about them is known, and most that is comes from hostile sources, which in historical terms means it is not often accurate. But determinist they were, and fate was their friend.

As mentioned before, most theistic religions saw determinism as abrogating moral responsibility away from humans, and so didn't really accept it as a belief system, other than in a few isolated groups here and there. From Buddha to Allah, the mainstream views were that, although God or other systems may strongly determine much in human life, ultimate responsibility lies with the human. As B. Alan Wallace (a famous American Buddhist practitioner, who specialises in many other disciplines) states, in the eyes of the Buddha, there is much in our lives that determines how we are, but through a pursuit of an ethical and spiritual life we can achieve liberation:

> *In pragmatic terms, as ordinary sentient beings we do not have free will to achieve what is of value within our range of circumstances insofar as our minds are dominated by mental afflictions. But the Buddha declared that these sources of bondage are not inherent to our very existence, that they may be dispelled through sustained, skilful spiritual practice.*
>
> *(Wallace, p.17)*

I had better get practicing, then.

PART IV – PROPHECY AND THEOLOGICAL

DETERMINISM

There was a young man who said, 'Damn,
It is borne upon me that I am
A creature that moves
In predestinate grooves
Not even a bus, but a tram.'
(From Simon Blackburn, 'Think')

Fear prophets...and those prepared to die for the
truth, for as a rule they make many others die with
them, often before them, at times instead of them.
(Umberto Eco)

Prophecy: The art and practice of selling one's
credibility for future delivery.
(Ambrose Bierce)

Prophecy: Two bull's eyes out of a possible million.
(Mark Twain)

Among all forms of mistake, prophecy is the most
gratuitous.
(George Eliot)

In this part of the book, I will be looking at what prophecy means to us now, and to the people of biblical times, and how this can affect the understanding of cause and effect, and determinism in general. I will look upon the biblical world, the issues of atonement and judgement, in the light of prophecy. Furthermore, I will consider the notion of theological determinism, inasmuch as God interfering with events on earth in order to achieve certain goals and ends. I will look to investigate how our freedom of choice can be affected by a God that is trying to determine a certain outcome for humanity, or a God who is trying to change things in the world to suit his own needs.

What, in the name of God, is prophecy?

Prophecy is a term that gets bandied about with relative ease in the spiritual world, and the practitioners of prophecy are often understood to do a wide variety of things to the point that your idea of a prophet might very well be different from the idea of a prophet in biblical times. Nowadays, you might be lucky to catch up with a soothsayer at the next circus that comes to town, paying her a quick buck to see into your future (if you're lucky, she might even have a comedy eye patch), to read the prophecies, and tell you weird and wonderful things that can be interpreted in all manner of different ways (Well at least there are some similarities here to biblical times...). Let us look at the term 'prophecy' and see what we can glean from some different sources. Over to you, Dictionary.com:

> *noun, plural -cies.*
> *1. the foretelling or prediction of what is to come.*
> *2. something that is declared by a prophet, esp. a divinely inspired prediction, instruction, or exhortation.*
> *3. a divinely inspired utterance or revelation: oracular prophecies.*
> *4. the action, function, or faculty of a prophet.*[1]

There are two characteristics to the term prophecy – it is both the foretelling of future events, but also the general

---

[1] http://dictionary.reference.com/browse/prophecy (10/2008)

declarations and actions of a prophet. So how do we understand what a prophet is and does? The catholic Encyclopaedia does a good job in explaining what a religious prophet does:

> *General Idea — The Hebrew Prophet was not merely, as the word commonly implies, a man enlightened by God to foretell events; he was the interpreter and supernaturally enlightened herald sent by Yahweh to communicate His will and designs to Israel. His mission consisted in preaching as well as in foretelling. He had to maintain and develop the knowledge of the Old Law among the Chosen People, lead them back when they strayed, and gradually prepare the way for the new kingdom of God, which the messias was to establish on earth. Prophecy, in general, signifies the supernatural message of the Prophet, and more especially, from custom, the predictive element of the prophetic message.[1]*

What is interesting about this definition is the idea that God is "communicating His will and designs" which explicitly decrees that God has a will and design about an outcome for the world. Is this just an idea about how he would like the world to be, such as if I decided to order a cake, I would have an idea about how it should be, but it does not necessarily mean it will turn out that way? Or does this assume that God has a design and will about the outcome of the world, and God will put into place the mechanism that will cause the outcome to be as he has designed. In other words, is God making the cake himself, or is God ordering other people to make the cake, and leaving it up to them to interpret his wishes and preferences?

The first person entitled prophet was Abraham, who is obviously a crucial cog in the religions of Judaism, Christianity and Islam (i.e. Ibrahim). Moses was probably the most heralded prophet, but there were many others, such as Balaam, Samuel, Isaiah, Elias and Eliseus. There were also prophetic writers, such as Isaias, Jeremias, Ezechiel and Daniel, as well as many others. But, as was warned a good few times, there were many

---

[1] http://www.newadvent.org/cathen/12477a.htm (10/2008)

false prophets – beware! Amongst the many jobs for these special people to do, there was the important function of the revelation of divine knowledge and inspiration. This revelation could be in the form of figures, words, signs and symbols, or all of them together. Their prophetic visions were obviously open to much interpretation, but they had the job of doing so, and communicating these ideas to God's chosen people: the Israelites. These visions took place, almost entirely, when the prophets were awake and often included angelic visions, and were often associated with a form of ecstasy.

For the purposes of this book, it is necessary to look at the predictive side of prophecy, and the many times when the prophets claim to foretell future events. They concern themselves, in the main, with the following:

> *...the constant subjects of the great prophetic predictions of Israel, the punishment of the guilty nations, and the realization for all of the ancient promises. Directly or indirectly all the prophecies are concerned with the obstacles to be removed before the coming of the new kingdom or with the preparation of the New and final Covenant. From the days of Amos, and clearly it was not even then a new expectation, Israel was awaiting a great day of Yahweh, a day, which it deemed one of extraordinary triumph for it and its God. The Prophets do not deny, but rather declare with absolute certainty that the day must come. They dispel the illusions concerning its nature. For Israel, faithless and burdened with crimes, the day of Yahweh will be "darkness and not light" (Amos 5:18 sqq.). The time is approaching when the house of Jacob will be sifted among the nations as wheat is shaken in the sieve and not a good seed drops to the ground [Amos 9:9]. Alas! the good seed is rare here. The bulk will perish. A remnant alone will be saved, a holy germ from which the Messianic kingdom will arise. The pagan nations will serve as sievers for Israel. But as they have wandered still further from the right path, the day of Yahweh will come for them in turn; finally the remnant of Israel and the converts*

*of the nations will unite to form a single people under
the great king, the Son of David.*[1]

Built into this general prediction, is (arguably, if you are
Jewish) Jesus, who as a prophet himself, represents the great
king, the Son of David. Jesus throws into the mix a number of
prophecies himself. Some prophecies from the Old and New
Testaments remain categorically unfulfilled, and many others
are claimed to have been fulfilled, mainly in the form of Jesus.

Many theologians will here differentiate between the nature
of foreknowledge and the nature of predestination. With
foreknowledge, it is claimed that it is the knowledge of future
events that depend upon free will. In context, foreknowledge
implies that God would know that Mr. Scelta would choose the
vegetarian pizza, whilst allowing him to choose it freely.
Predestination implies that God would choose (determine)
beforehand that Mr. Scelta would 'choose' the vegetarian pizza.
Of course, this presents many issues with which I will deal.
Predestination, in this sense, is the occurrence of events that
God has decreed and revealed that he will do, and which will
infallibly come to pass.

---

[1] http://www.newadvent.org/cathen/12477a.htm (10/2008)

Jonathan M.S. Pearce

How can we prove prophecies to be true?

There are many areas of prophecy that can engender fierce argument from many quarters, and this is not a book about prophecy, so I don't really want to go down that road. However, it is useful to have a bit of background knowledge about matters prophetical. The first problem is that prophecies in the bible can be read in a Jewish context, or a Christian context (some being also known as *eschatology* – concerning the impending end of the world, or end times). For example, there is a long running dispute over the meaning of the prophecy from Isaiah 7:14-17:

> ""Ask a sign for yourself from the LORD your God; make it deep as Sheol or high as heaven."
> But Ahaz said, "I will not ask, nor will I test the LORD!"
> Then he said, "Listen now, O house of David! Is it too slight a thing for you to try the patience of men, that you will try the patience of my God as well?
> "Therefore the Lord Himself will give you a sign: Behold, a virgin will be with child and bear a son, and she will call His name Immanuel.
> "He will eat curds and honey at the time He knows enough to refuse evil and choose good.
> "For before the boy will know enough to refuse evil and choose good, the land whose two kings you dread will be forsaken.
> "Te LORD will bring on you, on your people, and on your father's house such days as have never come since the day that Ephraim separated from Judah, the king of Assyria."

There are issues here that Christians and Jews wrangle over ad infinitum. Firstly, Christians reckon it is foretelling Jesus as the Messiah, and Jews think it is another Messiah, as yet to come to pass. Critics will say that Jesus was called Immanuel after the writing of the New Testament (he is not called Immanuel in the New Testament, it is only Matthew quoting Isaiah) to make it a self-fulfilling prophecy – a prophecy that you make come true by actively knowing about it and acting to fulfil it. Many scholars also assert that the translation of the word "almah" to mean virgin is incorrect, and it actually means young woman[1]. This has knock on affects, so that biblical critics now claim that the stories written of Jesus' birth, written some time after his death, were using this 'prophecy' to influence their accounting, after the events, of Jesus' birth and life. Since they were using a mistranslation of the word, then the claim that Jesus was born of a virgin birth is disputed. Other issues include the meaning of honey and butter; what the two kingdoms abandoned during his lifetime were; why was Jesus (who was sinless from birth) described as having to learn evil from good and choose the latter; who dreaded the Kingdom of Israel in the 1st century when there had not been one for 700 years; and so on?

To sceptics, the prophecies in the bible provide rich pickings for arguments of historicity, context and meaning. Robert Newman (1997), a Christian apologist, puts arguments against prophecy as follows. Firstly, many critics argue that the dating of many prophecies is incorrect, and they were originally dated as being written before the events they predict. However, it is argued, they were actually written after the events as correct 'prophecies' of events that had already taken place. These later authors may claim to be their more famous earlier counterparts. Newman says, "Daniel's prophecy of events leading up to the Maccabean revolt is so detailed that the whole book is removed from the traditional time of the prophet (sixth century B.C.) to the revolt some four centuries later" (Newman 1997, p.215).

In addition, it is argued that the prophets never actually meant to preach about events beyond their own immediate horizon. Thus, anything that is fulfilled as a prophecy centuries after it was preached could never have been meant to talk about such events. They were much more short-term than that. These prophecies may have actually happened in the era that they were talking about, but perhaps we don't know enough about those eras to prove that they were events that had already taken place. Thus, we attach new meanings to them.

---

[1] Matthew mistranslates the Hebrew word "almah", meaning young woman, into the Greek word "parthenos", meaning virgin. And now we have a virgin birth myth! The translation of "almah" in Isaiah is only found in Christian bibles (though some now show it as young woman) to harmonise it with Matthew's mistranslation. Jewish texts translate it differently.

Furthermore, it is often argued that a later writer, as in the Isaiah example, created events that fulfilled earlier prophecies, thus giving their own writing, and the person(s) they were talking about, much more authority. Even if the writer did not make up the accounts after the prophecy, there is the problem of self-fulfilling prophecies. If you know that there is a prophecy written about you that you will change your job to become a banker, and you do that on account of knowing that prophecy, is this then a true prophecy? It can be argued both ways, since you could say that you only did that action on account of already knowing the prophecy, that the prophecy itself was the only motivating factor, and so on. Newman continues that other methods of discounting prophecy include arguing that the prophecies were vague enough to read that which you like into them. Moreover, some say that there are so many prophecies that some were bound to come true. This is an interesting point when you consider that as according to 1 Kings 18, Elijah was up against 850 (false) prophets:

> *"Now then send and gather to me all Israel at Mount Carmel, together with 450 prophets of Baal and 400 prophets of the Asherah, who eat at Jezebel's table."*

Just look at the 850 (albeit false) prophets, and take into account that their main vocation is prophesying. They are going to be creating a good number of prophecies per year to earn their wage. Multiply that by 850, and you've got an awful lot of prophecies. So, statistically, there probably were a massive amount of prophecies, and it would be churlish to think that some might not come true, especially since they are so often open to a large amount of interpretation. Now, just in the bible, there were a large number of prophecies: "J. Barton Payne's Encyclopaedia of Biblical Prophecy lists 1,239 prophecies in the Old Testament and 578 prophecies in the New Testament, for a total of 1,817. These encompass 8,352 verses[1]". That's alotta prediction...

However, I am not here to debunk prophecies. In fact, I would go so far as to say, for the purposes of the experiment at hand, I need to assume that prophecies are true, that God often

---

[1] http://www.christiancourier.com/articles/318-how-many-prophecies-are-in-the-bible (10/2008)

popped down to Earth, or sent his messengers, to communicate that which would come to pass in the future. I will assume that Hosea's prophecy about the Israelites living for many days without king or prince did, indeed, refer to the Jewish people living without king for nearly 2000 years (apart from the Maccabean and Herodian descended kings). I will also assume all the Messianic prophecies are true, such as another Isaiah prophecy from Isaiah 53, which includes such lines as:

> *For He grew up before Him like a tender shoot,*
> *And like a root out of parched ground;*
> *He has no stately form or majesty*
> *That we should look upon Him,*
> *Nor appearance that we should be attracted to*
> *Him.*
> *He was despised and forsaken of men,*
> *A man of sorrows and acquainted with grief;*
> *And like one from whom men hide their face*
> *He was despised, and we did not esteem Him.*

I will ignore all the Jewish and sceptical protests that the whole prophecy refers to Israel, and not to a future Jesus. I am, for the meantime, a big fan of prophecies, and I believe them all wholeheartedly, and without a heartbeat of doubt. Let's hear it for prophecies!

Jonathan M.S. Pearce

God's diary is full of important dates and plans

So, assuming that all the prophecies were true in the bible, what is it that was so important that God wanted to make sure happened? What had God determined to happen to and for humanity? In the Old Testament, the prophets were mainly concerned with predicting the outcome of battles, the defeating of enemies, and towns that could or could not be destroyed. Moreover, the continuation of the line of David was foretold. David was so very important to the Jews that it was essential that Jesus was of the Davidic line. For Christians, though, the most important prophecies concerned the coming of Jesus himself, to atone for the sins of the world, and to start the new kingdom. There are many Messianic prophecies in the bible which herald the coming of the Messiah in the future, the person who will lead Israel into a new era (generally in a military sort of way). The ones that are harder to attribute to the coming of Jesus are seen as being Jewish prophecies, either unfulfilled or referring to someone or something else. Furthermore, after the Gospels, we have some startling divine revelations in, well, the aptly named Revelations, predicting the end times and other such exciting and happy events. We'll return to Jesus in a short while, but in the meantime, let us look at the other sorts of prophecy, and how this might affect free will.

Other than the Messianic prophecies, as mentioned, most of the prophecies were concerned with wars and politics in the context of Ancient Israel, or, since the nation of Israel didn't always exist, the twelve tribes of Israel. These are the sorts of prophecies that we will look at first.

So no matter what we did, we would always have won the battle?

There are many varying prophecies that predict all manner of political and military accomplishments in the context of the early Israelites. One could argue that God was ensuring the future of a very local people in a very parochial manner, without seemingly caring about appealing, or revealing himself, to the rest of the world. Thus, it seems that his chosen people were very important to him, and this is reflected in his intervening on a regular schedule.

So how does the fact that God had forecast certain eventualities affect the free will of those involved in the events? This is one such revelation to Jeremiah, in Jeremiah 34:2-5:

> *"This is what the LORD, the God of Israel, says: Go to Zedekiah king of Judah and tell him, 'This is what the LORD says: I am about to hand this city over to the king of Babylon, and he will burn it down. You will not escape from his grasp but will surely be captured and handed over to him. You will see the king of Babylon with your own eyes, and he will speak with you face to face. And you will go to Babylon.*
> *" 'Yet hear the promise of the LORD, O Zedekiah king of Judah. This is what the LORD says concerning you: You will not die by the sword; you will die peacefully. As people made a funeral fire in honor of your fathers, the former kings who preceded you, so they will make a fire in your honor and lament, "Alas, O master!" I myself make this promise, declares the LORD.' "*

What we have here is a king of Judah, a chap called Zedekiah, who is told that God has destined his city to be captured and burnt to the ground; he will be captured and taken to Babylon, where he will die peacefully. But he shouldn't worry too much, as people will surely be sad about his death. The implications here are that no matter what Zedekiah might do, no matter what stroke of military genius he might have, and despite the fact that his people are supposedly the chosen ones,

187

Zedekiah was going to lose his city, and many people would lose their lives. One assumes that this was destined to happen by God, because it all fits into the larger jigsaw puzzle of his intentions for Israel, and as such, the world.

Let us look at this episode in real-life context. God is decreeing that, no matter what happens, no matter what decisions are made, a good many people will die, and a whole city will burn to the ground. Perhaps God is not actually saying this, perhaps it is not a case of no matter what decisions are made, but is more a case that God knows *exactly* what decisions will be made. This then could potentially lead us to predestination, or determinism. In other words, God has either determined in advance what he wants, and has set all the variables up to achieve these ends, or he has set all the variables up with no particular design for the outcome, but can compute what the outcome will be. In either of these scenarios, there is left no opportunity for any of the protagonists to exercise anything that resembles a conventional form of free will. If Zedekiah had suddenly wanted to go on holiday to Egypt... well, he couldn't, since God had decreed exactly what was going to happen to him, and there was nothing anyone could do about it. This has moral implications for God himself, since this is not just simply a case of determining what I am going to eat for breakfast – toast with homemade raspberry jam, or Fruit and Fibre cereal – but it is a case of determining that tens of thousands of people are going to die horrible and painful deaths. Is this the behaviour of an omni-benevolent God? Could God have done otherwise? One of the classic defences that theologians use for the problem of evil[1] (the problem of death and suffering in the world), and of why God shouldn't just simply make there be less deaths, is that he has given us free will, and the suffering and deaths are a result of our

---

[1] We visited this earlier, but here is a piece of philosophical history for your enjoyment: Epicurus (341BCE-270 BCE) first formulated the dilemma dealing with God and his characteristics: "Is God willing to prevent evil, but not able?
Then he is not omnipotent.
Is he able, but not willing?
Then he is malevolent.
Is he both able and willing?
Then whence cometh evil?
Is he neither able nor willing?
Then why call him God?"

Free Will?

mismanagement of that free will. Evil and suffering come from humanity. However, in this case, the death and suffering come from our *lack* of free will[1]; God has determined that this will take place. The only way that this can be justified is by arguing that this is all for the better good. I would have to argue that I am sure that God could achieve this better good by setting up things a little more benignly, that the tens of thousands of people did not have to die so that Zedekiah would go into Babylonian captivity. Free will is simply not allowed to be exercised here. The future, for this corner of Judah, is in the hands of God, and no one else. If it is in the Judeans hands, then their hands are tied, and they are acting in the only way they can – and that is a way that results in the sacking of the city, and the capture of their king. The problem of evil remains a really fertile pasture for grazing philosophers, and the Tippling Philosophers are no exception, as we have vociferously and enjoyably argued the points at great length, costing many beers and pork scratchings.

Of course, as we discussed earlier, there are many potential difficulties with a system when one knows of a prediction of their own future. Knowing your own predicted choices (although in this particular prophecy, Zedekiah does not know how he comes by the outcomes of a burnt city and being captured) and outcomes could cause the protagonists to choose things that are contrary to the outcomes being achieved. However, since this is God saying that particular outcomes WILL happen, then one must assume that one cannot be contrary in such a set of decisions and events. God, in his omnipotence trumps all and everyone, and his predictions are infallible.

The question is, if God has stated that X or Y will happen, then how can he do this, and still operate a universe in which free will is an integral keystone to humanity? If God says X will happen, and then Y will happen, and there is nothing you can do about it, then this assumes that humans do not have free will.

---

[1] Remember when we talked about Augustine, and evil being a privation, or lack, of good. Thus, it doesn't come from God, as goodness does, but from a lack of his gift of goodness.

Jonathan M.S. Pearce

God is out of time

"Time don't fool me
no more"
I throw my watch to
the floor
(was so lazy).
"Time don't do it
again"
Now I'm stressed
and strained,
With my anger and
pain,
In the subway
train.

I think it's nine
When clock says
ten.
This girl wouldn't
wait
For the out of time
OUT OF TIME MAN.
(Mano Negra)

There does seem to be an issue for those that think God has foreknowledge of all that happens and that humans have free will. There is a necessity for these two things to be compatible. The Stanford Encyclopaedia of Philosophy states the following:

For any future act you will perform, if some being infallibly believed in the past that the act would occur, there is nothing you can do now about the fact that he believed what he believed since nobody has any control over past events; nor can you make him mistaken in his belief, given that he is infallible. Therefore, there is nothing you can do now about the fact that he believed in a way that cannot be mistaken that you would do what you will do. But if so, you cannot do otherwise than what he believed

190

*you would do. And if you cannot do otherwise, you
will not perform the act freely.*[1]

This kind of fatalism presents some major problems for the Christian who maintains prophecies to be accurate. There are many arguments that have been set out using modern logic, but we don't need to explore the logical intricacies of the arguments here. Suffice it to say, there are some premises of the fatalism of foreknowledge argument that many theologians have tried to take issue with. These seem to have been refuted over the years[2].

One of the most seemingly appealing arguments that theists often use, is the argument that God is outside of time, as we understand it. One of the first problems associated with stating that God somehow exists in a timeless realm, and that he can therefore see future events by being in a different temporal reality, is that it is incoherent with some of the other properties of God, such as his personhood (i.e. any personal characteristic that would require time to exist, such as thinking, acting, perceiving, etc.). Most people claim of God a set of human-like characteristics like thinking. But to think, you need time, otherwise things just are – there is no thinking, deliberating, choosing, getting angry etc. You would essentially have all characteristics at one instance – time would be one instant. Moreover, if God existed outside of our temporal reality and saw all of our futures and pasts, then it doesn't actually affect the outcomes of our temporal reality – we are still determined, whether God can see it from outside our own time or not. This solution simply moves the problem, and does nothing to solve it.

The other, and for me, even more compelling, argument against the notion of an out-of-time God, is the idea that an a-temporal (out-of-time) God cannot logically interfere with a temporal universe in a temporal fashion. In other words, if God wants to be able to ensure that Zedekiah is sent into Babylonian custody, then he needs to make sure that, prior to this, his city is burnt down by the Babylonians and he is captured. In order for this to happen, he needs to know when to

---

[1] http://plato.stanford.edu/entries/free-will-foreknowledge/ (10/2008)

[2] Please see http://plato.stanford.edu/entries/free-will-foreknowledge/ (10/2008) to see discussions of infallibility and truth values, and refutations of theories expounded to invalidate the logical argument for fatalism.

be able to interfere in this temporal system. If you are living in a timeless system, there is no logical way that you could integrate into a temporal system. How would God know exactly when to pop down and reveal or ensure certain things happened, without being a part of that time? You simply can't logically decide to pop down to earth at Time X or Time Y when the system you exist in has no concept of Time X or Time Y. In order to interfere with our system, you have to be connected to our system, at least temporally. God would need to be temporal himself to have any notion of when to act in our world.

If we refer back to our theories of causation, there is always a temporal aspect to causality – things are always caused by preceding events, within their own temporality. If we look at the well documented idea of Creation, of God creating our cosmos, then it is inherently illogical to posit that God is a-temporal. For him to have caused, to have created, our cosmos, he has to be in the same temporality as that which he has created. This commonly held logical position[1] is relatively straightforward as a powerful rebuttal to theologians insisting on the out-of-time thesis.

Theologians such as Aquinas and Augustine often relate the time argument to an eternalism, that God is eternal and thus there is no *fore*knowledge, since there is not past or future but an eternal present (for God). This line of reasoning can simply be boiled down to the previous points, and has many detractors, arguing that, for example, Aquinas' arguments are incoherent[2].

Some theologians also argue over the facts of the past, in terms of God's beliefs, and differentiating God's beliefs from an actual earthly event. This argument was started with William of Ockham (as in Ockham's Razor) and was more recently taken up by Alvin Plantinga, a more modern Christian philosopher. These people have argued that God having a belief in the past is not really in the past, because they are beliefs about the future, which affects the logical argument[3]. For example, if God

---

[1] For a good synopsis of this argument, see (amongst many others) Paul Almond's article 'Can God Exist Outside of Space-time?' -
http://machineslikeus.com/articles/CanGodExist.html (12/2009).

[2] Hasker in Kane 2001

[3] I didn't want to get into the logical intricacies of what is called the Ockhamist Solution here, but if you feel like researching it, there are many good refutations, but it is obviously worth seeing the logical argument in the first place that Ockham (and

believed yesterday that I would buy Andy a pint at 9pm today, then we would normally assume that because God believed this yesterday, and he is infallible, then I *must* buy the pint tonight. However, people try to get round this by saying that the belief that God had yesterday is not a true fact – it has no truth value – because it is about something in the future. It only has a truth value when that action actually happens.

A past belief about the future is, in part, a sort-of fact (known as a *soft fact*) about the future. Yet, for God to only be omniscient in things that have truth values, and not about future events, calls into doubt the range of his omniscience. Again, without getting a little bogged down about it all, in the 1990s, Dale Brant (amongst others) has shown the logical deficiencies of Plantinga's arguments[1].

Another slightly dubious argument is that of backward causation. This is the argument that since you can see time going forwards, with one event causing another, one could theoretically see time going backwards, with a kind of reverse causation. There has been limited research into this, and the philosophy of time that is associated with it, but most people seem to think it makes little intuitive sense.

In the modern era of science and philosophy, time has come under the microscope and attracted a good deal of attention. Most people understand time in a linear fashion so that time in the past has happened, we live in the now, and future events are undetermined and yet to happen. In other words, we live at a spot on a timeline that moves through us, with future events not yet fact. This is most certainly the intuitive view of most of the world's population. However, much to the distress of the average person's ability to comprehend

---

Plantinga) refute themselves with their solution. The refutation of the solution can be roughly summed up as follows:

The problem is that God's past beliefs seem to be as good a candidate for something that is strictly past as almost anything we can think of, such as an explosion last week. If we have counterfactual power over God's past beliefs, but not the past explosion, that must be because of something special about God's past beliefs that is intuitively plausible apart from the attempt to avoid theological fatalism. If it is not independently plausible, it is hard to avoid the conclusion that the Ockhamist solution is ad hoc. (http://plato.stanford.edu/entries/free-will-foreknowledge/#2.3 (01/2009)

[1] See Robert Kane in his 2002 book *'The Oxford Handbook of Free Will'*, p.54. As mentioned above, many pages have been scribbled on in this fight, and it would be ill-advised to contain them here.

seemingly simple concepts, the seas of change are washing over our approach to time. We can call this first version of time A Time (A-series / A-theory of time). There is a second school of thought that views time with no tense, but as relational, or in a manner that some event is earlier or later than another event. This B Time sees time as tenseless; that your birth is earlier than your death. Yet 'earlier' is a word used differently to the common sense definition, more in a lesser than / greater than sense of number. This means that things in the 'future', and 'past' and 'present' are not really described in those terms, but all exist as fact. This sounds confusing, but it seems to be backed up with what we are discovering in modern physics, especially in the field of special relativity.

So the A-theory of time believes that the past doesn't exist anymore, the present is fact and that the future is a potentiality. The B-theory dictates that the difference between past, present and future is an illusion of the mind, that the past is as real as the present, which is as real as the future. Our brains interpret, according to B-theorists, reality as a subjective psychological illusion, unbeknownst to us. This may seem crazy, but as mentioned, it is very prevalent amongst many physicists, who see reality (including time as part of space-time) as a 4 dimensional block. The universe, in this case, is a block (Block Universe or Block Time are often used as terms) that is unchanging. The most substantive point I will make in this section is this: many physicists now seem to think we live in a Block Time universe. Block Time is entirely deterministic. Therefore, our existence, if the Block Universe is to be believed, is deterministic. This point cannot be laboured enough – determinism is seemingly borne out by modern physics, with regards to relativity and time. The past, present and future, as seen by the human brain, are all facts, all part of a 4 dimensional block that is our universe. This is why Christian philosophers, such as William Lane Craig, who have studied time in great detail, shy away from accepting Block Time, or the B-theory, in the presence of much evidence to support it. A Christian belief (outside of Calvinism) simply necessitates that A-theory is true, and that Block Universe is a figment of physicists' imaginations. Who says Science and Religion don't get on...?

Personally, if a very clever person tells me that the universe works on a Block Theory of time, I am likely to take their word for it, though I will always have an agnostic space in my brain for doubt: scientists used to think the earth was flat, I am sure. Nevertheless, I will continue the book from an A-theory point of view, as if we do experience time in the way in which our brains interpret. However, bear in mind that if physicists are correct in their speculation over the properties of time and the universe, and that existence is deterministic, then the rest of this book is completely unnecessary, and I should have just concentrated on these last few pages!

Looking at the standard notion of time, theologians such as the aforementioned Craig claim that God entered time at the creation of the universe; that he was timeless before the Big Bang, but at the universe's inception, he entered time. This also seems to imply that God cannot now stop the universe, or destroy it (is he not now omnipotent?) or possibly even have the power to create another simultaneous universe where he is required to be in another dimension of time at the same moment. Moreover, though I will not go off on a tangent here, the fact that God was outside of time before the Big Bang implies that he could not have had a personality or emotions, such as we know them, because they require time[1]. God could not develop or change in any way. However, on entering time at the beginning of time, God cannot change either, if one has God adhering to being immutable or unchanging, as many theists do. Time and the Big Bang create many issues for God and the characteristics that he is supposed to have. He is on shaky ground, indeed.

We will now look, in a little depth, at one of the main arguments in support of God's foreknowledge, how it happens, and how it supposedly enables free will.

---

[1] As hinted at earlier, to be angry, one must know a different time of being calm. The change that emotions involve requires time. There are also issues with the claim that God cannot suffer, or that his omnipotence or maximal perfection would also assume that he cannot get angry, or have other such emotions.

Jonathan M.S. Pearce

Somewhere in the Middle

One of the big defences of divine foreknowledge is known as Molinism (after Luis de Molina, the 16th century Jesuit who originally thought all this up), or Middle Knowledge, and is favoured by some of the more prominent modern Christian theologians. It tells us *how* God might well be able to know the future. In basic terms, it asserts that God knows everything that happens and that will happen in the future, but he also knows what would happen if he acted differently. God's knowledge is separated into three types. Necessary truths are those which have to be true, independent of God's doings, such as tautologies and the like – "all bachelors are unmarried". The second type consists of what are known as contingent truths, and these depend on the will of God. Such examples might include God appearing to Moses, or God creating the universe. Good old Middle Knowledge comprises the third type. These are things that are contingently true (things that are not necessarily true, and not necessarily false, or as Blackburn (2008) says, "a contingent truth is one that is true as it happens, or as things are, but that did not have to be true"[1]) but they do not depend on the will of God. In other words, God is not the primary agent in these events. "If I had taught my children the song instead of letting them draw a picture, then the lesson would have run late". Since it was me who made the children draw, and not God, this is middle knowledge, and the song taking longer than the drawing is not a logical necessity, but contingent if true. It is not necessarily true that a song takes longer than drawing in every possible world, but in that particular situation, it was true.

God, in this theory, knows of all necessary truths (laws and immutable facts) but also all *counterfactuals*. In other words, God would know that if Jimmy went to the park, he would go on the see-saw first (this is a counterfactual, a kind of *if* statement). Even if Jimmy didn't go down the park, God knows that he would still have chosen that *had he actually gone*, because God can look into all *possible worlds*, and work out which one he wants to actualise. God's knowledge of all these counterfactuals, all these possible actions and choices, leads him to actualise a particular world, making the fact that he

---

[1] See the glossary for another explanation.

knows these things, before they are in existence, very important.

This is how the ordering of the process that involves Middle Knowledge goes:

> *Step 1. God's knowledge of necessary truths.*
> *Step 2. God's middle knowledge, (including*
> *counterfactuals).*
> *Step 3 The Creation of the World*
> *Step 4. God's free knowledge (the actual ontology[1] of*
> *the world).*
> *Hence, God's middle knowledge plays an important*
> *role in the actualization of the world. In fact, it seems*
> *as if God's middle knowledge of counterfactuals*
> *plays a more immediate role in creation than God's*
> *foreknowledge.[2]*

This supposedly ensures that free will is still possible by actualising a world whereby he knows what will be freely chosen by everyone. To clarify, God knows all possibilities of what might happen in all possible worlds. God decides on which world he wants and creates it (this one). God then knows the future of this world.

There are many aspects of Molinism that are and have been debated over the years. One such prominent criticism is the "grounding objection", which is based on the following points. If God knows that if I were in circumstance C, I would do X, then this is inconsistent with me choosing to refrain from doing X in circumstance C (in other words, God cannot have two opposite things X, and not X, as truths in circumstance C). To put this in plain English, Jimmy goes to the park on Tuesday at 9am: this is his circumstance. It cannot be true at the same time that he would choose to go on the see-saw first, and be true that he would refrain from going on the see-saw. Therefore, the choice that he does not refrain from going on the see-saw first, and actually goes on it must be defined or caused by some preceding influence (such as the fact that the other piece of equipment, the roundabout, scared him the last time he was on it). This means that he is not effectively *freely*

---

[1] Ontology means having to do with the nature of existence.
[2] Adapted from http://en.wikipedia.org/wiki/Middle_knowledge (10/2009)

choosing to go on the see-saw first. Therefore, this argument shows that there is an inconsistency in acting freely in circumstance C. It, therefore, allows for deterministic values to slip through the door. By saying, "When Jimmy goes to the park he will go on the see-saw first", by definition you are denying the alternative possibility of not going on the see-saw first. Jimmy is determined. Defenders of Middle Knowledge claim that because God knows Jimmy will do this will not make him do this, but that knowledge simply 'corresponds' with his action. However, this says little about how the causal circumstance affects the decision. God is simply calculating the causal circumstance.[1]

So let us recap. God knows all the facts about the universe, and all its truths. He also, before deciding to do or create anything, knows all the possibilities of all the possible creatures that he may or may not create in any possible universe. Using this knowledge, he then decides to create, in one massive choice, the universe, having accounted for all the possibilities: a universe that is settled from start to finish. And for Molinists who believe that God is doing this to also allow us free will, it must be assumed that God has no control over our conditional choices, our counterfactuals. It must therefore be that he sort of discovers them (the counterfactuals) in his knowledge before he creates everything. They cannot be determined choices by him, otherwise there would be no free will.

God knows all the potential choices and counterfactuals of all the possible creatures and then 'chooses' an actual world to create. This actual world, incidentally, with God being omniscient, omnipotent and omni-benevolent, must surely be the maximally best world he can choose; otherwise he is not being omni-benevolent. Therefore, with God-given free will, the present world we live in must be the very best possible world there can be, since if it is not, God would have the power and goodwill to have it otherwise, and to actualise or choose a better world with a better combination of counterfactuals. It seems that, with God's defining triplet characteristics, he is as straight-jacketed in his ability to freely create whatever world he wants. In order to earn the "maximally good" title, he has to

---

[1] "…even though the theory of Middle Knowledge is a powerful theory of divine knowledge and providence, it is neither necessary nor sufficient to avoid theological fatalism by itself." Stanford Encyclopedia of Philosophy - http://plato.stanford.edu/entries/free-will-foreknowledge/#2.4 (10/2009)

have created this world in such a manner as to obtain the most benevolent outcomes, and that gives God no free will in his own creation. God's own free will is curtailed in arguably the biggest decision of his existence.

Moreover, let us consider previously mentioned theologies which involved people being damned in this world from the outset. Since people in this world are damned, and God chooses which world to actualise, God is choosing to damn certain people (or being forced to damn people by his maximal goodness!) – some people are damned who might not be damned had God chosen another possible world with slightly different counterfactuals. Kane (2002) has called this "religious luck", and Molina himself believed this. Modern Middle Knowledge proponents aren't so sure that this is a terribly likeable state of affairs, since there is some intuitive lack of free will in saying that certain people are damned before they have a chance to live their lives. God has chosen a certain world with a certain set of counterfactuals that means they are for the high jump. This smacks, as some have said, of Calvinism that we explained earlier. From Hitler down to an aspiring writer stealing a chopper bicycle, we are all doomed to our 'choices' from the world that has been actualised. Since God knew all the counterfactuals and necessary truths from the start of the universe that led up to Hitler coming to power, God knew from the start that he was going to actualise a world with the Holocaust.

Hasker, in Kane (2001), explains the issues with Middle Knowledge as follows, showing how Middle Knowledge could use true statements, but only if you accept determinist qualities into the theist's account of libertarian free will:

> *But the weakness of the suggestion becomes apparent when the following question is asked: Are the psychological facts about the agent, together with a description of the situation, plus relevant psychological laws, supposed to entail that the agent would respond as indicated? If the answer is yes, then the counterfactual may be true but it is not a counterfactual of freedom; the agent is not then free in the relevant (libertarian) sense. If on the other hand the answer is no, then how can those psychological facts provide good grounds for the*

> *assertion that the agent definitely would (as opposed,*
> *say, to very probably would) respond in that way?*
> > *(Kane 2001, p.278)*

Some more thorns arise when we consider that God supposedly 'chooses' which world, of all the infinite possibilities, to actualise. The three problems I can foresee (pun fully intended) are as follows. Firstly, if these worlds and futures and counterfactuals concern all creatures (all their possible actions) and all possible but not actually created creatures (and all their possible actions) then the list of possibilities and possible worlds is actually infinite. It is all up to God's imagination. Being omnipotent, he could create a universe with a trillion people in it, no...a trillion and one, no...a trillion and two...and so on. I could move a millimetre to my left on Tuesday morning at 09:36:05am, or half that distance, or half that distance and so on ad infinitum. God's possibilities for created creatures and possible actions for them are limitless, infinite. And infinity creates all sorts of issues that I have neither the time or space to get into, but suffice it to say, it would really cock up any kind of logical theory, or, even, God's ability to compute future contingent events. If you think that God has personhood (i.e. characteristics such as thinking, acting, deliberating etc.) that fundamentally requires time / temporality, and he needs to know counterfactuals, which are infinite, how does he come by thinking or knowing them if computing them is temporally endless? Can infinities be computed? Even by God? Is this logically incoherent?

The second problem that I can see is the idea that God 'chooses' to actualise a world that he would already know he would choose due to his foreknowledge. Foreknowledge of all creatures and their possible actions must surely extend to foreknowledge of himself, and foreknowledge of what the maximally best choice of universe would be, thus negating the need to 'choose' or even to calculate all other 'non-events'. It is potentially a chicken and egg situation with what God knows and what he chooses, creating some mind-boggling head scratches. If you believe that God is a-temporal before the creation of time, then this is not relevant, but God can do no choosing, no deliberating and no calculating – everything is instant and without any type of temporality. God would not have the personhood that we would imagine a 'mind' to have.

Thirdly, and again focusing on time, if God is a-temporal, then there is no differentiating between steps 1, 2 and 3 in the sequence. There is no knowing the counterfactuals *and then* deciding to create, as Molina and others stipulate.

It is apparent that there are many people who give in-depth refutations of Middle Knowledge, and those who also try to defend it, and philosophical and logical battles have been taking place over the last few decades that have involved some incredibly long winded pages of eye-drooping writing, with logical swerves, shimmies and side-steps. In addition, there is no biblical evidence of Middle Knowledge – there is no discussion or quote that confirms that God had the certain order of knowledge that Molina claimed. There are some instances of counterfactuals, of conditionals, such that if someone did this, then this would happen. From these instances, one can even claim that they are self-fulfilling prophecies and suchlike. The idea of Middle Knowledge assumes that the decision about what world is actualised, from all the possible choices, takes place before the creation decision.

However, the bible talks of events where people interact, argue and barter with God, such as Abraham at Sodom. These instances seem to be incoherent with Middle Knowledge. Middle Knowledge, in order to allow for Godly interaction with the world, must allow for the idea that God knows his future actions, through his omniscience, and this is built into knowing his interactions with the world and ultimately influencing his choice of possible worlds to create. God knowing his own future actions can be fraught with issues in itself.

I also find it amusing that people like William Lane Craig talk about God's knowledge and how he got that knowledge and how he uses it as if they are good friends that spend a lot of time with him, getting to know how he thinks, which is completely unfalsifiable, and a little presumptive to say the least. As I have said, God gets involved rather a lot in the Old Testament, and he also knows exactly what he will do in the future. He, at the point of creation, knows all *his own* future actions on earth. This surely invalidates the whole notion of Middle Knowledge, since it argues that God can know things before they are created, but he knows his own actions after having been existent. This then begs the question of how he can know his own actions: what is the mechanism for that if Middle

Knowledge cannot answer it? It is one thing having foreknowledge of that which you create, and thus impacting whether your creations have free will or not, and it is another thing entirely to have prefect foreknowledge of *your own* actions. This would surely mean your own actions would be fully determined. You can't start talking about being outside of time, or having Middle Knowledge, when you are talking about yourself! God sees his own actions on Earth ahead of time – he is determining himself! This all seems rather logically nonsensical.

So what I conclude here is that, in order to find a theory that allows for God to have foreknowledge of all things and still create a humanity that has full free will, one has to have a PhD in logic (and all the arguments have been refuted in one way or another, anyway) and implausibility. The simpler, more obvious solutions to these issues are that God does not exist; or if he does, he does not have divine foreknowledge; or that humans do not have free will. This more plausible and simple accounting is trumped by the faithful in favour of some highly difficult and arguable logic. Here we return to cognitive dissonance, since in light of good solid arguments against faith, or certain aspects of faith, and in order to allow the conditions of their faith to remain, the believer has to find defensive arguments that are intuitively less plausible than the alternatives that they simply don't want to face. This idea of God, and the understanding of how he operates is, more often the not, not borne out by the Scriptures themselves. The risk-taking personality of God as seen in the bible is inconsistent with the God of dubious and contrived logical arguments. These arguments themselves are seriously doubted and critiqued by the many logicians and philosophers who feel similarly.

The classic "well, it's *possible* and it allows me to retain my faith so therefore it's the most *probable explanation*" is so counter-intuitively frustrating that it annoys me. Surely, at some point, the more plausible explanation has to trump the less-plausible-but-just-about-logically-possible one.

Are there any Alternative Possibilities?

Some philosophers argue for the existence of, or lack thereof, alternative possibilities to chosen events. Known as the Principle of Alternative Possibilities (PAP), there is much written on whether humans have alternative possibilities to their actions. I, throughout this book, favour the (deterministic) account that there are no possibilities to act differently, since there are reasons to act in any given way. If I had sufficient reason to act differently, then I would act differently. Any choice I make is dependent upon my reasons, which are both nature and nurture, genetic and environmental. I would have to be a different person in order to choose differently. If I choose to steal a bike, then that is because, at the moment of choosing, I am defined by who I presently am, and choose accordingly. If I were several molecules different, or had a slightly different past, then I might choose alternatively, but at that moment, I am who I am, to the very molecule and to every millisecond of my life up to that moment. If I chose to steal that bike, as mentioned before, and then carried on life for five minutes, and then life stopped and rewound to that very millisecond, then I would always choose to steal that bike. Any different choice at that moment, everything else remaining the same, would have to mean that there were random elements to my choosing mechanism. Any choice that does not rely on determining reasoning must, therefore, be random. And my feelings on random have been clearly expressed!

To put this another way, imagine I commit an action, such as stealing the bike (X) as opposed to not stealing the bike (Y), and you ask me why I did this. If there is any answer at all ('because...') then this implies determining reasoning for X over Y. It is only when 'why?' is met with no answer, or 'just because', that there is no determining, and room for an alternative possibility. But this is clearly random or totally unreasoned behaviour. I *could* have done otherwise (Y), but it would have been for a reason to do Y and not X. Given an answer, it is essential to continue to ask 'why?' like a persistent child. Most theists and libertarians think that just being 'able' to do otherwise is good enough and that enquiry stops there, but it doesn't. For each action you must question 'why?' and for each answer and reason you must also question 'why?' This situation will leave you understanding that the Principle of

Alternative Possibilities is incoherent. People do everything for a reason, and that reason exists itself for a reason, and so on. Until the Big Bang.

I absolutely dispute the claim that God can know the future of any part of this world if the future depended on true random variables. The argument that God simply knows all possible worlds is, quite frankly, irrelevant. He needs to know, for divine prophecy to be accurate, the events that will happen in *this* world, not all possible worlds. They are two very different kettles of fish. For God to prophesise something happening 200 years later, he cannot account for random chance to occur, since the true nature of random means that the outcome of random chance is unknowable. Randomness is incoherent with foreknowledge.

In this fashion, and whether you believe in random or not, I refute alternative possibilities.

So by knowing our actions, does God cause them to be?

Depending on what you believe, yes and no, and here is the whole crux of the argument about whether we have free will or not in a religious context. We have looked at a few ways in which it is claimed *how* God can know of our future actions. By this knowledge, does this mean that we have no free will? If God infallibly knows Mr. Scelta will choose to call the waiter over at 21.33, does that mean there is nothing else that could happen, that his will is not free to choose otherwise? In strict causal sense, God may not be responsible for our actions, but if you take into account that God created the world, or even chose which world to actualise out of all possible worlds, and knew what Mr. Scelta would do at that time, then Mr Scelta would always do that. He was determined to do so. Although it might appear that his 'free will' was unaffected by God's knowing, we are still in a position of causal determinism. If there is random, and if there is true free choice, then God would not know our choices. Which is where Middle Knowledge and a timeless God come in, but they have serious issues, and don't actually refute determinism.

If God were to omnisciently know that I was to do something that warranted eternal damnation before I was born, before, even, the creation of the world, then why create me at all? Why, as mentioned with Calvinism, create me in the knowledge that I will be damned due to the choices that I will make? If I was to create a new life-form (a dooberry) in the laboratory, and set about multiplying their number, knowing what each of them would get up to, such as knocking over a test tube in the lab on purpose, can I them blame the dooberry for doing so? It was my choice to create them in the first place. If I then knowingly create them, and see the test tube get knocked over as predicted and then punish the dooberry that does so, or worse, punish all the dooberries, is this fair? I am simply carrying out my own set of dominoes and then erupting in anger at a set time upon an action of a creation over which I am responsible, which I knew I was going to do anyway. It is simply an incoherent and unfair approach to being a god.

Another analogy to our human world that might describe how God can see all our actions might be one of watching my favourite DVD. By watching the DVD, I am not causing the events on the DVD to happen, but I know that if I rewound the

DVD five minutes and watched it again, the same thing would happen. Although I am not directly causing the actions to happen, it doesn't mean that the causality of those actions is not fixed. God, however, is the film-maker, the DVD manufacturer and the energy producer, so in affect, the buck stops there.

Consequentially, there appears to be a simple state of affairs:

God has omniscience, in some way, and knows all our actions. They are determined.

Or

God does not know our future actions (with or without random). We have free will.

Or

God does not know our future actions. We are determined (with or without aspects of random).

Despite the attempts of many great theologians, no one, as far as I am concerned, has produced anything like a universal and plausible method of making omniscience (foreknowledge) and free will compatible. I can understand omniscience, but only with determinism as a natural consequence.

What about Jesus?

When we are talking about Christian prophecy, there is a clue in the name as to who we should be talking about. Christ, who is also God, was prophesied to come down to earth long before he actually came down (for example, in the Book of Daniel). Let us think about why Jesus needed to come down to earth, if we assume that he is the Son of God, or actually is God himself. Here is a typical reason:

The main reason Jesus came to earth was to be the final sacrifice for our sins. The simple truth of the matter is that we are not good, and Jesus came to be our salvation, to atone for our sins.

With this accepted (of course, you could say that he had other ancillary missions too), let us look at the notion of prophesying this need to save our souls. In order for Jesus to be prophesied up to a thousand years before his arrival, what are the implications?

In order for God to need to send Jesus down for our salvation, we needed to be pretty sinful. So, at the time of, say, Daniel, some 600 years before Jesus came, we had prophecies dictating that Jesus was to come and rebuild Israel and destroy the wicked, amongst other things. Leaving aside arguments over Daniel's historicity, and claims that it was written in the second century B.C.E., it seems there was a 600 year time-span from the prophecy to the moment of Jesus' arrival. What this implies, is that in that 600 years, there is nothing that, not just one person, but the whole of humanity, could do to avoid needing Jesus to come down and atone for our sins. This means that all of humanity was without the possibility, without the ability, to be able to act in any way to divert the necessity for Jesus to atone for our sins; we were going to be evil, and that's that.

Even with the idea that God could have Middle Knowledge, and that we were still freely choosing to be sinful, there is an onus on God here that he chose the world to actualise that meant that he would have to send Jesus to atone for our sins. He chose the world that, even with 600 years forewarning, humanity would do nothing to avert. The difficult issue for Christians is if one believes that this is the best possible world that God could create, then his design is a little poor, since even with such foreknowledge, we would be unable to divert imminent sinfulness and atonement. If we, with God's best choosing, still could not act differently, given God's foreknowledge that we wouldn't, then God simply didn't do a good enough job at designing us. If we are the apex of God's creation, as the bible leads us to believe, then God is responsible for our design when we find ourselves unable to act in any other way than sinful enough to deserve atonement. It seems odd that, as the apex of creation, we are so poor as to constantly incur the wrath of God. But he chose this world to create, knowing full well we would act like this! How can God be angry if he knows what is coming? If he has divine foreknowledge?

One imagines that in another possible world that God could have chosen to create, there could be a humanity that did not necessitate Jesus coming down to pay for our bad behaviour and evil ways. In this world, humans would be better behaved, though, one would assume, have less free will. If we did have the same amount of free will and could avert the sacrifice of Jesus, then why did God not create that particular world?

In the world in which we live, Jesus supposedly knew and indicated the main perpetrator of his betrayal – Judas Iscariot - and it seems that there was nothing that Judas could do to avert his own, desperate, and condemned future. There was no way he would sit at the Last Supper and say, "You know what, Jesus, I'm really going to surprise you, with my ability to choose freely, and not leave the table now and report you. Instead, I really fancy some more bread and a glug of wine. Incidentally, I am considering supporting you to the death now, in case any nasty traitors decide to report you. You've really made an impression on me, and I've had a change of heart." Unfortunately, it seems his path was chosen many years before. It really puts the Principle of Alternative Possibilities to the test. He could have chosen otherwise, but then why didn't he? I would state that he would have to be someone just a little bit different to have chosen differently.

Crucially, it is vital to note that 600 years of foreknowledge is no small undertaking. Knowing what will take place in 600 years time does not entail simply adding the odd thing here and there to the potion of life. Not a bit. To do that, with the massive enormity of variables that exist in the universe, you have to lay in place something of such intricacy that it is nothing other than deterministic. The classic mantra of chaos theory is that of the butterfly effect: if a butterfly flaps its wings on one side of the world, does it set off a tornado on the other? The theory entails the small variation in a system having a large effect on the variations of that system in the long term, such that:

> *The phrase refers to the idea that a butterfly's wings might create tiny changes in the atmosphere that may ultimately alter the path of a tornado or delay, accelerate or even prevent the occurrence of a tornado in a certain location. The flapping wing represents a small change in the initial condition of the system, which causes a chain of events leading to large-scale alterations of events. Had the butterfly not flapped its wings, the trajectory of the system might have been vastly different. While the butterfly does not "cause" the tornado in the sense of providing the energy for the tornado, it does "cause" it in the sense that the flap of its wings is an essential part of the initial conditions resulting in a tornado, and without that flap that particular tornado would not have existed.[1]*

The causal connection between events in a system can mean that the variation in initial conditions can have truly profound effects, for which there are also in-depth mathematical definitions too. So, in order to know that Jesus is to come down in 600 years and atone, in order to know that humans will not be able to act in any way but evil enough to necessitate Jesus' arrival, God has to know and manage the world on a micro scale. And I mean manage, because, according to the Old Testament, God manages the world an awful lot. The Old Testament is filled to brimming with accounts of the times that God has intervened, interfered and got generally involved with events on earth. This idea that God has simply chosen the world with its freely willing humans happily doing as God has actualised is somewhat negated by the fact that God spent some three thousand years or so intervening, and making sure

---

[1] http://en.wikipedia.org/wiki/Butterfly_effect (10/2009)

cities got burnt here; armies got massacred there; entire tribes and nations were killed there, right down to their women, children and animals; a man was struck down there for picking up sticks on a Sabbath; or, over there, making sure that 42 children got mauled by two bears for calling Elisha "bald". On the evidence of the last one, all the children in my class deserve to get mauled...

So for Jesus to be prophesied, God has to ensure that he has the right parents, who have to be, for prophetic reasons and reasons of Jewish authority, in the lineage of David. This is no small organisational feat – the family line must be kept alive throughout the years. In fact, the order is taller than you might think since it is often not a case of ensuring things *do* happen, but ensuring that things *don't* happen. Mary, for example, cannot be bitten by that poisonous snake when she was 12, must not have injured her uterus when the plough skewed into her abdomen at 14, must not have slipped off the wall she was walking along a week later, must not have starved due to a poverty stricken lifestyle, must not have been miscarried, must not have contracted an early form of cancer, must not have... the list is tremendous. And that is just for Mary in her short life. One has to map out the entire history of the world to ensure the rest. It has to be ensured that Jesus doesn't die in some way before his time of preaching and atonement. The entire ancestral line of his parents must be preserved (well, he actually only has one parent – quite where his genetic makeup on his father's side came from, we'll never know. There are many issues that if Jesus was fully man, who selected the male parental genome, since it was a virgin birth, and if it was God, on what basis did he select those genes? The lineage of Joseph set out in the Gospels seems irrelevant in the light of biological understanding). The Egyptians must not have been allowed to kill their Hebrew slaves, the surrounding empires must not have obliterated the Israelites in a major conquest, a volcanic eruption must not have wiped out the Middle East, a meteorite must not hit earth, man must have evolved in a certain way from the original life-form. So on, and so on, to the point that, in order to ensure that Jesus would come down in the fashion predicted, some 600 years later, God has to micro-manage the entire universe, and this smacks, just a little, of determinism. In order for something to happen with any kind of certainty later down the causal chain, God, pretty much literally, has to make the butterfly flap its wings.

There is no other way that a freely intervening God can be explained, other than for achieving certain ends, for managing his world and universe, otherwise he would simply not have bothered intervening.

All too often, people view prophecy and foreknowledge with a relatively benign outlook, without thinking about the implications involved. The example of prophesying Jesus arriving to atone for the sins of mankind concerns itself, predominantly, with foreknowledge, but intertwined with this is the difficult idea of theological determinism. Let's examine, for a while, this other can of worms.

Jonathan M.S. Pearce

Of hardening of hearts

Normally, there are two ways of seeing theological determinism. Firstly, the soft type, called soft theological determinism, allows for humans to have free will, even though God knows what they are going to do. The hard type means that humans do not have any free will, and God, in one way or another, determines their each and every action. However, this is remarkably similar to the previous discussion. I want to now talk about the intervening God, and how God can force people's hands.

It seems to me that Christians quite often have their cakes, and then eat them too! How greedy (though I often wonder what the point of having a cake is, if not to eat it...)! I mean this by the fact that they will always argue the virtues of free will, and the wonderful gift that it is, and then allow God to punish us for using it, and then intervene willy-nilly and lessen its potency as a gift. That is like me giving you a gun for Christmas and you firing it and me shouting, "You silly bugger, what are you doing firing it!? You've gone and hurt someone! I'm going to have to punish you now! You should have used the gun to do something nice like bake a cake! And then we could ALL eat it!" I would then continue to intervene whenever you got the gun out to make sure you knew the rules, or that you used the gun to do something that I wanted. Furthermore, I would often do things that would allow you not to use the gun. In view of this, what is the point of giving you the gun in the first place? It's a complete waste of time, unless seen as a tool for my own selfish gratification?

Take Moses, for example. He was given the unenviable task of mustering all the Hebrews in Egypt and leading them out of slavery, back to their promised land. Leaving aside all the historical, archaeological and commonsensical issues of this story (how bad at Geography must you be to take two million people[1] and assorted livestock into the wilderness and not find

---

[1] Taking the figures in the bible of 603,550 fighting men, that gives an estimate of 2 million people in total. There is no archaeological evidence for the exodus, the number of Egyptians in Egypt only numbered some 3-6 million. With a more plausible estimate of 20,000 people, all the same issues still remain. There has also been found no archaeological evidence of anyone in the wilderness area, especially requiring settlements of the size necessary to support such large numbers.

your way out for forty years? Where were the pastures and food to support this multitude? Marching ten abreast would have meant a line 150 miles long etc), let us assume it is true. The issues concerning God interfering start when Moses is a shepherd in exile from his Hebrew brethren, in Sinai or Midian. He sees a burning bush that will not burn out, and God speaks to him from there revealing his name. God orders Moses to go to Egypt and free his brethren from Egyptian bondage. So much for *freely* tending to his sheep! Moses is then almost killed by God because his son was not circumcised. Free will was fine, but if you chose freely not to cut the skin at the end of your son's penis off in the name of God, then you were in really deep trouble. Meanwhile, tribes all around the world happily existed with their own moral and legal systems without necessarily resorting to self genital harm.

Now, in all of Moses' life, there existed some three or so Pharaohs who had incredible power and renown, but none of whom were named. Strange, since historically we tend to name all our kings when talking about them. Moses and Aaron managed to hold court with the Pharaoh and ask him to allow Moses to take the Israelites for a feast in the wilderness, which was denied. At the second asking, Moses and Aaron turned Moses' rod into a snake, which the Pharaoh's magicians did too, and they were denied again. The third meeting allowed Moses to prove himself by having Aaron turn the Nile to blood, but the magicians did the same, so he was not seen as that clever. At the next meeting, he opted to make Aaron bring all the frogs from the Nile to overrun Egypt, but those pesky magicians copied. When Moses said he could get rid of the frogs, Pharaoh decided to submit, but when the frogs died in a horrible mess, Pharaoh took back his allowance. As a side point, it is funny to note how no Christian ever seems to doubt the fact that the pagan magicians of the Pharaoh could do these amazing acts to match Aaron and Moses. I know of no other humans outside of Christianity that we, in the Western world, believe could do these things. Either one is naturally capable to do these things, or you need supernatural aid. Since God is the only agent with such supernatural abilities (or agents under God's control), then one must assume these were either natural occurrences or God was enabling the magicians to do thusly. Which then means that God is setting up the whole situation, and forcing more people's hands. He is completely creating the backdrop for the next truly tragic events to unfold.

Now this is where God unashamedly affects the people of Egypt with his actions. In order to force the Pharaoh's hand and allow the Hebrews to depart, God sends the ten plagues down. Now let's think about these plagues:

- All the rivers and streams throughout Egypt are turned to blood.
- Frogs run rampant throughout the land, from border to border.
- All the land of Egypt is infested with lice or gnats.
- Egypt and the houses of Egyptians are attacked by swarms of flies.
- Diseases are meted out upon horses, asses, camels, oxen and sheep. All Egyptian livestock die.
- Boils are inflicted upon man and beast alike.
- Egypt has its first ever hailstorm.
- The pitiful remaining crops are devastated by a massive plague of locusts.
- Three days of thick darkness ensue.
- The first born of every family and beast in the land of Egypt dies.[1]

Now, correct me if I'm wrong, but is this not hideous? Is this really the behaviour of an all-loving God? Really? There are millions of Egyptians living the length and breadth of Egypt who have nothing to do with the Hebrews, who have likely never met one, who have their crops destroyed, their animals diseased and covered in boils, who have their firstborn die, and those of their livestock and so on. The life of these people is a *determined* misery. And these influences are out of their control and in the hands of an all-powerful, all-loving God. God could have simply, and very easily, in all his power, appeared to the Pharaoh and made him say "Yes". One simple word would have averted all this pain and suffering. The course of the lives of all those Egyptians was changed forever, and they were punished for the transgression of one, single person – the Pharaoh. This

---

[1] It is interesting that in the early plagues the bible explicitly states that all Egyptian cattle died bar none, and then in the hail plague cattle are mentioned again, and then in the final plague, the firstborn cattle die. Again. Yes, the cattle seem to be able to die multiple times. This is either a biblical contradiction, or cattle have multiple lives.

is no tectonic plate movement, no natural disaster, this is a set of direct actions from an all-loving God.

But the most disturbing part about this story is the declaration made earlier in the biblical text, in Exodus 4:21-23:

> *The LORD said to Moses, "When you return to Egypt, see that you perform before Pharaoh all the wonders I have given you the power to do. But I will harden his heart so that he will not let the people go. Then say to Pharaoh, 'This is what the LORD says: Israel is my firstborn son, and I told you, "Let my son go, so he may worship me." But you refused to let him go; so I will kill your firstborn son.' "*

Not only did God cause the horrible plagues that came down upon Egypt as a result of the decision made by Pharaoh (and thus you could say that Pharaoh caused the plagues), but he actually made up Pharaoh's mind. Thus, the whole incident, the whole catalogue of events, was based on God reducing Pharaoh's actions to a determined outcome. God determined that Pharaoh was not going to let Moses take the Hebrews away by declaring that his hand was to be forced, and that the answer he was always going to give would be a resounding "No". The sheer number of deaths and the pain and suffering caused by this determined outcome, by this constraint of free will, make a mockery of the gift that God has supposedly given us, and the moral responsibility for these tragic events lies squarely on the shoulders of God.

God is seen to harden hearts elsewhere, too, such as this passage from Paul in his letter to the Romans, which he draws on earlier Old Testament[1] scripture:

> *What then? What Israel is seeking, it has not obtained, but those who were chosen obtained it, and the rest were hardened; just as it is written,*
> *"God gave them a spirit of stupor,*
> > *eyes to see not and ears to hear not,*
> > *down to this very day."*
> *and David says,*
> > *"let their table become a snare and a trap,*

---

[1] Deuteronomy 29:4, Isaiah 29:10 and Psalms69:22-23.

> *and a stumbling block and a retribution to them.*
> *"let their eyes be darkened to see not, and bend their backs forever."*
>
> *(Romans 11:7-10)*

We return again to the idea of having a chosen elect, and the rest of the people being unfairly disadvantaged in their actions by having their faculties unfairly tinkered with. These are the sort of passages that give people who argue for free will, of the fairness of God, so much trouble in explaining away, until eventually, many theologians simply say that Original Sin allows God to punish whomsoever he chooses.

Such divine interventions are, more often than not, seen as miracles. The implications are that God intervenes for a reason – it is not as if he is sitting in heaven bored, with nothing better to do (although, who am I to say that this isn't the case?). God gets involved to achieve an end. The idea that God needs to achieve a certain outcome to his own creation (that he has supposedly designed to achieve a particular end) has implications for his design ability. Moreover, there are similar implications for believers in the fact that God used Middle Knowledge to create the world. Of all the possible worlds that God could have created, knowing all the possible counterfactuals and options, God has chosen a world that still requires him to intervene on a regular basis, seemingly in one particular area of the world, and over one particular epoch. The usefulness of Middle Knowledge is perhaps rendered impotent as God finds it a necessity to get his hands dirty sorting out the causal chain on earth. He has chosen to actualise the maximally best world, and yet he still produces one that requires a few thousand years of constant intervention in the Middle East. One must remember that every time that God intervenes on earth, there are implications for the free will of those involved: people are being used as pawns, being moved around the chessboard of the Ancient Near East, in a one-sided game that God simply cannot lose.

And don't forget that God has foreknowledge, and, therefore, foreknowledge of his own actions. Or is it simply that God's intervening actions ensure that the prophecies that he communicated come true – a set of self-fulfilling prophecies? Maybe it is the case that God does not know all possible futures, but that he predicts something to happen hundreds of years down the line, and if it doesn't look like it is going to come about, then he goes about his business to make sure it does, by moving his chess pieces around, or sending the odd plague.

Philosopher James Keller[1] has stated that miracles are inherently unfair, and show that a supposedly all-loving and all-powerful God is unjust in singling out a person or people for preferential treatment. To be fair, I think he has a good point. God could quite easily divert dangerous volcano eruptions or tsunamis yet deems it more important to maul 42 children with a lion for jeering at a man, as seen in 2 Kings 2:23-24:

> *Then he went up from there to Bethel; and as he was going up by the way, young lads came out from the city and mocked him and said to him, "Go up, you baldhead; go up, you baldhead!"*
> *When he looked behind him and saw them, he cursed them in the name of the LORD. Then two female bears came out of the woods and tore up forty-two lads of their number.*

There is definitely evidence of an unbalanced approach to intervention policy for sorting out the world's problems. Our imminent climate change problems and mass reduction of biodiversity seem like more pressing matters than the pride of a prophet. This is surely not evidence of an all-loving God, given the reality of 42 extremely upset families.

To get back to the point at hand in a more direct fashion, if we define miracles as perceptible interruptions of the laws of nature which can be explained by divine intervention; and if we define free will as the power of making choices unconstrained by external agencies, then there is evidently a contradiction in the existence of both in the same system. Defenders of evil existing in the world as a result of having to allow for free will, as discussed earlier in the book, must answer this, then: Why does God, on the one hand, allow evil to happen in the world (apparently as a cost of free will), and on the other hand, intervene at times, denying free will to those involved to achieve ends that are resultant from free will caused sinning? It all seems so confused and contradictory. To simplify:

---

[1] Keller (1995).

"*Why does God not intervene more often to minimise suffering?*"

"To allow for us to use free will."

"*Why did God send Jesus down to be sacrificed?*"

"To pay for us using our free will incorrectly."

"*Well then, why not intervene earlier?*"

"Er, because he had a plan for 600 years that Jesus would come down and pay for all the free will sins that he knew were going to happen. But he did intervene for other reasons."

"*What were the other reasons?*"

"To create a chosen people who lived in awe and fear of the law-giving God by destroying their enemies for using free will, and also punishing the chosen people themselves for using free will."

To further the point, let me remind you that the Catholic Encyclopaedia included the telling words:

> The Hebrew Prophet was not merely, as the word commonly implies, a man enlightened by God to foretell events; he was the interpreter and supernaturally enlightened herald sent by Yahweh to communicate His will and designs to Israel.[1]

This explicitly talks about the will and designs that God had for Israel that he would intervene to ensure they came to pass. God knew he would have to intervene, and he knew that he would be curbing the will of his creations at a regular frequency.

Somehow there appears to be an incoherent use of intervention in the biblical era. Jesus, as a tool for intervention, is sent down as a foreknown penalty for our use of free will, and, ultimately, didn't have any impact on the way humans act. We still sin in exactly the same way we did before Jesus' arrival. It becomes a guessing game as to what the ends were that God wanted to achieve in the carrying out of all these interventions. Since they seem to predominantly fall before the arrival of Jesus, one must assume that they were, in some way, preparation for Jesus. The interventions seem to be directed

---

[1] http://www.newadvent.org/cathen/12477a.htm (10/2009)

towards showing that the Israelites were the chosen ones, to ensuring certain (and at times bizarre) military and political situations that Jesus can then come and, essentially, supersede with his new covenant.

I have to confess, it seems like an awful lot of interventional effort was expended by God in the direction of the Israelites, and their seemingly petty (on the scale of the history of the world) politics. The rest of the world seemed to exist perfectly well, developing their own moral and legal systems, co-operative farming techniques, civilisations and cultures, *without* the necessity for God to intervene. And they did this more freely, by definition of the fact that there was no influence from external agencies, from God / Jesus / the Holy Spirit.

And crucially, we have yet to take into account end times, and the revelations explained at the end of the New Testament. New Testament Eschatology is the study into the events that are prophesied at the end of days. Now, it must be stressed that many Christians differ on their understanding of the prophecies described in Revelations and elsewhere, from literal to liberal, from concrete to symbolic, but let us look a little at the more literal interpretations to start to get a feel for that which is supposedly inevitable. (Also let us remember that End Time movements are also gaining massively in general support, but also in political power and economic power throughout the world, from the US to Uganda.) This is what can be said of one particular literal interpretation[1]:

> *It predicts that Christ's second coming will inaugurate a literal 1,000-year earthly Kingdom, at the conclusion of which will be the final judgment. Upon Christ's return many anticipate a partial resurrection, only of the faithful, who will reign with Christ for one thousand years. During this time Satan will be imprisoned or restrained in the Abyss or Bottomless Pit. At the end of the thousand years, Satan will be released to deceive the godless people of Gog and Magog, who will have re-accumulated during the Millennium.*

---

[1] http://en.wikipedia.org/wiki/Christian_eschatology (10/2009)

> *The wicked will attempt to surround the Holy City once more during this Millennial rebellion. Again they will be defeated and for all time. The Great White Throne Judgment will follow, and Satan will be cast into the Lake of Fire. The Devil will be condemned to hell for all eternity, together with those who have trusted in him rather than in God.*

> *This penultimate event is the Last Judgment of the Great White Throne. Each person will be consigned to either hell or heaven. The end of all things is a new heaven and a new earth...*

This then assumes that it is inevitable, it is written in God's plans that these events will come to pass upon a second coming of the Messiah. Admittedly, the disciples of Jesus, at the time, must have been pretty upset that their hopefully eternal Messiah was suddenly crucified, and must have sought ways of allowing his return. However, God has declared through these prophecies that such events will come to pass. There is nothing we can do to avoid them, and we will be judged, even though, if you believe in Middle Knowledge, there is *absolutely no need* to judge, since God already knew the outcomes of people's lives and choices prior to creating the world (here we can see more incoherence with Middle Knowledge). God doesn't have to judge at the end of people's lives, but he can judge as he creates the universe as he foretells all their actions.

Theoretically, we could all, as a humanity, live peacefully and wonderfully together in perfect Christian belief (especially those of Gog and Magog), so that there would be no need for the release of Satan, like a caged beast, to exact his destruction. However, God already knows that we will not do this, that humans will inevitably be judged, and many will be found wanting.

As hinted, the power of End Time followers is gaining momentum year by year, and this is an entirely scary prospect. The inevitability of their beliefs mean that they actively welcome crises, destruction and doom, thinking that it is all part of the End Times foretold in Revelations. This breeds a very dangerous form of fatalism, such that global warming is actively encouraged, or that Israel is financially and politically assisted in resisting peaceful reconciliation with her neighbours. It is a depressingly dangerous game to play. To welcome wanton destruction and the end of the world is absolutely no different from an Islamic extremist terrorist welcoming seventy-two heavenly virgins after blowing himself and a thousand others up. It is nihilism at its most despicable.

221

So what can we conclude?

After all that, where does it leave us? Well, confused, I imagine. God knows everything in advance, either by Middle Knowledge, or sitting outside of time, or by determining things in advance. All of these options have issues, no matter how you look at them. Either they are incompatible with the texts of the Scriptures themselves; or they have logical, philosophical and scientific issues; or they are incoherent with other beliefs about God. I see this as a fundamental weakness of Christianity as a whole, and, to be fair, can understand why Calivinism and such similar sects exist – at least they follow a clear, logical path (though having their own crucial problems).

The victim, in any notion of Christianity where God intervenes regularly, and where God knows how we will act, seems, inexorably, to be free will. Additionally, God has granted us the ability and option of using our free will, and has then laid down hundreds and hundreds of rules to constrain the use of that free will. This is a very conditional gift, indeed, and in some understandings of Scripture, can lead to eternal damnation. Not really much of a gift. I would prefer the odds involved in being prescribed actions and going to heaven for eternity, rather than chancing it with a very dangerous free will, and quite possibly ending up being eternally damned.

Whatever you believe about the bible, you cannot argue at all with the knowledge of God's many interventions, that (at least for the duration of biblical times) God has at least determined a good deal of what has happened, and not simply left it up to his freely willing humans. If we include the end times, then much more of human history is defined by God, and as a result, one can argue (as I would, if I were a Christian) that every aspect of the universe could well be micro-managed by the Creator. A Christian would concur that God clearly has plans, and clearly has intervened to realise those plans, and one can surmise that no matter what we do, God will ensure that the end times happen as foreknown.

Do we have free will in the world that God has created for us? I would claim that on the evidence shown, we do not, and this is certainly the case if we start erring away from God's intended plans, because we can't err away from God's intended plans, since he already knows everything that we will do. He has actualised this particular world in order that what he wants will actually happen. Therefore, the fact that he keeps having to intervene in order that we get back on his intended path makes little sense, because he has actualised that particular path anyway. There is effectively a contradiction here that requires some impossible logical gymnastics to untangle. It appears to me that you cannot have both God knowing all our actions in the future and having created the best possible world to achieve his aims, and God needing to intervene regularly to force different people's hands in order to achieve his aims. Coupled with the fact that foreknowledge is incompatible with free will, unless you are willing to sacrifice logical plausibility and common-sense integrity, it seems that the case for free will within the scriptural context is highly contentious.

Jonathan M.S. Pearce

PART V – RESPONSIBILITY AND HOW TO LIVE

IN A DETERMINED REALITY

You cannot hope to build a better world without improving the individuals. To that end, each of us must work for our own improvement and, at the same time, share a general responsibility for all humanity, our particular duty being to aid those to whom we think we can be most useful.
(Marie Curie)

In making judgments, the Early Kings were perfect, because they made moral principles the starting point of all their undertakings and the root of everything that was beneficial. This principle, however, is something that persons of mediocre intellect never grasp. Not grasping it, they lack awareness, and lacking awareness, they pursue profit. But while they pursue profit, it is absolutely impossible for them to be certain of attaining it.
(Lü Bu-wei 246 B.C.)

Jonathan M.S. Pearce

Moral responsibility. So what is it, anyway?

In Italy in 2007, an Algerian man by the name of Abdelmalek Bayout confessed to the murder of Walter Perez, who had racially taunted him. He received a sentence of 9 years and 2 months. This was a low sentence due to the mitigating factors of Bayout being mentally imbalanced, and having a history of psychiatric illness. In 2009, an appeal court judge reduced this sentence by a year. Why? In simple terms, some of the moral responsibility of Bayout committing this crime was absolved when it was found out that he had a gene variant linked to aggression. The counsel maintained that he had five genes linked to violent behaviour. As The Times, reporting on this case, noted:

> *Some believe that the link between antisocial behaviour and genes is so strong that genetic information should be accorded the same status as mental illness or an abusive childhood in deciding punishment. In a 2002 report, for example, the influential Nuffield Council on Bioethics concluded that the use of genetic information to help determine custodial sentences (along with other information such as previous convictions) should not be ruled out.*[1]

Of course, the danger here is assuming that genes = behaviour = causation, when we all know it is a combination of any number of factors (though a deterministic combination at that) that result in a given behaviour or action. It is now understood that, mainly in the US, behavioural genetics has been invoked in over two hundred cases. With a greater understanding of the human genome, one can imagine this number can only rise vigorously. When we couple this with biological influences on causation, as opposed to genetic, such as low serotonin levels[2] (thus causing depression etc.), we can

---

[1] http://www.timesonline.co.uk/tol/news/science/genetics/article6919130.ece (01/2010)

[2] Dion Sanders escaped a death sentence for shooting his grandparents dead based on low serotonin levels - http://www.timesonline.co.uk/tol/news/science/genetics/article6919130.ece (01/2010)

226

see that the legal system is adopting a thoroughly deterministic framework.

When we talk about moral responsibility for an action, we talk about an action which garners a certain kind of reaction which would usually take the form of praise or blame, or of something similar. "Responsible" is a difficult term in the circumstances because it can mean something of which we have been talking about, that of a simple cause for an effect. For example, one could say that it is my responsibility to carry out a class register in the morning, or that the earth's rotation around the sun is responsible for day and nightfall. However, we need to be a little more sophisticated when dealing with moral responsibility.

Morality is a characteristic that seems to be far more human a trait than universal throughout the animal kingdom. This, though, is an often held thought that I find a little incorrect. It is my opinion, along with many a behavioural psychologist, anthropologist and zoologist, that morality is derived from evolutionary processes that have been formed over millennia and more. It was only the other day that I was at an environmental education centre when I spotted a beehive and asked what the bees did over winter. I was told that they came out on a warm day still, but in the main, they gather into a tight ball to keep the queen bee warm in the centre. Many of the bees on the outside die in their valiant and altruistic efforts to keep the queen, and thus their species, safe from death and available to reproduce the next season. This is morality on a very much simpler, but no less important scale – a matter of life and death for the species. If I perished, knowingly, by pushing my child away from a passing bus, and saved my child's life, then I would no doubt be lauded as a hero. In a beehive, there are many heroes every year. Moreover, if the bees were clever enough to rationalise their thoughts, a bee that buzzed off from the hive and selfishly struck out on its own path, would be seen by the hive as morally irresponsible, I would wager.

Morality is a huge and satisfyingly fascinating subject, and I have no chance of doing it the sort of justice that I would like in such a short space, but It needs to be discussed in this context. Those that believe, such as I do, that morality is derived from evolutionary processes, believe that it developed as a result of providing reproductive and survival benefits. Every social animal has developed distinct behaviours that have adapted their lifestyles and helped them to restrain selfishness in order to promote a better group situation. Humans are incredibly social, and we have the crucial advantage of a huge set of languages at our tongue-tips. Morals are essentially socially constructed because they achieve a successful species, and as a result, they are not watertight, they are flexible. This is reflected in the moral zeitgeist, the moral shift that we have seen over the thousands of years of our known history. What we find unacceptable now, may well have been acceptable hundreds of years ago, and vice versa. What we may find acceptable now, is often unacceptable in another society *now*, and vice versa. Objective morality remains a fiercely debated ideal in theological and philosophical circles. Many non-philosophically literate religious people argue that morals only exist as a result of divine guidance, that without a God there would be no morals, and yet not many modern day Christians will happily go out and slaughter a goat and burn it on an altar to God, as was done in the bible. Likewise, I find it morally abhorrent that God demanded Abraham to sacrifice his only son, and then rescinded the command as some kind of amoral test. This is hardly the benchmark, in my opinion, that we humans should be using to deal with each other. Morals have changed, even in biblical terms[1], and this only goes to back up evolutionary theories of morality. Moreover, this religious approach does nothing to explain, say in Mosaic terms (about Moses, not tiled Roman floors), that humans still had morals before the Ten Commandments were given. Primitive societies clearly had morals before organised religion eventuated, whether they were codified on tablet or not. And what's more, hunter gatherer societies successfully created moral and legal systems that were not passed down from, or anything to do with, their gods[2]. The Piraha tribe, for example, have existed atheistically in the depths of the Amazon rainforest for ages. A good number of Christian missionaries have tried, unsuccessfully, to convert them. One such example was Daniel Everett who, over a thirty year period, eventually deconverted from Christianity, finding the tribe of atheists to be the happiest

---

[1] For example, circumcision is seen by Christians as unnecessary, moving away from the Old Testament Covenant. Likewise, animal sacrifice (and, arguably, human sacrifice in the case of Jepthah's daughter, amongst others) is no longer seen as apt.
[2] See Wright (2009)

people he had met[1]! Morality can quite successfully come from sources other than deities[2].

As I have mentioned earlier in this book, one of the cornerstones of morality is the nature of repricocity, the 'you scratch my back and I'll scratch yours' approach to the efficient distribution of skills and resources. Empathy, altruism, cooperation and a sense of fairness also feature. Morality has also been linked to *mirror neurons* which are neurons in your brain that fire when you empathise in certain situations and make you more likely to do altruistic things. This was found out when some Italian scientists were experimenting on a monkey (and its brain) when one of the scientists walked in to the lab with an ice cream. On seeing this, some particular neurons in the monkey's brain started to fire. This is because mirror neurons fire when they see an act by another animal as if they were carrying out that act themselves – a mirror of the act. In context, this might be seen when you are sent junk mail through the post asking you to donate £100 to an African family to save them from starving to death. You might not part with the money due to the lack of empathy felt, since it seems so far away, and so out of touch (the mirror neurons don't particularly fire). However, if you are driving past a road accident and see a man with a broken and bloody leg, you are more likely to act, since your mirror neurons would be firing, producing empathy (imagining yourself lying on the ground in pain, blood pouring out). This might lead to you generously put the person in the back of your car knowing that it will cause more than £100 of damage to your seats. Thus, the money has little to do with it, the empathy has much more. And one can then argue that, the more effective your mirror neurons, the more 'kind' and 'altruistic' you might become. So here we have another example of biological determinism – your behaviour being determined by your biology[3].

If you remember the earlier examples used of automatic reactions of prosocial people, we can increase the evidence for

---

[1] See Everett (2008)

[2] The argument usually revolves around whether morality can be grounded objectively. Whether raping a child is bad, no matter who does it and when it takes place, and no matter whether the culture at the time thinks it is fine.

[3] Research into mirror neurons is still in its infancy, and there is a small minority of scientists who refute their importance. Others herald it as the most important discovery in neuroscience in years.

biological determinism. Not only is our generosity determined by our mirror neuron capability, but also our kindness is determined by the automatic reactions of our amygdalas, which are, in turn, determined by our genotype, and previous experience up until a given moment.

Whether or not you believe the theories put forward about mirror neurons, one has to agree that empathy is a crucial aspect of moral behaviour. It then follows that there must be a reason for your empathy, and for the differences in empathy between people – empathy doesn't differ due to randomness, but must surely come from what makes you, well, you. One of the best arguments to back up the fact that, in this case, it is the brain that defines your empathy and that there is good foundation in the mirror neuron theory, is autism. I have taught a good few autistic (note, though, that autism can manifest itself in many different ways) kids, and their main problem is their inability to empathise. This anecdotal observation is backed up by scientific findings: autistic children's mirror neuron areas are anatomically different, and they have less activity in the brain when imitating other actions[1], among other fundamental differences.

Let us return to evolution (though mirror neurons are the products of evolution themselves). It is known that chimpanzees are a good study for morality, and they illustrate reciprocity well. Oliver Curry from the London School of Economics described human and chimp morality in this way: "Humans have much more sophisticated versions of the kinds of social instincts you see in chimps and other creatures. Really, there's no great leap ... You can think of chimps as MS-DOS and humans as Windows 2000."[2] This illustrates the theory that we naturally have a more complex version of the simple primate morality, though with our many annoying problems and glitches that come with it. Macaque monkeys are interesting since they show an ability to deceive other monkeys particularly well, in order to make sure that they get more food[3]. Different monkeys vary in their abilities to deceive each

---

[1] University Of California, San Diego. "Autism Linked To Mirror Neuron Dysfunction." ScienceDaily 18 April 2005.
http://www.sciencedaily.com/releases/2005/04/050411204511.htm (10/2009)
[2] Oliver Curry, L.S.E., interviewed by Richard Dawkins in his Channel 4 documentary 'Root Of All Evil?' (IWC Media Limited 2006)
[3] Amici et al (2009)

other for their own gain. You could argue that monkeys and other animals have souls or dualistic minds, but I prefer the notion that they, like humans, have brains, and their consciousnesses are created thereof. These animals possess, like humans, the ability to deceive, but also to act for the benefit of others, and in reciprocation, showing that they, too, have morals. These morals weren't defined to them by God, but seem to have developed to serve them beneficially, either as an individual, or as a species. In fact, literally as I am writing this very sentence, Sir Richard Attenborough is on the television waxing lyrical about the co-operative effectiveness of a clan of hyenas as they work together as a team to steal a carcass from a pride of lions and back them into a retreat. These animals are using rudimentary group morality, working for each other, just as humans might at a church fête, working together for a collective goal. Soldiers rotating their watches to achieve a co-operative group goal is matched by Meer cats rotating their own watch from their burrow for the same end goal of safety. Sometimes I get the impression that we like to see human behaviour as inherently different, separate from and higher order to, the behaviour of other species of animals. More accurately, though, our behaviours are pretty well mirrored by these other species, though with less language and perceived complexity.

Like with many things in evolution, we, as humans, can take characteristics or behaviours and use them for different purposes, in different situations. A simple example of this theory is shown when we understand how moths don't fly into candles and burn themselves purposefully. They are using navigation techniques that they have picked up over a huge amount of evolutionary time, and they use these genetically inherited behaviours in different situations (and in this case, suicidally) in a sort of 'mis-firing' of genes. Instead of navigating in relation to the moon, that vital navigational ability is used so that they can accidentally kill themselves[1]. Consequently, we can see that this happens throughout the animal world, and in particular, the human world, as we (arguably) are outmanoeuvring our Darwinian constraints. Some argue that religion itself is a mis-firing of genetic traits, of other human behaviours. How we view our morals, and organise ourselves in

---

[1] Dawkins 2006

our modern society is quite possibly a mis-firing of genes that were developed for a different reason throughout our evolutionary history.

Arguers against evolutionary morality will normally argue that morality is, therefore, entirely subjective. We have seen how this is certainly the case to some degree, no matter what you believe, as even Christians have changed their moral attitudes over the last few thousand years - I don't see too many people stoning others for transgressions, and there seems to be rather a lot of people working on the Sabbath. People unarguably subjectively adapt morals to suit their own needs, to achieve personal benefit in some way.

One of the keystones of moral responsibility is the idea that it can only be ascribed to those, and by those, who have the ability to reason. This is exemplified by the fact that if animals commit certain behaviours, we don't necessarily hold them as morally responsible since they cannot reason their behaviours. For example, male ducks often 'gang-rape' female ducks, mobbing them for sex, to the point that the female ducks sometimes drown. Now, we don't sit at the park and watch this in horror, and then incarcerate the ducks for amoral conduct after putting them on trial. We simply say, "That's the way ducks do it; it's nature. So be it." If they could communicate like humans, and reason their own behaviour, then we would likely have duck prisons[1]. We seem to have ascribed much more emotion and rationalising to actions, and judge them accordingly. Morality seems to depend upon our ability to reason and to assume that humans have morality, but all other animals do not seems to deny animals access to any kind of ability to reason. We actually know that some animals, such as ravens, dogs and chimpanzees can reason to a lesser degree than humans. And they have a morality to a lesser degree. It certainly seems that the more social and complex (especially linguistically) a creature is, the more morality becomes a vital tool to use to succeed cooperatively in that society.

We humans can communicate our actions, and seem to assign to them more 'ownership' and 'authorship'. As we will now see, the actions that a human commits, as is reasoned by someone judging them, can usually be viewed in two separate ways.

---

[1] And have British Members of Parliament claim them on expenses.

Merit and consequentialism

There are essentially two sides to moral responsibility: 1) the view based on merit and 2) consequentialism. The first view is that actions somehow *deserve* either praise or blame, based on assessing the merit of the action. The second approach, as was talked about at the beginning of the book, is concerned with apportioning praise or blame in order to affect future behaviour, either that of the agent committing the action, or of others who may learn from the consequences.

No matter what you believe about whether humans have free will, or whether we are entirely determined in our actions, a consequential aspect to moral responsibility has a very important job to do. The fact that one might get their hands chopped off for stealing a loaf of bread will have an affect on the choice a person makes whether to steal a loaf of bread or not, irrespective of whether the person's choices are determined or freely willed. The variable of the possible punishment is still effective, and is a variable that is considered in both options. For the determinist, it is a very important determining factor that will act with all the other variables to produce an outcome that is the person's decision to steal or not. For the Free Willer, it is a determining factor, but ultimately the person has free will to override the determining influences. Likewise, the praise I can give a child for not calling out in class, and patiently putting up their hand, informs their future behaviour over whether they put their hand up, or call out in the next lesson. I can honestly say that children can often work like computers in this respect, with me giving them the input and them giving the output in deterministic fashion. It all goes to ratchet, however, when you have thirty of them, all with a seemingly infinite amount of variables, and very different brains (some autistic, some behaviourally challenged – oh, for smaller classes!). The butterfly flapping its wings on the other side of the class can cause untold chaos by the whiteboard...

Therefore, the consequential aspect of moral responsibility can hardly be underplayed, for both sides of the argument. The merit-based view, on the other hand, is where the philosophical battles rage. Fatalism, whether it be theological determinism or naturalistic determinism, does not lend itself easily to producing actions that, in and of themselves, deserve praise or blame. How can you blame the Pharaoh for saying "no", when

233

God hardened his heart? How can you praise a child with more merit than another for trying hard at a maths problem and producing good work, when she had a brain that was more mathematically able, was neurologically programmed to be able to concentrate better, and who had such an upbringing that made her more likely to work with more effort, and so on? One famous philosopher, John Rawls, argued that it was a 'natural lottery' in life that decided whether one person had a higher natural talent in something than another person, and as a result, the talented person does not intrinsically deserve the possible rewards of his skills. This would simply equate reward with a sort of 'random' chance of being dealt the right genes and the right environment. World record holding Australian swimmer Ian Thorpe has a lot to thank for his massive size 17 feet. Not decrying his hard work and commitment, he has a natural advantage over most of his other rivals. This sort of achievement based on naturally gained advantages filters right throughout society and institutions.

The merit-based view, for the Free Willer is a no-brainer; the agent that carries out a morally corrupt (or good) action *could have done otherwise at the time*. However, as we have discussed, in order for the agent to have done differently, in the view of the determinist, they would have had to have been an ever-so-slightly different person, or the same person in an ever-so-slightly different causal circumstance. Remember, if we rewind the world to the exact millisecond of the decision to carry out that act, the agent, with every variable remaining the same, will always choose that act. So for the Free Willer, the agent *can* be held responsible in a deserving way, because he *originated* the action – there is no prior reason or circumstance that causes that choice. Also remember that a compatibilist believes that though the situation was determined, the agent somehow still had free will.

Determinists and near-determinists will insist that people carry out actions for specific reasons and those reasons are outside of their control, so where does this leave them? First of all, as alluded to earlier in the book, retributive theories (whereby people are punished for their crimes because they deserve it, in a vengeful sort of way) are scrutinized by the determinist and usually found wanting (under their worldview). As we have seen, consequential aspects of blame are very useful, but the other side of the coin is the feelings that humans normally have when annoyed with someone for doing something morally reprehensible. For example, if Doug, after serving time in prison for dealing drugs, gets out and shockingly rapes your daughter, the feeling of rage and desire to exact revenge will be palpable. What this raging desire will boil down to is revenge and balancing the books for the action committed. In other words, you would undoubtedly feel that Doug *deserves* some retributive vengeance, and this would manifest itself in the demand that he be incarcerated forever, or worse, the death penalty, depending on your beliefs. Humans have a very measure for measure approach to life, and our brains love to balance things – we don't like living in imbalance. Whether as a child, when you span round clockwise three times, you felt the need to do so anticlockwise 3 times, or having all the tins in your cupboard facing the right way, it's all in the name of balance, patterns and 'fairness'. The point is, retributive punishment is an emotional way of balancing the scales, which is a great phrase, since legal systems throughout the world sensibly use the scales as their representational symbol.

This is illustrated by the following example. Imagine the Oklahoma building explosion was not caused by Timothy McVeigh, but by a mouse chewing through some electrical cables. The initial feelings of resentment and blame, of retribution and revenge, if McVeigh had planted a bomb through his own free will, would be somewhat diminished in the case that the mouse did it[1]. Humans engender a real sense of vindictiveness and blame when they do something that truly impinges upon our perceived rights.

This would be a good opportunity to return to the earlier section in the book that dealt with this, and *The Reader*. We talked about the more you knew and understood someone, the less you could judge them in this retributive manner. The hauntingly powerful words echo, "When I tried to understand it, I had the feeling that I was failing to condemn it as it must be condemned." Thus, retributive approaches to punishment and just deserts are the first theories to suffer when considering life as a determinist. Punishment is not about retribution; it is about looking at the reasons for the offence and understanding

---

[1] See the interview with Galen Strawson, P.F. Strawson's son, http://www.naturalism.org/strawson_interview.htm (10/2009)

them in order to correct them so that there is no repeat from the offender.

These days, Many people arguing over moral responsibility spend much energy disputing what it means to be morally responsible, and redefining the terms of the argument, and even redefining the definition of freedom, as previously discussed. A chap called P. F. Strawson is often drawn into the debate here. He sees moral responsibility as a more subjective set of attitudes; that objective morality is an unrealistic ideal; and that we see everything, as humans, as an outcome of complex interpersonal relationships. As the Stanford Encyclopaedia of Philosophy says of his views:

> *That is, unlike most former consequentialist forms of*
> *compatibilism, it helps to explain why we feel that*
> *some agents deserve our censure or merit our praise.*
> *They do so because they have violated, met, or*
> *exceeded our demand for a reasonable degree of*
> *good will.*[1]

One of the cornerstones of a traditional view of moral responsibility is willpower. Having spoken with members of the Tippling Philosophers, I have boiled moral responsibility down to a very simple equation, especially when considering the consequences of judgement from God (always light and fun conversations at the round table). If it comes down to me walking past that chopper bike, and deciding whether to steal it or not, or if I have the choice of shooting up some heroin or not, or having a beer or not, then my decision will often come down to a matter of willpower. In addiction cases, this is obvious, but it is also highly prevalent in so many other situations. Do I have the willpower to resist the temptation, the pull of that "one more beer"? Fascinating research has been carried out by Walter Mischel, psychology professor at Columbia University. He has tested some 650 pre-school (4-year-olds) by putting them in a room with a cookie or marshmallow. They could either eat the treat immediately or wait until he got back and have two. The reactions of the children were then measured and analysed. Some children could hardly last a minute, others twenty minutes. The ones that held off from the temptation

---

[1] http://plato.stanford.edu/entries/moral-responsibility/ (10/2009)

were seen as having good 'self-regulation' (will?). Those that were good at self-regulation were good at using distraction tactics, whilst others could resist because they could think about the object in a cold or cognitive way. In other words, that the marshmallows were not yummy and chewy.

The vital research, in view of this book, came next. Mischel returned to these children later in their lives, particularly at adolescence. As Carducci (2009) says:

> *...the ability to delay gratification is associated with a number of favourable consequences for adolescents. Mischel and his colleagues examined the academic and social competencies of adolescents whose ability to delay gratification was first assessed when they were in preschool. In comparison to those adolescents who demonstrated a lack of delay of gratification when measured in preschool, those who had an ability to delay gratification had higher Scholastic Aptitude Test (SAT) scores and were rated by their parents as being more mature, better able to cope with stress and frustration, more likely to respond to and use reason, more likely to think and plan ahead (Shoda, Mischel and Peake 1990).*
>
> *(Carducci 2009, p.444)*

These children able to delay gratification were able to cope much better at times of rejection, as well. There are many real-world applications to this characteristic which really do stand you in good stead, from the obvious ones of delaying gratification by not stealing the bicycle now, but saving up to obtain one in a year's time; to having the self-regulation to abstain from watching the television now, and going down to the library to study, and indeed to study for a longer time. Moreover, other abilities outside of the agent's immediate control might come into play here. In the case of, say, Millie going to library, let's assume she has a greater ability to delay gratification, and can see the benefits down the line of going to the library rather than watching television. Let us now also assume she has a predisposition to enjoy reading more, inherent from her high cognitive abilities given to her by her parents, and the amount of time they spent reading with her and promoting the enjoyment of reading. This not only will affect her willpower to go to the library, since she might still actually get enjoyment through her delayed gratification (the fun of reading and studying), but will also illustrate how she might embrace her own education more, allowing her to sidestep issues of poor literacy and antisocial behaviour. A lack of delayed gratification seems to be a shortcut to antisocial behaviour.

Bringing God into the picture, if he is judging us absolutely, and on the merit of the actions we do, and the actions we do are effectively hard-wired, at the very least, to a large degree, then where is the fairness in this? We are returning to Rawls' natural lottery. Imagine a Christian (Mark) turning to Doug, with his lack of ability to self-regulate and delay gratification, and with his physical and mental predispositions, and saying, "You will deservedly go to Hell for the transgressions, for your sins, that you have done in this world". This is evidently wrong, when Mark was lucky enough to be born and brought up with all the tools that allowed him to adequately deal with all of the issues that life threw at him. This seems so very inadequate and unfair. To me, this is one of the most powerful arguments against a personal and judgemental God. Forget the bible, forget the higher level theology: if we are dealt different cards that biologically or environmentally determine our willpower, our motivation, our cognitive abilities, our behaviour, our predisposition to believe in the supernatural more than someone else, then by what mechanism, and by what right, does God have to judge us?

To produce more evidence to support this outlook, and there is a plethora of different evidences to pull on, let me refer to some very recent findings from Gao et al (2009) of the University of Pennsylvania. These researchers have found a driving force behind criminal behaviour in the neurological networks of 3 year-olds. They have collected data from children in the 1970s, allowing them to find out which children were susceptible to fear, and which weren't. The 137 children with criminal records some 20 years later were all found to have significantly less receptiveness to fear than those who had no criminal record. As the conclusions to the paper state:

Poor fear conditioning at age 3 predisposes to crime at age 23. Poor fear conditioning early in life implicates amygdala and ventral prefrontal cortex dysfunction and a lack of fear of socializing punishments in children who grow up to become criminals. These findings are consistent with a neurodevelopmental contribution to crime causation. [1]

Thus, it seems that certain conditions innate amongst certain children make them more likely, more predisposed, to become criminals later in their lives. This is scary, but unsurprising to the determinist. There are obviously many, many other variables that can interfere with such indicators, but there is certainly more and more evidence emerging that shows that our characteristics and the way in which we react to the world around us, and the way we develop, is determined by our physical make-up. As the years go by, the more the variables are mapped and analysed.

On a personal note, I have grappled with the implications that determinism has, as it is something that I have come to accept from the evidence given The more that I have researched this book, the more sure I have become. Determinism can be, in equal measures, both challenging and enlightening. I have started to look at people's transgressions, both against me, and in general, and have started to approach them with a desire to understand them, and to try to help them not make the same mistake in the future – to be a positive variable in their lives. This seems to be basic psychology. I know that, sometimes, all my work in teaching is undone at three o'clock when the child goes home, but I am aware that there is no use, especially at their young ages, in retribution for transgressions, that there should only be help to ensure that they learn from their mistakes. Moral responsibility, in my opinion, is not about judging other people, but judging how best to personally ensure people don't commit antisocial behaviour again, and work towards a better society.

---

[1] See Gao et al (2009)

Jonathan M.S. Pearce

Neurocriminology

Over the last several decades, research into, and the understanding of, the brain and our genetic makeup have initiated the development of the field of neurocriminology. Whereas in the early and mid part of the last century there was a movement away from this sort of area on ethical grounds, nowadays we really do understand a lot more about ourselves, and what drives us. Neurocriminology puts together genetic and biological research and couples them with criminology to try to understand what drives people to commit crimes. In effect, it looks at the causal circumstances, from a biological point of view, and works out the determining factors in a criminal's activities. It is these researchers who have been prevalent in the outcomes of cases such as Abdelmalek Bayout, and such scientists have been called upon to testify in court as to the defendant's mitigating circumstances.

This understanding is a double-edged sword. On the one hand, we can work out the drivers behind anti-social behaviour, understanding why criminals have acted in the way they have (why Abdelmalek Bayout murdered someone in a given circumstance, but why Joe Bloggs, in the same situation, would likely not have murdered someone). On the other hand, this understanding acts to mitigate the responsibility of the defendant, allowing them to say "Look, I'm not responsible for killing this person, my genes made me do it". This is a dangerous place to be, a moral tightrope to walk, with the consequences of falling into abrogating the responsibility of everyone that commits a crime. Essentially, we are getting ever closer to being within the knowledge realm of Laplace's Demon, knowing more and more of the causal circumstances that determine our behaviour. Surely, extrapolating this will get us to the position of saying about anyone, committing any crime, "Well, they were bound to do this horrible act, because we know X, Y and Z about their behaviour and makeup".

Where do we go from here? One can approach the findings of neurocriminology in two different ways. This was patently obvious when I was having a chat to my partner over a cup of tea about Abdelmalek Bayout. Most people might well be passing the time of day talking with their partners about what they are going to buy from the supermarket that week. Not me, I prefer to discuss the outcomes of deterministic research in the

240

field of crime over a brew and a chocolate Hob-Nob. Discussing this matter, I concluded in agreement with the judge of the crime that, knowing Bayout's genetic makeup (to a degree), and understanding his psychological condition, it would be unfair to incarcerate him for so long because he was less responsible for the crime he committed – it wasn't *so* freely willed. My partner, on the other hand, had a completely different approach. She declared that, since we knew he had a predisposition for violence, and since he had a history of psychological issues that meant he was less likely to be able to deal rationally and calmly in certain situations, he actually could be predicted to be less safe in society, and should therefore be incarcerated for longer. Letting him out earlier would lead to a greater likelihood of committing similar offences, irrespective of responsibility. In her eyes, it is actually society's responsibility to safeguard its own safety by insuring people like Bayout are kept away from positions of being likely and able to cause harm.

This smacks of a fine moral dilemma. Are we more bound to look after the rights of an individual over the rights of the society as a whole? One would intuitively say that the greater amount of people should be satisfied in this case, and my partner's views are arguably more powerful. The discipline of neurocriminology has opened up a veritable can of worms, and a moral conundrum has materialised. We are edging closer to the reality of films such as *Vanilla Sky* which pose questions about whether we should punish criminals for crimes that we know they are likely to commit, based on their genomes and environment, before they have even committed them. As ever, science fiction metamorphoses inexorably into science fact. Should Andy send me an email ahead of the next Tippling Philosophers meeting accusing me of being tight, and not buying him a beer on the night ahead? Probably. Guilt does wonders to influence behaviour!

Jonathan M.S. Pearce

A better society

The nature of the beast, especially when considering actions on a determinist footing, is to assess really what is best for society, to set out a mission statement for humanity. This is something that the U.N. has attempted to do[1], but it needs to be done with the buy-in of everybody. People really need to know, especially in a global society of so many religions, and lack thereof, what direction humanity needs to head in and why. From a secular point of view, and almost an evolutionary perspective, we (as a global society) need to set a clear mission statement in order to get a sense of clear morality and direction to a species that is, at present, making a damn good mess of the planet. You can say what you like about absolute morals defined by this god or that god, but something is not working, population is spiralling out of control[2], biodiversity is collapsing[3], pollution is escalating, social depravity is rife, the gap between rich and poor is bigger than ever[4], and prison populations are growing[5]. It can be quite depressing when you look at it.

Perhaps, at this stage, it is worth redirecting people to theories such as those of John Stuart Mill and Jeremy Bentham (philosophers of the 19th century who devoted themselves to the philosophy of happiness), and all their modern counterparts. Happiness has been debated, (as *utilitarianism* which is a swanky word for happiness), and these theories could be put to good use (and arguably have, by some)

---

[1] The Charter of the United Nations is available here to peruse:
http://www.un.org/en/documents/charter/index.shtml (02/2010)
[2] Set to reach seven billion in 2011, from a much smaller number of just over two billion in 1950, according to the UN -
http://www.un.org/esa/population/publications/popnews/Newsltr_87.pdf (02/2010)
[3] For example, the number of invertebrate species fell by nearly a third between 1976 and 2006. See the Convention of Biological Diversity / United Nations Environment Program's report Global Biodiversity Outlook 3 (May 2010) available at
http://gbo3.cbd.int/the-outlook/gbo3/foreword/foreword-by-the-united-nations-secretary-general.aspx (05/2010)
[4] See 'Income gap between rich and poor is huge and growing, warns UN report', UN News Centre, 2008, (05/2010)
[5] See World Prison Population List (8th edition), Roy Walmsley, International Centre for Prison Studies &King's College London – School of Law, (2008)
http://www.kcl.ac.uk/depsta/law/research/icps/downloads/wppl-8th_41.pdf (05/2010)

242

to devise a society that would be optimal for everybody involved. I would advise researching the area of utilitarianism for a better idea. In basic terms, Mill, for example, thought that societies should act to produce the greatest amount of happiness for the greatest amount of people, within a reasonable framework. Happiness and contentment were (are still can be) seen as different notions, such that intellectual and moral pleasures were seen as more important than tangible and physical pleasures (learning from reading a book as opposed to drinking a bottle of wine in the park). But Mill didn't necessarily (as opposed to Bentham's approach) stipulate that if a society garnered more enjoyment playing Monopoly than from going and watching a play at the theatre, then the society should facilitate the promotion and propagation of Monopoly playing. Therefore, an investigation into what really makes society happy would be of great value (Mill greatly advocated education since an educated person was in a better position to judge these things on a personal and societal level).

Let us return to the idea of consequentialist punishment. As a determinist, consequential punishment is crucial, and it needs to be effective. Rolled in with this, it might be worth considering agreement theories, where criminals agree to go to prison, understanding what they have done in the context of society as a whole, and helping to encourage rehabilitation. Of course, rehabilitation has got to be a central component of the justice system. I would posit here that we are moving, inexorably, to a more determinist approach to crime and punishment, to welfare and society in general. The victims of the natural lottery, that gives so many less fortunate and less-abled (in body and mind) people in society, no longer have to suffer in places such as Bedlam, but are rightfully included amongst society as a whole. Our much improved understanding of the wide variety of different people in our society has led to a much more inclusive society. Criminal punishment does take into account mitigating circumstances, and sentences vary accordingly. It is this understanding of each other (with the help of scientific studies) and the understanding of variables and consequences in society as a whole that are vital components of our modern society, and play such a role in consequentialism. Retributive punishment, on the other hand, holds less and less value in modern state systems, though still permeates through our everyday lives and human emotions.

Although it might be easy to regard a purely consequential system in society as acceptable in obvious cases of why a criminal committed a particular crime, how does one explain a seemingly normal person suddenly committing an atrocious crime? Take Lynddie England in the Abu Ghraib prison – how did that come about, and what were her mitigating circumstances? Well, to move to darker areas of human psyche, it would be prudent to mention that all of us are closer to truly dark acts than we might like to admit. This is the conclusion of the very famous Stanford Prison Experiment that took place in 1971. Psychology professor Philip Zambardo, together with 24 students, set about creating a prison in the basement of the psychology block. The students, on a coin toss, were chosen as either prisoners, or guards, and went through the process of recreating a prison environment to measure psychological phenomena. The experiment had to be abandoned after six days because a third of the guards had been exhibiting genuine sadistic tendencies. Basically, the guards had allowed unethical behaviour to take place under their supervision. Consequently, many of the prisoners were emotionally traumatised. As well as influencing cognitive dissonance theory, and theories on authority, what it sadly showed is that the darker side of human nature is dangerously close to the surface and can break out given the right circumstances. If those buttons are pressed, all hell can break loose, and this was seen in the horrific context of Abu Ghraib[1].

As far as retributive punishment is concerned, it might be worth dwelling a short while on the Old Testament. Biblical critics have long levelled at God his vengeful and retributive nature in the Old Testament, and the deaths that came aplenty as a result of his wrath are fearful evidence. Judaism is well acknowledged as having a very high regard for measure for measure accounting, originating in the sacrifice of Isaac and culminating in the atonement for sins offered in the death of Jesus. Modern society, perhaps more in tune with the New Testament, finds itself to be a far more forgiving society than five hundred years ago or more. Why is this? Simply put,

---

[1] Philip Zamabrdo has compared the experiment to Abu Ghraib in his well received book *The Lucifer Effect: Understanding How Good People Turn Evil.* It is also very well worth seeing his TED talk at
http://www.ted.com/talks/philip_zimbardo_on_the_psychology_of_evil.html
(10/2009)

because we embrace more deterministic ideals. We *understand* that a child with autism or any mental disorder has different needs and different computations in the brain, and as such is *not worthy* of punishment for failing to do X or Y. We can judge with more understanding, without creating one rule fits all to people. We are starting to personalise society much more, and this is no more evident than in education, where we strive to provide a personalised education as much as possible (they are the buzzwords in the discipline at the moment).

I have often wondered how God acts in judgement. By reading the bible, there is not often mention of mitigating circumstances, and, in fact, there is an inherent misunderstanding of medical and psychological issues. Demonic possession is now epilepsy and so on. One of the most fascinating insights into the world of biblical biological understanding is the approach to menstruation. God declared menstruating women unclean, stating that no one should have contact with her for seven days or until the bleeding has stops. From the Levitican text, God deems anyone or anything that touches her unclean. If she touches another person, god deems them unclean until they bathe. In fact, the same goes for anything that she has *previously* touched (Lev 15:19-30). All this uncleanliness is resolved by needlessly killing two doves:

> 'Then on the eighth day she shall take for herself two turtledoves or two young pigeons and bring them in to the priest, to the doorway of the tent of meeting.
> 'The priest shall offer the one for a sin offering and the other for a burnt offering. So the priest shall make atonement on her behalf before the LORD because of her impure discharge.'
>
> *(Leviticus 15:29-30)*

If this is the sort of approach, set out as a benchmark in the bible, that we should adopt towards women and biology, then I fail to see the relevance of such passages and scripture. Why should they be held in such high esteem in our modern society. Back to the point, though. When God judges, how does he judge the following?

1) someone with very low I.Q., say, lower than 50?
2) someone with downs syndrome, for example?

245

3) a chimpanzee or orang-utan?

4) someone with a psychological disorder, personality disorder or suchlike?

5) someone with an extreme cognitive disorder such as Alzheimer's or another dementia?

6) someone with a neural cognitive disorder such as autism?

7) someone with brain damage through an accident or stroke?

8) someone who was indoctrinated as a child?

9) someone who is living in a hell on earth, such as Darfur, Somalia or Hull?

10) someone who is a product of a broken, dysfunctional and violent family?

11) someone who was born addicted to heroin and was fostered out?

12) someone genetically predisposed to anger?

And so on, the list is almost limitless. If one resigns themselves to the idea that God does in fact do this, then one is admitting that God judges everyone on a case by case basis, and effectively has a matrix of judgement (a bit like a computer program that demands an input of the person's details, genetic and experiential, that then gives the output of judgement / punishment) that he puts you up against. Indeed, you are saying God admits determinism, that there are mitigating circumstances (causal circumstances) for everyone.

I was at a training course recently where I met two people working for a youth group in a large secondary school nearby. They have to deal with all the difficult children who are about to be excluded, do some sessions with them, and then throw them back into lessons with the hope that they have developed a few more skills. I asked them what the overriding factor was in the children's lives that appeared to be responsible for their wayward behaviours. (I recognise this as anecdotal, but no less important since it is frontline opinion) They indicated that for some 85-90% of the misbehaving children, the factors were poor literacy skills and poor parenting. It is well documented that children with poor literacy skills find it almost impossible to access most other lessons. Imagine barely being able to read and write and going into a Chemistry lesson and being faced with work on the board about covalent bonding, or chemical formulae. Their only apparent option is to misbehave in order to communicate or hide their own anxieties – they don't have a repertoire of tools to call upon in their emotional toolbox such as someone else more highly emotionally literate. These are the children that are then marginalised in society in their adolescences and later lives. These are the children that end up being judged by society, and end up in prison (I am obviously generalising here, and there are many exceptions to the rule who have slightly different causal circumstances). And why? Not because they chose to misbehave per se, but because their literacy skills were poor, and because they had broken families that took little interest in their education, or passed on poor cognitive ability genes. We need to move away from declaring "These children chose to misbehave" towards "Why did these children choose to misbehave?" if we have any hope of improving the situation going forward[1]. But, according to what is exemplified in the bible, all of these determining factors are irrelevant, since the judgement is in the action. God didn't show any evidence of understanding why the man might have been picking up sticks on a Sabbath when he struck him down – one assumes for firewood to heat or feed his family, which hardly seems to be a crime. A right-minded determinist would[2], I maintain, act to pursue solutions to the problems of crime and literacy, rather than expend energy throwing blame and retribution around. "What do I need to do, as an omnipotent God, to stop you from perpetrating this heinous Sabbath crime again? How can I help you, going forward, improve your behaviour, and show you that trying to heat your family is less important than breaking a banal heavenly decree?" It could be argued that the poor chap was merely the unfortunate collateral damage in expressing and enforcing consequentialist judgement for the rest of the community[3].

---

[1] "Going forward?" It's like playing 'Buzzword Bingo' in a management meeting...

[2] Obviously a fatalist who is the sort of person who 'gives in' to the vagaries of fate would not.

[3] Numbers 15:32-36:

Now while the sons of Israel were in the wilderness, they found a man gathering wood on the sabbath day.

Those who found him gathering wood brought him to Moses and Aaron and to all the congregation;

and they put him in custody because it had not been declared what should be done to him.

Jonathan M.S. Pearce

The Old Testament biblical rules are, in many people's eyes, archaic and irrelevant to today's society, with our understanding of physiology and behaviour. I no longer need to know that I cannot boil a goat in its mother's milk[1], or that I shouldn't mix clothing of two different materials[2]. As a result, I think we need to move on, and not see it as any kind of a benchmark for organising society.

So what we need to concentrate on is creating a circumstance where the people do not have the desire to commit crime – and this is the vital cog. It is almost a truism to say that if there is no desire to commit a crime, then there will be no crime, so we have to go about investigating what a society would look like if there was no desire to commit a crime. We then need to set up the systems to achieve this utopia. And that has been the ideal for everyone from Keynes to Marx. I would say that one of the core reasons for crime is inequality, and the problem is that inequality is the basis of Western societies, of capitalism and making a fortune. The American Dream is at loggerheads with equality (for which, in their eyes, you can read socialism / communism). However, in deterministic terms, one could debate that being born into money is inherently 'unfair', that a redistribution of money is the way forward (for example). And yet, one could also argue that, from an evolutionary point of view, making a fortune and ensuring the success of your offspring is right on the money, so to speak. There are always two sides to every coin. It is frustrating that, in life, there seems to be no right answer! Though this might be a flippant remark,

---

Then the LORD said to Moses, "The man shall surely be put to death; all the congregation shall stone him with stones outside the camp."
So all the congregation brought him outside the camp and stoned him to death with stones, just as the LORD had commanded Moses.
Not that God had the decency to mete out the punishment himself, but ordered the man's peers and neighbours to carry out the stoning. Do you know how horrible it is to be stoned to death? It is despicable (I have seen it in a propaganda video against the Saudi Arabian justice system. This, in no way, and with all the logic and morality I have been graced with, is or could ever be the actions of an all-loving God.

[1] Exodus 23:29:
You are not to boil a young goat in the milk of its mother.
It's not something that was top of my to-do list...
[2] Leviticus 19:19: *'You are to keep my statutes. You shall not breed together two kinds of your cattle; you shall not sow your field with two kinds of seed, nor wear a garment upon you of two kinds of material mixed together.'*

248

the notion that there is a right answer implies there are actions that we *ought* to do and ones that we *ought not* do. This requires an establishment of your worldview, since if you are religious, your *oughts* and *ought nots* might well come from God. Otherwise, you have to go through this very process of working out what the meaning or purpose to life is, if there really is one.

There are perhaps more avant-garde, original and leftfield approaches that could be adopted to take our society forward, to the next level. One such example might be the approach of Jacque Fresco with his Venus Project suggestions, indicating that it would be better to move away from a profit driven economy to a resource-based economy:

> *The Venus Project presents a bold, new direction for humanity that entails nothing less than the total redesign of our culture. There are many people today who are concerned with the serious problems that face our modern society: unemployment, violent crime, replacement of humans by technology, over-population and a decline in the Earth's ecosystems.*
>
> *... The Venus Project is dedicated to confronting all of these problems by actively engaging in the research, development, and application of workable solutions. Through the use of innovative approaches to social awareness, educational incentives, and the consistent application of the best that science and technology can offer directly to the social system, The Venus Project offers a comprehensive plan for social reclamation in which human beings, technology, and nature will be able to coexist in a long-term, sustainable state of dynamic equilibrium.* [1]

This is just one example of how we could work towards understanding our relationships with the world around us, and all other species upon which we rely, living together more harmoniously, and potentially more happily.

To balance the rather challenging feelings of dismay involved with determinism, it is wise to note that determinism

---

[1] http://www.thevenusproject.com/ (11/2009)

still allows for hope. Hope is just as valid an emotion in a deterministic framework as it is in the libertarian world. Hope depends upon a lack of knowledge of an outcome, and with regards to our knowledge of our own lives, we are quite dense in comparison to a foreknowing omniscient God. Prophecies are depressing in the feeling of inevitability that they engender, but hope still stands strong in mortal determinism. Just because it is determined by the myriad of variables that Mr. Frisky Fingers will win the 3.10 at Ascot, it will not stop me putting £10 on Sir Gallopahead in the hope that *he* will win instead. I have no idea what the variables are, though I can become slightly more informed upon reading the form guides and getting insider information, and no idea of what might happen in the race, and so hope still encourages me to shout at the television in the betting shop (not that I ever bet on anything anyway!). And hope for a better society is probably one of my greatest hopes, and one that the world desperately needs to come through.

Conclusion

I have come to accept determinism for several reasons. It has the benefit that with all the evidence that backs it up, it also remains the case that nothing has yet proven it to be a false doctrine. As Honderich says[1] , it takes into account neuroscience, quantum theory, science in general, and common sense, and is *"very strongly supported"* and has *"not been shown to be false"*. No theory in the world has ever been proven – theories, by their own definition, are theories, a best fit for all the information we know. The theory of gravity is still a theory, though it is universally accepted as "fact". People often dismiss evolution, since it is "only a theory" without understanding that every law they think of as fact is "only a theory". I suggest they start investigating the theory of... theories. In fact, as Descartes said, nothing in the world can be proven, only that I exist, because I think. Determinism does seem to fit all the knowledge and evidence that I have learnt and experienced.

The question for me to answer, which is what I have discovered through writing this book, is whether I should live my life under the illusion of having free will (along Wegnerian lines), and thus continue much as if nothing was any different; or whether I should think about the deterministic qualities of life in all that I do every day. If evolution has created us to live life under the illusion of free will (and many will say there is certainly an 'if' there), then perhaps that illusion is a useful one? One could say that our sight is an illusion, in many ways, and yet it is useful to us, and serves a purpose very well. We cannot see other light in the spectrum, from infra-red to gamma rays, and yet other animals can. Other animals see differently to us in other ways, too (such as a fly or spider), and yet is there an absolute truth to sight? Just because we (the animal world) interpret the visual world around us in different ways, does that make one animal right, or more right, and another animal wrong, or less right? Our interpretation of intention and will might be along these lines; it might be useful, but not the absolute truth. Do we adhere to truth, or that which is useful? Are they mutually exclusive? Is the truth of our intention and will, of determinism, more or less useful than the illusion that

---

[1] Honderich (2002), p.90

we might be living under? These are questions to which I have no answer, but upon which I will certainly deliberate further.

As I have said, it is both challenging and enlightening, and it does affect the way you view things. But rather than start with a conclusion, and massage the evidence to fit it, I like to think that, throughout life, I have started with the evidence, and seen where that has taken me. All too often in life, we look at things we want to be true, whether that be souls, or life after death, or an all-caring God, and we like the idea so much, that these conclusions are our starting points, and we create or massage the evidence so as to fit the conclusion. The truth to life, any absolute truth, is no less true because it is unpalatable. Many a philosopher has dismissed determinism, simply because they don't like it, or it conflicts with other beliefs that they have. This is the same mechanism that Creationists use to disbelieve evolution. They start with a conclusion, that every word in the bible is inerrantly true, and then massage all the evidence to fit that conclusion – whether it be ignoring geology, or biology, physics, human geography, palaeontology, statistics and genetics – or using spurious and poor science. This is a case of arguing *from* the bible rather than *to* the bible. In other words, using the bible as truth, and then using that to influence all the evidence and learning around you, rather than using all the evidence and learning around you to argue the validity of the bible. This, to me, is the most disheartening of human traits. We must continually question, discover new knowledge, seek answers, and I will always consider evidence in the determinism debate, whether it contradicts the position of determinism or not, and weigh it up in light of what I know[1] and experience. At least, that is what my brain has told me to say, and has made me tap, as I sit here at my laptop.

With regards to my own personal beliefs in a god of any religion, I think the findings on my travels have led to a definite assertion that that which makes us what we are is inherently incompatible with the notion of a personal and judgemental god. Views on what sin really is, on how God has delivered justice biblically, and for what motivates us to do the things we do, all lead me to believe that there really is not the God that most people would believe there to be. There may well still be a

---

[1] The epistemological question of "what is knowledge?" naturally follows. Oh how philosophy is so interconnected!

God, just one that is totally incoherent with the one offered in the bible, or any other Holy Book in existence.

Determinism has also allowed me to approach the world, and my day-to-day activities, in a calmer and more calculated way. It is not that I am fatalist, as an emotional disposition, but that determinism promotes understanding and this allows for a sense of connection to everything around me. I search, constantly, for reasons to things, to other people's actions, to why that person got angry there, to why I didn't make that tackle in a game of rugby, to why this thing happened in the news, or to why that person doesn't care about the environment. All this is in the hope that I can understand more of the causal circumstances that surround us all, to understand where I fit in and what causes and effects I produce, and, as I am programmed, to work out a way in which I can make the world a better place.

And I hope, that in some kind of way, this book will act as a positive variable in your casual circumstance; that it might act to make you search for reason and understanding in a world in which variables fly at you from every direction, every second, and in which your senses take it all in, continually computing; that it might pique your interest, when you next look at your hand reaching for the kettle, as to whether you consciously decided to move that hand, or whether your non-conscious brain 'decided' for you. Go on, go and make yourself a nice cup of tea.

P.S. – I was always going to write this book.

GLOSSARY

Automatism – A type of automatic behaviour whose functions are accompanied but not controlled by consciousness.

Begging the question – when what you are trying to prove in an argument is implicitly assumed in one of the premises.

Causality – the relationship between a cause and an effect, or a first event and a second event whereby the second event is a direct consequence of the first event.

Causal circumstance – the entire universe, if you will, at the time of a decision. This entails all the causal variables of the agent(s) involved and the external variables that determine the decision.

Circular Argument – a logical fallacy that ends up assuming what it is trying to prove. An example might be: It says in the bible that God exists. Since the bible is God's word, and God never speaks falsely, then everything in the bible must be true. So, God must exist.

Compatibilism – the belief that free will and determinism can exist in a system together, that free will and determinism are somehow compatible with each other.

Compatibilist – someone that believes in compatibilism.

Contingent – an event that is neither logically necessary (i.e. it *has to happen*) nor logically impossible. For example, "The car is red" is a contingent truth, since the car does not have to be red; it is not red in all possible worlds.

Counterfactual – an 'if-then' statement such as "If Peter goes into the garden then he will see that it is raining".

Deist – someone who believes in a usually impersonal god who does not interfere in the universe after creation.

Determinism – the belief that all variables in an agents life are outside of their control, thus rendering any of their decisions causally determined and not free.

Dualism – the belief that mental phenomena, as in consciousness, are non-physical. That mind and body are distinct substances with distinct properties.

Epistemology – philosophy dealing with the theory, nature and scope of knowledge.

Fatalism – the notion that all events are inevitably victim to fate, or predetermination.

Hard determinism – the belief in the full implications and veracity of determinism – no exceptions!

Incompatibilism – the belief that free will and determinism cannot exist in the same system together, that they are mutually exclusive.

Incompatibilist – someone that adheres to incompatibilism.

Indeterminism – the belief that the world is not fully determined, that determinism is incorrect. This might be due to free will, or due to chance.

Indeterminist – some one that believes in indeterminism, of course!

Libertarian – someone who believes in the notion of free will, that an agent can be the originator for a choice, without that choice being fully determined by things outside of their control.

Materialism – the belief that everything in the universe is made of matter (or energy). It is akin to physicalism.

Methodological naturalism - an epistemological view concerned with practical methods for acquiring knowledge, irrespective of one's metaphysical or religious views

Monism (in philosophy of mind) – that mind and body are one, that the mind is not separate from body.

Naturalism – the belief that everything in the world (universe) can be explained in natural terms, without invoking anything supernatural or miraculous.

Near–determinist – a determinist that allows for indeterminacy on a micro-level, allowing for some interpretations of quantum theory that factor in indeterminate events. Other than this small exception, they are determinist in nature.

Ontology – The study of the nature of existence.

Physicalism – akin to materialism, but a preferred term to some scientists. It is the belief that there are no other kinds of things other than physical things, such that in the philosophy of mind, it constitutes monism.

Predestination – the idea that God ordains, before existence, what will happen to his creations. A little like fate.

Soft determinism – another name given, sometimes, to compatibilists.

Jonathan M.S. Pearce

Special pleading - an argument that ignores all unfavourable evidence or a pleading that alleges new facts in avoidance of the opposing allegations.

Theist – someone who believes in a usually personal god.

BIBLIOGRAPHY

Books:

Armstrong, K. (2002), *'ISLAM: A Short History'*, London ; Phoenix

Armstrong. K. (2008), *'The Bible: The Biography'*, London ; Atlantic Books

Ashton, J. (2006), 'The Big Argument: Twenty-Four Scholars Explore How Science, Archaeology, and Philosophy Have Proven the Existence of God', Green Forest, AR ; Master Books

Audi, R. (Ed.)(1999 2nd edition), *'The Cambridge Dictionary Of Philosophy'*, Cambridge ; Cambridge University Press

Baggini, J. (2006), *'The Pig that Wants to be Eaten'*, London ; Granta

Barrow, J. D. (1998), *'Impossibility'*, London ; Vintage

Belby, J. K. and Eddy, P. R. (2001), *'Divine Foreknowledge: Four Views'*, Westmont, IL ; InterVarsity Press

Blackburn, S. (1994;2008), *'Oxford Dictionary of Philosophy'*, Oxford ; Oxford University Press

Blackburn, S. (1999), *'Think'*, Oxford ; Oxford University Press

Boa, K. and Bowman, R. M. (2002), '20 Compelling Evidences That God Exists: Discover Why Believing in God Makes So Much Sense', Colorado Springs ; RiverOak Publishing

Brown, Dr. J. (2005), *'Biblical Nonsense'*, Lincoln, NE ; iUniverse

Callahan, T. (2002), *'Secret Origins of the Bible'*, California ; Millennium Press

Carducci, A. (2009 ; 2nd edition), *'The Psychology of Personality: Viewpoints, Research, and Applications'*, Chichester ; John Wiley and Sons (now Wiley-Blackwell)

Carson, D. A. (2000), *'The Difficult Doctrine Of The Love Of God'*, UK ; Intervarsity Press

Dawkins, R. (2006), *'The God Delusion'*, London ; Bantam Press

Dennett, D. C. (2004), *Freedom Evolves'*, London ; Penguin

Drescher, G. (1991), 'Made-Up Minds: A Constructivist Approach to Artificial Intelligence', Cambridge, MA ; MIT Press

Everett, D. (2008), 'Don't Sleep, There are Snakes : Life and Language in the Amazonian Jungle', New York ; Pantheon Books

Geivett, R. D. and Habermas, G. (Eds) (1997), *'In Defense of Miracles'*, Westmont, IL ; InterVarsity Press

Hitchens, C. (2007), 'The Portable Atheist: Essential Readings for the Nonbeliever', London ; Da Capo Press

Honderich, T. (2002, 2nd edition), *'How Free Are You?'*, Oxford ; Oxford University Press

Hume, D. (Edited by L. A. Selby-Bigge) (1975), 'Enquiries concerning Human Understanding and concerning the Principles of Morals', Oxford ; Clarendon Press

Hume, D. (Edited by L. A. Selby-Bigge) (1975), *'A Treatise of Human Nature'*, Oxford ; Clarendon Press

Kane, R. (1996), *'The Significance of Free Will'*, New York : Oxford University Press

Kane, R. (2001), *'Free Will'*, Malden, Mass. ; Wiley-Blackwell

Kane, R. (2002), *'The Oxford Handbook of Free Will'*, Oxford ; Oxford University Press

Kolazowski, L. (2008), Why Is There Something Rather Than Nothing?', London ; Penguin

Loftus, J. W., (2008), 'Why I Became An Atheist: A Former Preacher Rejects Christianity', New York ; Prometheus Books

Luria, A. R. (1961), 'The role of private speech in the regulation of normal and abnormal behaviour', London ; Pergamaon

Moll, A. (1889), *'Hynoptism'*, London ; Walter Scott

Russell, B. (1961, 2nd edition), *'The History Of Western Philosophy'*, London ; Routledge

Ruthven, M. (1997), *'Islam: A Very Short Introduction'*, Oxford ; Oxford University Press

Schlink, B. (2008), *'The Reader"*, London ; Phoenix

Schwartz, B. (2004), *'The Paradox of Choice: Why More is Less'*, New York ; HarperCollins

Tabensky, T. A. (2006), 'Judging and Understanding: Essays on Free Will, Justice, Forgiveness and Love', Farbham ; Ashgate

Thompson, M. (1995;2006), *'Teach Yourself Philosophy'*, London ; Hachette Livre UK

Vivekananda, S. (1977), *'Complete Works of Swami Vivekananda Vol. 1'*, Calcutta ; Advaita Ashrama

Vygotsky, L. S. (1934), *'Thought and language'*, ed. And translated E. Hanfmann and G. Vakar, Cambridge, MA ; MIT Press (1962)

Wegner, D. M. (2002), *'The Illusion of Conscious Will"* Cambridge, Mass. ; MIT Press / Bradford Books

Wright, R. (2009), *'The Evolution of God'*, New York ; Little, Brown and Company

Papers:

Amici, F., Call, J., Aureli, F. (2009), 'Variation in withholding of information in three monkey species', *Proceedings of the Royal Society*, Volume 276: no. 1671, 3311-3318 (22 September)

Barash, D. P. (2003), 'Dennett and the Darwinizing of Free Will', *Human Nature Review* 2003, Volume 3: 222-225 (22 March), http://human-nature.com/nibbs/03/dcdennett.html (retrieved 08/2009)

Bargh, J. A., M. Chen and L. Burrows (1996), 'Automaticity of social behavior : Direct effects of trait construct and stereotype activation on action', *Journal of Personality and Social Psychology,* 71: 230-244

Craig, W. L. (1998), 'Divine Timelessness and Personhood', *International Journal for Philosophy of Religion,* Volume 43, Number 2 / April, 1998 : 109-124

Dennett, Daniel (2006), 'Knowledge Argument', in Alter, Torin, Phenomenal Concepts and Phenomenal Knowledge, Oxford Oxfordshire: Oxford University Press,

http://ase.tufts.edu/cogstud/papers/RoboMaryfinal.htm
#_ftn1 (retrieved 11/2009)

Dijksterhuis, A. and A. van Knippenberg (1998), 'The relation between perception and behavior, or how to win a game of Trivial Pursuit', *Journal of Personality and Social Psychology*, 74: 865-877

Gazzaniga, M.S. (1983), 'Right hemisphere language following brain bisection: A 20-year perspective', *American Psychologist*, 38:525-537

Gao, Y., Raine, A., Venables, P.H., Dawson, M.E. and Sarnoff Mednick, A. (2009), 'Association of Poor Childhood Fear Conditioning and Adult Crime' , *The American Journal of Psychiatry*, Nov 16, 2009 as doi: doi:10.1176/appi.ajp.2009.09040499

Gilman, R. W., (2004), 'Daniel Dennett's Choice', http://www.logosjournal.com/gilman.htm (retrieved 09/2009)

Gopnik, A., and Astington, J. W. (1988) 'Children's understanding of representational change and its relation to the understanding of false belief and the appearance-reality distinction'. *Child Development*, 48: 26-37

Hamilton, R. L. (2002), 'Philosophical Reflections on Free Will', http://evangelicalarminians.org/files/Hamilton.%20Philo sophical%20Reflections%20on%20Free%20Will.pdf (retrieved 08/2009)

Haruno, M. and Frith, C. (2009), 'Activity in the amygdala elicited by unfair divisions predicts social value orientation', *Nature Neuroscience*, 13 (160-161), journal published 2010; Published online: 20 December 2009 | doi:10.1038/nn.2468

Jacobson, E. (1932), 'The electrophysiology of mental activities', *American Journal of Psychology*, 44: 677-694

Kapogiannisa, D., Barbeya, A. K., Sua, M., Zambonia, G., Kruegera, F. and Grafmana, J. (2009), 'Cognitive and neural foundations of religious belief', *Proceedings of the National Academy of Sciences of the United States of America*, March 24, 2009 vol. 106 no. 12 4876-4881

Keller, J. (1995), 'A Moral Argument against Miracles', *Faith and Philosophy*, vol. 12, no 1. Jan 1995. 54-78

Lhermitte, F. (1983), 'Utilization behavior and its relation to lesions of the frontal lobes', *Brain*, 106: 237-255

Lhermitte, F. (1986), 'Human anatomy and the frontal lobes. II. Patient behavior in complex social situations: The environmental dependency syndrome', *Annals of Neurology*, 19: 335-343

Linder, D.E., Cooper, J. and Jones, E.E. (1967), 'Decision freedom as a determinant of the role of incentive magnitude in attitude change', *Journal of Personality and Social Psychology*, 6:245-254

Logan, G. D., and W. Cowan (1984), 'On the ability to inhibit thought and action: A theory of an act of control', *Psychological Review* 91: 295-327

Macrae, C. N. and L. Johnston (1998), 'Help, I need somebody: Automatic action and inaction', *Social Cognotion*, 16: 400

Shoda, Y., Mischel, W., & Peake, P. K. (1990). 'Predicting adolescent cognitive and social competence from preschool delay of gratification: Identifying diagnostic conditions', *Developmental Psychology*, 26:978-986

Mozes, E. (2003), 'The Dogmatic Determinism of Daniel Dennett', *Navigator*, Dec 2003, http://www.objectivistcenter.org/showcontent.aspx?ct=766&h=51 (retrieved 09/2009)

Newman, R. C. (1997), 'Fulfilled Prophecy as Miracle', *In Defense of Miracles*, p.214-225

Perner, J., Leekam, S. R. and Wimmer, H. (1987), 'Three-yearOolds' difficulty with false belief', *British Journal of Developmental Psychology*, 5:125-137

Peterson, B. (added 2009), '*Augustine: Advocate of Free Will, Defender of Predestination*', *http*://www.scribd.com/doc/17202864/Augustine-Advocate-of-Free-Will-Defender-of-Predestination (retrieved 08/2009)

M. Reuter, C. Frenzel, N. T. Walter, S. Markett, C. Montag. (2010), 'Investigating the genetic basis of altruism: the role of the COMT Val158Met polymorphism.' *Social Cognitive and Affective Neuroscience,* 2010; DOI:10.1093/scan/nsq083

Soon, C.S., Brass, M., Heinze, H., and Haynes, J. (2008), 'Unconscious determinants of free decisions in the human brain', *Nature Neuroscience* DOSteele, C. M., and Aronson, J. (1995), 'Stereotype threat and the intellectual test performance of African Americans, *Journal of Personality and Social Psychology,* 69:797-811

Wallace, B.A. (unknown date), '*A Buddhist View of Free Will Beyond Determinism and Indeterminism*' http://www.alanwallace.org/PDF%20NEW/Buddhist%20 View%20of%20Free%20Will.pdf (retrieved 09/2009)

Weisberger, A. (1995), 'Depravity, Divine Responsibility and Moral Evil: A Critique of a New Free Will Defence', *Religious Studies,* Vol. 31 (1995), pp. 375-390

Whitson, J.A. and Galinsky, A.D. (2008) 'Lacking Control Increases Illusory Pattern Perception', *Science* 3 October 2008: Vol. 322. no. 5898, pp. 115 – 117

Lightning Source UK Ltd.
Milton Keynes UK
24 November 2010

163377UK00002B/106/P

9 780956 694805